Adolescent Crime
Individual differences and lifestyles

Per-Olof H. Wikström and David A. Butterworth

WILLAN
PUBLISHING

Published by

Willan Publishing
Culmcott House
Mill Street, Uffculme
Cullompton, Devon
EX15 3AT, UK
Tel: +44(0)1884 840337
Fax: +44(0)1884 840251
e-mail: info@willanpublishing.co.uk
website: www.willanpublishing.co.uk

Published simultaneously in the USA and Canada by

Willan Publishing
c/o ISBS, 920 NE 58th Ave, Suite 300
Portland, Oregon 97213-3786, USA
Tel: +001(0)503 287 3093
Fax: +001(0)503 280 8832
e-mail: info@isbs.com
website: www.isbs.com

Reprinted 2007

ISBN 13: 978-1-84392-369-5 (Paper)
ISBN-13: 978-1-84392-177-6 (Cased)

British Library Cataloguing-in-Publication Data

A catalogue record for this book is available from the British Library

Typeset by GCS, Leighton Buzzard, Beds
Project management by Deer Park Productions, Tavistock, Devon
Printed and bound by TJI Digital, Padstow, Cornwall

Contents

List of figures and tables

Figures

Tables

Acknowledgements

In this book, we present the key findings of the cross-sectional Peterborough Youth Study (PYS). The study focuses on the role of individual differences and lifestyles, particularly their interaction, in the explanation of adolescent offending. The study was financed by a grant from the Home Office Innovative Research Challenge Fund. Some additional funding was provided by the Cambridge Institute of Criminology.

The Peterborough Youth Study is a forerunner to the current longitudinal Peterborough Adolescent Development Study (PADS). Many of the topics we take forward and the methodologies we use in PADS emerged out of our experiences of conducting PYS.

The basic PYS research team consisted of myself, Charlotte Read (research assistant) and Suzanna Wikström (part-time research assistant) and I would like to thank both Charlotte and Suzanna for doing an excellent job. In addition, a number of other people helped with the data collection (e.g. administration of questionnaires, conducting interviews, inputting of data). There are too many to mention them all, but special mention should be made of Linda Harte (Peterborough), Vicky Wright (M.Phil student at the time at the Cambridge Institute of Criminology), Jon Olafsson, Stephen Boxford and Joel Harvey (all Ph.D students at the time at the Cambridge Institute of Criminology), who carried a larger share of the work (they have of course been paid for their effort, although at a modest rate, which makes their contribution even more appreciated).

We would especially like to thank all the Peterborough young people who took time to share some of their life experience with us, and the Peterborough schools and their staff who allowed us some of their time and assistance to carry out the school questionnaire study.

Chief Superintendent David Harvey played a pivotal role in my decision to locate this study to Peterborough. His continued support and help in facilitating local contacts necessary for this study are acknowledged and much appreciated.

After completing his Ph.D and working for several years as a research associate with PADS, David Butterworth agreed to help me turn the initial PYS report to the Home Office (Wikström 2002) into a book manuscript. This book is the result of a fruitful collaboration between the two of us.

In the final stages of editing, Charlotte Christie and Kyle Treiber helped us consolidate and trim the rough edges of the manuscript.

Per-Olof Wikström
University of Cambridge

Chapter 1

Introduction

There is a lack of current research on young people's offending and its causes in the UK. The main source of information on current juvenile offending comes from two recent national self-report studies (Graham and Bowling 1995; Flood-Page et al. 2000; and see Chapter 4).[1] However, very few academic studies have explored the prevalence and patterns of juvenile offending in UK cities. The only more recent exceptions known to us, of which none have been carried out in England or Wales, are a study of about 1,200 11–15-year-olds from five selected schools in Edinburgh by Anderson et al. (1994), an ongoing (longitudinal) study of 4,300 juveniles, covering most schools in Edinburgh, from which some initial findings are available (e.g. Smith et al. 2001) and some research carried out in the city of Belfast based on a random sample of about 900 14–21-year-olds (McQuoid and Lockhart 1994). These city-based studies, with some exceptions in the Smith et al. study, do not consider explanatory factors in any depth.

In addition to this, there are a few older longitudinal studies (for an overview, see Loeber and Farrington 2001: app. C), of which the most prominent is the so-called Cambridge Study in Delinquent Development, a study of a 1953 male cohort from a London working-class area (see e.g. Farrington 1989, 1992). In this context, also McDonald's (1969) 1964 cross-sectional study of male juvenile delinquency in four different areas of England, and Belson's (1975) 1967–8 cross-sectional study of juvenile theft in London should be mentioned.

Although the British Crime Survey (BCS) has supplied a wealth of information on victimisation, its regular sweeps do not cover young victims (under the age of 16). However, one special study has been made of 12–15 year-olds' victimisation using a special sample from the sample of one of the BCS waves (Maung 1995). Studies of young people's victimisation in particular cities are rare. The already mentioned studies in Edinburgh (Anderson *et al.* 1994; Smith *et al.* 2001) and Belfast (McQuoid and Lockhart 1994), in addition to a study of six schools in Middlesborough (Brown 1995), are the prime examples of studies of young people's victimisation conducted in particular cities.

In search of patterns and explanations

The starting point for this research is the sometimes controversial idea that a key objective of social science is to study *patterns* in social life and to try to offer *explanations* of these patterns. To do so we need to map out the correlates of social action and to try to understand the causal mechanisms at work. Some of the correlates may be just correlates; others may help to identify what mechanisms cause a particular social action. An important task is therefore to evaluate the correlates (their potential as representing causal mechanisms at work) in relation to theories of what constitutes social action.

The basic position taken here is that social actions, like offending, 1) ultimately are a result of an individual's perception of action alternatives and process of choice, and that 2) a key challenge for social science research is to understand how an individual's wider social situation influences his or her individual characteristics and experiences and exposure to environmental features that, in turn, independently or in interaction, cause action (e.g. acts of crime) through their influence on how an individual perceives ac-tion alternatives and makes choices (Wikström and Sampson 2003; Wikström 2004, 2005, 2006). This is, of course, a monumental task, and no single research project can hope to be able to provide more than a small contribution towards this goal.

In the Peterborough Youth Study we attempt to move knowledge a little further forward by studying the relationship between individual characteristics (social bonds and morality and self-control) and lifestyles (as defined by delinquent peers, substance use and exposure to risky behaviour settings) and their joint influence on juvenile involvement in crime, against the backdrop of the juveniles' social context (their family's social position and, to some extent, their wider social context as represented by their neighbourhood and school contexts). We assume that individuals' social lives will differ and interact with their individual characteristics and that this will have some bearing on their involvement in crime as offenders or victims. However, it is out of the scope of this research *empirically* to address the role of individual perception of action alternatives and the processes of choice (although we will *theoretically* discuss this as the main mechanism linking individuals and behavioural contexts to their actions).

The problem of correlation and causation

Criminological research has demonstrated hundreds, if not thousands, of stable correlates to adolescent crime involvement. These correlates are commonly referred to as risk (or protective) factors, and sometimes treated as established causes rather than mere correlates for which causation has to be established. This problem has increasingly been recognised as one that has to be dealt with in order to advance our knowledge about the causes and explanation of crime involvement.

Farrington (2002a: 664) has defined 'risk factors' as 'prior factors that increase the risk of occurrence of the onset, frequency, persistence, or duration of offending'. There appears to be an increasing consensus in discussions of risk (and protective) factors, with regard to their associations with offending, that there is a need for a framework by which one can distinguish risk factors that are 1) causally related to offending from those that are 2) symptomatic of offending and, finally, those that may be 3) both symptoms as well as causes, such as excessive alcohol use (Farrington 2002a). Farrington (2002a) reviewed the criminological literature on temperament and personality factors (e.g. impulsivity; see also Tremblay and LeMarquand 2001), family factors (e.g. parental supervision; see also Wasserman and Seracini 2001) and school factors (see also Herrenkohl *et al.* 2001), which have been found to be risk factors in the development of offending, and noted:

> In explaining the development of offending, a major problem is that most risk factors tend to coincide and tend to be interrelated. For example, adolescents living in physically deteriorated and socially disorganized neighbourhoods disproportionately tend also to come from families with poor parental supervision and

3

erratic parental discipline, and tend also to have high impulsivity and low intelligence. The concentration and co-occurrence of these kind of adversities make it difficult to establish their independent, interactive, and sequential influences on offending and antisocial behaviour (2002a: 680).

Therefore, one point which seems to be widely accepted by those working within this criminological tradition is that *'a major problem of the risk factor prevention paradigm is to determine those risk factors that are causes from those that are merely markers or correlated with causes'* (Farrington 2000: 7, emphasis added).

Conversely to risk factors, 'protective factors' are characteristics that are seen in some way as operating to reduce the likelihood of offending. Farrington (1998) has suggested that there are three distinct definitions of what constitutes a 'protective' factor. The first of these is that a protective factor is just the opposite of a risk factor. Hence if low self-control were a risk factor for offending, then high self-control could be a protective factor. Secondly, protective factors may simply 'stand-alone' – that is, they do not have a linear relationship with offending. Thirdly, protective factors may operate in interaction to mitigate the effects of other risk factors (see also Lösel and Bender 2003).

It seems entirely plausible to suggest that a fruitful way to sort true risk and protective factors (i.e. causes) from correlates is through greater theoretical attention being paid to what actually puts the 'risk' into risk factor, or what it is about protective factors that actually provides the 'protection'. For example, Sampson and Laub (1993) suggest that marriage, *per se*, does not act as a 'protective' factor but, rather, it is the strength of the attachment to one's partner that accompanies marriage which acts to lessen the likelihood of offending. As Rutter (1987: 329, emphasis in original) concludes in his discussion of protective factors, 'The focus of attention should be on the protective *processes* or mechanisms, rather than on variables' (see also Hedström and Swedberg 1998; Wikström 2004).

Perhaps therefore the fundamental issue that arises as a result of the rather atheoretical nature of the risk and protective factor paradigm is the question of their underlying cause or causes. As Farrington (1998: 262) notes: 'What is needed is a coordinated program of research to determine how many key theoretical constructs underlie all these variables, what they are, how they are causally related, and how they should best be operationally defined and measured.' Furthermore, while person-centred risk factors have been the focus of extensive investigation, Farrington (2003: 227) highlighted that much less is known about peer, school and neighbourhood risk factors.

Although the consistency of between-individual differences is frequently accepted (for example, the chronic/non-chronic offender dichotomy), the possible reasons for such continue to appear to be hypothesised as being the result of stable individual traits. This individual-oriented view has diverted attention from the social contexts within which individuals actually live their lives. As Magnusson (1988: 23) has commented, there is a 'dynamic, continuous, and reciprocal process of interaction between the individual and the environment'. While self-selection is no doubt likely to play a role in determining the social contexts in which individuals choose to engage as they age, there can be little doubt that such ability to choose those contexts is severely limited during the early years of individual development.

Hence the risk and protective factor approach has not only tended to downplay the consideration of the environment in producing *contexts of action* which lead to *within-individual* differences in the likelihood of criminal propensity becoming substantiated as (criminal) acts at different times (Farrington 2000; Wikström 2004), it has also largely ignored the influence of environmental factors as a *context of development* in the acquisition of characteristics (e.g. see Bronfenbrenner 1979; Martens 1993; Wikström 2005) that give rise to *between-individual* differences in offending.

In this study we will demonstrate associations (correlations) between variables and show how they independently, jointly and through interaction can predict outcomes (e.g. crime involvement). It is important to stress once again, as discussed above, that correlation (and prediction) do not necessarily imply causation and that findings of statistical studies, like the present one, cannot by themselves establish causation and offer explanation. One of the authors has elsewhere argued that causation can only be established through experimentation, and that explanation can only be offered by analytic work aimed at specifying plausible mechanisms (processes) that link the putative cause to the effect (Wikström 2006). In the concluding chapter we will discuss the empirical findings of this study in relation to a theoretical framework (*the Situational Action Theory of Crime Causation*) that will allow us to interpret the findings in terms of how they may contribute to the explanation of adolescent offending.

Aims of the research: key questions and constructs

The overall aim of this research is to contribute to a better understanding of adolescent involvement in crime (primarily as offenders but, to some degree, also as victims). We aim to achieve this by studying the relationships between *family social position* (parents' occupational social class, family structure and family ethnicity), the *adolescents' social situation* (family and school bonds), their *individual dispositions* (morality and ability to exercise self-control) and *lifestyles* (as implicated by their peers' delinquency, their own activities and alcohol and drug use) and how these factors relate to their involvement in crime as offenders (and partly as victims). We are particularly interested in testing the idea that the adolescents' individual characteristics (their social situation and dispositions) *interact* with their lifestyle in producing crime involvement. Specifically, we hypothesise that the impact of adolescent lifestyles on their crime involvement is dependent on their individual characteristics. We are also interested in exploring the influence by the adolescents' family social position on their individual characteristics (morality and self-control) and lifestyle. We are postulating, and aim to test whether the data are consistent with the assumption, that any impact of the adolescents' family social position on their crime involvement is mediated through an impact on key individual characteristics and lifestyles. Finally, we are also interested in exploring any influences of the wider social context (as defined by neighbourhood and school contexts), although we do acknowledge that the data we have on these two aspects are far from perfect. Our general approach is summarised in Figure 1.1, where the double arrow indicates an anticipated interaction effect – that is, that the impact of lifestyle on offending is dependent on an individual's characteristics.

Outline of chapters

After presenting the design of the PYS study, its data and discussing various key methodological issues (Chapter 2), we turn to familiarising the reader with the broader context in which the study is set. The findings chapters start with a presentation of Peterborough and its neighbourhoods (Chapter 3). Chapter 4 gives a detailed presentation of the prevalence, frequency and characteristics of offending and victimisation and includes basic data about substance use. The next four chapters deal with potential explanatory factors.

Social context (neighbourhood and school)

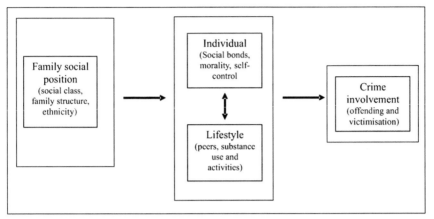

Figure 1.1 Overview of key hypothesised relationships between key studied constructs.

In Chapter 5 we explore adolescents' family social position (family social class, family composition and family ethnicity) and analyse its relationship to their offending and victimisation. Statistical analyses performed in this and other chapters include tests of significance,[2] factor analysis, OLS and logistic regression. In Chapter 6 we deal with the adolescents' individual characteristics (social bonds, self-control and morality). Key constructs referring to social bonds, self-control and morality, and an overall risk-protective scale (a composite measure of all the individual constructs), are presented. Statistical analyses are performed to see how these relate to the adolescents' family social position, and to their involvement in offending and victimisation.

In Chapter 7 the focus is on the role of neighbourhood and school contexts. Constructs of area of residence structural risk and school structural risk are created and discussed. The relationship between neighbourhood and school context and the youths' offending and victimisation is studied. The focus of the statistical analyses of the role of the neighbourhood context is on its impact on locally committed crimes and local victimisation, while the focus in the statistical analyses of the role of the school context is on offending and victimisation taking place in the school environment. The impact on offending and victimisation by the neighbourhood and school context is also analysed in relation to the youths' family social position and their individual risk-protective characteristics.

Individual lifestyles are the topic of Chapter 8. We explore how these relate to the youths' individual characteristics and their neighbourhoods and in turn how all this is related to their offending in particular, but also their victimisation. A special analysis of interaction effects is also performed. Main groups of offender types are suggested.

In Chapter 9, the study of lifestyles is taken one step forward by introducing data from the special space-time-budget study. We explore in detail the 'last week' activities of the youths to give an in-depth picture of adolescent routines, and conclude with a comparison of how these vary by structural contexts and by types of offender groups.

In the concluding Chapter 10 we summarise key findings, provide a theoretical interpretation of the findings in relation to the Situational Action Theory of Crime Causation (Wikström 2005; 2006), and finally discuss the implication for strategies and policies to prevent adolescent offending.

Notes

1 A number of other, recent, self-report studies have been identified, but these have not been included for discussion here. Youth surveys conducted by Communities that Care (2002) and MORI (2002, 2003, 2004) have been excluded due to the rather disappointing response rates secured by these studies, and the On-track Youth Lifestyles Surveys (Armstrong *et al.* 2005) have also been excluded, in this instance due to the composition of the sampling frame for these studies which, following the On-track initiative, targeted only neighbourhoods with high levels of disadvantage and crime (see Armstrong *et al.* 2005: 5) and are therefore not directly comparable with the PYS.

2 To avoid repetition, whenever we talk about significant findings in this report, unless otherwise stated, we refer to findings statistically significant at the 5 per cent level or better. When referring to *significant group differences*, the tests used are chi-square when analysing differences in prevalence, and *F-Tests* (ANOVA) when analysing differences in mean frequences.

Chapter 2

The Peterborough Youth Study

The Peterborough Youth Study (PYS) is a cross-sectional study of 1) all juveniles who started Year 10 (aged 14–15 years) in autumn 2000 in the 13 Peterborough state schools (the questionnaire study) and 2) a random sample thereof who participated in a space and time-budget study concerning their last week activities (the interview study). The questionnaire study was carried out during late 2000 and early 2001. The interview study was carried out in spring and early summer 2001. In addition, data from 1998–9 on neighbourhood disadvantage and enumeration district data on population characteristics from the 1991 census were utilised to classify the structural context of the youths' area of residence (see Chapter 3).

The questionnaire study

In order to ameliorate the problem of the 'dark figure' of crime inherent in analyses of official crime data, criminological surveys over the past 50 years or so have turned to self-report methodologies to reveal the 'true' prevalence and frequency of offending (Short and Nye 1957–8; Hindelang *et al.* 1979; Thornberry and Krohn 2000; Farrington undated). As Farrington (undated: 9) has noted, 'Most attempts to test delinquency theories in the last 30 years have used the self-report method' (and see, for example, Hirschi 1969).

This method is not without its detractors. Elliott and Ageton (1980) identified three areas for which self-report surveys have been criticised, namely: 1) that the method is inherently unreliable and does not provide valid data due to such problems as the falsification of responses or inaccurate recall; 2) that there have been problems with the research instruments and the ways they have been employed in self-report research; and 3) problems of generalisation due to the use of small and unrepresentative samples.

Addressing these issues in reverse order with regard to the PYS, the sample used in the study – at nearly two thousand young people – makes this one of only a handful of large-scale surveys investigating the causes of crime conducted to date in the UK. The use of virtually the entire population of 14–15-year-olds in Peterborough in the survey and the very low rates of non-response (see below) give us confidence that there is no great problem regarding the representativeness of our sample that would meaningfully affect the research findings.

With regard to the research instruments, the questionnaire used was based on a translation of a questionnaire tested and modified over a 15-year period in a number of different studies of Swedish young people (see Wikström 1990 for the first version of this questionnaire). The questionnaire was further modified for this study and piloted in a Cambridge school. The questionnaires were administered to six pupils in Year 10 who filled it in and then discussed the questions with one of the project staff to make sure the participants understood the questions as intended. This resulted in some changes in the wording of a few questions and their response categories. The pilot study also reassured us that one hour was sufficient time for completion of the questionnaire. Throughout the presentation of the findings from the study, the items used to construct scales have been identified and reliability tests on the constructs reported.

Regarding the way the questionnaire was deployed in the field, every attempt was made to maximise the validity of responses obtained. All the questions referred to events and conditions during the year 2000 (the last two terms of Year 9, the summer holidays and the first term of Year 10). To help the subjects place their answers in the correct timeframe, the questions started by asking about what they had done to celebrate the new millennium. This was followed by three questions which asked them to mention what they remembered most readily that happened to themselves, their family or friends during the last two terms of Year 9, the summer holidays and since they started Year 10.

The study was kindly supported by Peterborough City Council and the local education authority (LEA). The head of the LEA wrote to the heads of the 13 state schools in Peterborough to encourage them to take part in the study. To our great pleasure no school refused to take part. The only Peterborough school with Year 10 pupils not included in the study was a small, private, day and boarding school for girls. However, we did include the Link programme, which is an alternative educational programme for pupils who have been excluded from school or who in some cases refuse to go to ordinary schools.

In total there were 2,118 pupils enrolled in the 13 schools and the Link programme. Letters were sent out (in most cases by the participating school) to all parents informing them of the purpose of the study and giving them the opportunity to withdraw their child from the study if they so wished. Overall, 33 parents withdrew their child from the study (see Table 2.1). The number of males and females

Table 2.1 Questionnaire and interview samples and non-response rates

	No.	%	Comment
Questionnaires			
Sample	2,118	100.0	All Year 10 pupils in Peterborough
Included in study	1,957	92.4	
Non-responses	161	7.6	
Thereof:			
Withdrawn by parents	33	1.6	
Refused to take part	8	0.4	
Absentees	120	5.7	
Interviews			
Sample	409	100.0	Random sample of Year 10 pupils (every fifth pupil)
Included in study	339	82.9	
Non-responses	70	17.1	
Thereof:			
Moved out of Peterborough	7	1.7	
Moved school/class	5	1.2	
Withdrawn by parents	5	1.2	
Subject refused interview	18	4.4	
Non-English speaker	1	0.2	
Unable to make contact	34	8.3	Pupils who did not fill in questionnaire (absentees)

among the withdrawn pupils was about the same, although the proportion of withdrawn pupils was higher among ethnic minorities. Arrangements were made between project staff and the individual schools for convenient times for data collection. The questionnaires were administered by project staff in classroom settings and the time set for completion of the questionnaire was about one hour (50 minutes). The project staff reassured the pupils that their answers would be treated in absolute confidence and that they would remain completely anonymous in the reporting and presentation of any findings. Only eight pupils declined to take part (see Table 2.1). The pupils were instructed not to talk to anyone else during completion of the questionnaire and to remain quiet until all the pupils in the class had finished.

With regard to non-responses, Farrington (2002: 3) noted that:

Attrition is important because of evidence that the persons who are most difficult to find and to interview tend to commit the most offences. Hence, a survey with a high attrition rate will tend to miss out a relatively large number of frequent offenders and to underestimate the true number of offences committed.

To increase motivation to participate and to keep good order in the classroom the pupils were informed that all who completed the questionnaire and remained calm throughout the session would be entered into a draw in which one pupil in the class would win a £15 record-store voucher. The draw was administered after all pupils had completed the questionnaires.

Members of the project staff were available during the completion of the questionnaire to answer any questions that the pupils may have had. In a small number of cases (about ten) the pupils could not fill in the questionnaire by themselves due to learning or language difficulties. In these cases they were asked whether they would like to have their learning support assistant or one of the project staff help them fill in the questionnaire. Most who agreed to do so opted for help from a member of the project staff.

All schools were visited twice. The revisits were made to pick up those students who were absent at the original data collection. At the first data collection, 1,817 pupils completed the questionnaire, and the revisit added 140 pupils who were absent at the first data collection. However, 120 pupils were absent at both data collections and were therefore not included in the study (see Table 2.1). The absentees make up the main part (74 per cent) of the total non-response rate (7.6 per cent). Although the overall response rate is very good (92.4 per cent), it is likely that the non-responses may include a higher number of pupils with different kinds of social problems and higher rates of criminality, and we therefore may somewhat underestimate the rates of such problems and the number of high-frequency offenders. For example, the zero-order correlation in this study between frequency of truancy and frequency of offending is $r. = 0.39$ ($p = 0.000$).

Finally there is the issue of the validity and reliability of responses obtained through self-report data. Farrington (1973) examined the reliability of the self-report instrument used in the Cambridge Study of Delinquent Development and found it overall to be broadly reliable, although there was some not inconsiderable variation in the likelihood of respondents continuing to admit ever having committed some offences at the ages of 16–17 in comparison with their responses at 14–15. However, as Farrington reported (1973: 107), 'The percentage of obviously inconsistent responses out of all responses was only 6.4%'.

Summarising their review of the reliability of self-report studies, Thornberry and Krohn (2000: 49) stated: 'Overall these studies suggest that the self-report possesses acceptable reliability for most analytic purposes. Test–retest correlations are often 0.80 or higher, and self-reported delinquency responses are no less reliable than other social science measures.' Turning to the validity of self-reports, Thornberry and Krohn (2000: 34) comment on what seems likely to be the most persistent fear among those unfamiliar with self-report methodology: 'There was great scepticism about whether respondents would agree to tell researchers about their participation in illegal behaviours. However, early studies found that not only were respondents willing to self-report their delinquency and criminal behaviour, they did so in surprising numbers' (internal references removed).

Unfortunately, there is no rock-solid way to assess the veracity of the responses given in self-reports. One approach frequently taken is to see whether those who have self-reported offending also have an official police record (although, of course, it should be remembered that one reason self-reports have increased in popularity is precisely because such 'official' records are inadequate).

Hirschi (1969) found that those respondents with an official record were more likely to self-report delinquency. Farrington (1973) found that self-reported delinquency scores at the age of 14–15 possessed concurrent validity (those who had official records self-reporting more delinquency on average than those without) and also predictive validity in that those without an official record at the age of 14–15

13

and who self-reported higher rates of offending were more likely to go on to acquire a criminal record.

Gold (1966: 31–4) utilised reports by teenage 'relevant informants' regarding the delinquency of peers to assess the validity of self-reports and found that 72 per cent of those respondents who had been said by the informants to have engaged in delinquent behaviour self-reported delinquent behaviour, with 17 per cent concealing and 11 per cent classified as giving 'questionable' responses.

Overall, there seems little reason to believe that self-report findings provide anything other than a reasonable portrait of young people's involvement in crime. However, studies have raised two areas where the validity of self-reports is more in question: the issue of differential validity by race/ethnicity and gender. In a work that so comprehensively supports the use of self-reports, Farrington (2002: 10) has commented 'this landmark book tended to kill methodological [self-reported offending] research stone dead. Researchers assumed that the validity of SRO surveys had been established for all time'. Hindelang *et al.* (1981: 175, emphasis in original) found that: 'The self-report scores of blacks are not as valid as those of whites using the official record as the criterion (among both males and females) *and* blacks are less likely to report delinquent offences at all levels of official delinquency.' However, Jolliffe *et al.* (2003), using data collected from the Seattle Social Development Project, found little in the way of an overall differential validity distinction between white and black respondents, but suggested that Asian females did exhibit low validity of responses. Jolliffe *et al.* (2003: 193) state: 'The self-reports of Asian and black females had the lowest predictive validity. The low validity of Asian females is an important result, which to our knowledge has not been found (or investigated) previously.'

In their reviews, both Farrington (2002: 15) and Thornberry and Krohn (2000: 58) comment that the research in this area has led to contradictory findings and that, hence, the truth of the 'differential validity' hypothesis has yet to be ascertained. It is worth commenting that the Jolliffe *et al.*'s (2003) finding of differential validity (i.e. increased concealment of delinquency) by Asian females challenges the findings of this study. An interesting salient finding of the present study is a low rate of offending by Asian females. Is this finding substantive or likely to be the result of Asian females' concealment?

There is no way for us to answer definitively this question from the data that we have; however, we do not yet feel sufficiently persuaded to accept the differential validity explanation. We will briefly try to explain why. First, the low rate of self-reported offending by Asian females was theoretically in accordance with their self-reported more protective individual characteristics and their lower-risk lifestyles. This would mean that not only did the Asian females in our sample conceal their offending, but that they also systematically answered questions throughout the questionnaire in a fashion that would prove consistent with the reported low levels of offending. Secondly, as Thornberry and Krohn (2000: 58) note, if there is differential validity, then 'the processes that bring it about frankly are not understood'. We are unable to think of an adequate theoretical explanation for why Asian females would be more likely to conceal and, given the lack of consistent empirical findings on differential validity in the past, it seems too early to assume the Jolliffe *et al*. finding is relevant to our study. It might be suggested that Asian females are less likely to self-report offending for 'cultural reasons' (such as higher levels of shame), yet this is also the kind of characteristic which we would expect to lead to less offending in the first place. Therefore it remains unclear why such characteristics should differentially affect reporting but not actual offending behaviour.

Furthermore, other analyses indicate that not only do Asian females report lower rates of offending, they also report lower rates of victimisation. Given the link between offending and victimisation, this is as would be expected. However, whereas reasons may be postulated as to why Asian females might conceal offending, it is less clear to us that such explanations would also apply equally to victimisation.

Finally, as part of PYS, a random sample (20 per cent) of the young people in the study were interviewed using a 'space-time budget' (on average conducted six months after the subjects took part in the questionnaire study) where they were asked to account for every hour (location, company, activities, etc.) in the previous week (see next section for details). Given the low number of Asian youths it was not considered reliable to disaggregate the analyses by gender. However, the results indicated that, overall, Asian youths reported spending significantly more time at home, sleeping, doing homework or other educational activities, at meetings of clubs and societies and with family members only, and less time on the streets, in transit, walking around or on public transport, by themselves, alone with peers, doing hobbies or playing games, in pubs and nightclubs and consuming alcohol than their non-Asian peers. It therefore appears that the Asians youths, and we would predict especially the Asian females, spend significantly more time engaged in conventional activities and less time in behaviour settings and/or with companions that might be considered to increase their exposure to criminogenic situations. These findings are both consistent with the overall picture of the Asian youths built up through their questionnaire study responses and also suggest, in terms of the differential validity argument, that not only would Asian females have had consistently to falsify their responses for the questionnaire study, but also similarly systematically mislead interviewers as to their whereabouts and activities over the week previous to the time-space budget interview. Once again, without a good theoretical reason, this is not an assumption that we are willing to make.

Therefore, while it is difficult to disagree with Thornberry and Krohn's (2000: 58) suggestion regarding differential validity that 'This is perhaps the most important methodological issue concerning the self-report method and should be a high priority for future research efforts', we do not consider that the present state of knowledge is such that we should dismiss the findings for the Asian females in our study.

The interview study

The main purpose of the interview study was to map out the juveniles' day-to-day activities and movements. To do so we used a time-budget technique and added on a geographical component in what can be called a 'Space-Time Budget Study'. As far as we are aware, this is the first time such a technique has been used to study the relationship between individuals' routine activities and their crime involvement.

This research was, for financial reasons, restricted to a sample of all Year 10 juveniles. These were selected from class lists by randomly picking a starting number between one and five, and thereafter choosing every fifth student. The class lists are in alphabetical order and there is therefore no reason to suspect that they are in anyway systematic in relation to the characteristics measured in this study. By this method 409 pupils were selected for interview. Of those selected, 34 were absent at both visits when questionnaires were collected and therefore we were unable to make contact with them. An additional five had already been withdrawn from the study by their parents.

The pupils chosen for interview were approached at the collection of the questionnaires and, if they agreed to participate, handed a form to fill out their contact details. A small number declined to take part in the interview (18 pupils) and were hence excluded from the study. The selected pupils were informed about the purpose of the interview, that they would be paid £10 for their time and effort, and that the interview was likely to last for about half an hour. At a later stage they were contacted to set up a date for the interview. All interviews took place in their school in a private room. Interviews were carried out with only project staff present. Each interview took about half an hour in which the subject was talked through his or her last week retrospectively starting with the day before the interview. For example, if the interview was done on a Tuesday, it started with questions about Monday and then moved on to Sunday, etc. For each hour they were asked to indicate on a map of Peterborough where they were (coded for the study by enumeration district) and then asked what place they were in (e.g. in a shopping-mall), what they were doing and with whom, and whether they used any alcohol or drugs, carried any weapons, were truant, entered into any risk situation (e.g. were harassed or witnessed an act of violence), committed a crime or were a victim of one (see Appendix B).

The general impression from the interviewers was that the pupils had a very good recollection of their last week whereabouts, although it is reasonable to assume that the accuracy may have been somewhat less when asked about activities several days ago. Of those selected for interview we were unable to carry out the interview in one case because the pupil did not speak English and we had no funds available for an interpreter (see Table 2.1). An additional seven subjects had moved out of Peterborough between the time they filled in the questionnaire and agreed to the interview and the time for which the interview was scheduled. We had no funds available to trace these subjects and therefore they were excluded from the study. Finally, five subjects had moved school/class between the time of the questionnaire collection and the interview date and we were therefore unable to locate them. The response rate for the interview study was good (82.9 per cent) but not as good as for the questionnaire study (see Table 2.1). The higher non-response rate was predominantly due to a higher number of refusals and absentees in the interview sample as well as the fact that some had moved to another school/class or out of Peterborough.

A comparison of 10 selected key characteristics (gender, family social position and involvement in crime and substance use) between those included in the interview study and the rest of the questionnaire sample showed no significant differences at the 10 per cent level. We may therefore conclude that there is no reason to assume that the interview sample is a biased subsample of the questionnaire sample (see Table 2.2).

Table 2.2 A comparison of those selected for interview with the rest of the questionnaire sample. Probability value (chi-square)

Compared characteristic	Probability value
Gender	n.s.
Family social class	n.s.
Family structure	n.s.
Family ethnicity	n.s.
Offending prevalence	n.s.
Victimisation prevalence	n.s.
Alcohol use	n.s.
Cannabis use	n.s.
Inhalants use	n.s.
Hard drug use	n.s.

Notes:
n.s. = not significant at the 10 per cent level; ($p > = 0.1$).

Chapter 3

The City of Peterborough and its neighbourhoods

Given that the PYS is a single-city study, an obvious question is to what extent the results obtained are specific to Peterborough or applicable to other locations. This issue can be addressed in two ways. First, is there anything specific about Peterborough as a research site that would lead to a particular bias in the results obtained by the study and, secondly, are the results broadly concordant with extant criminological research on a national and international basis?

Situated in East Anglia, 80 miles north of London, Peterborough is one of two large cities in Cambridgeshire (the other is Cambridge). The Peterborough urban area has approximately 134,000 inhabitants (1997). Peterborough was a small market town until the Industrial Revolution. With the advent of the railway, Peterborough became a major junction point and consequently attracted heavy industry to the city. More contemporaneously, in 1968 Peterborough was included in the 'New Towns' programme and a master plan drawn up to double the population of the city through the development of four new residential townships. As a result of this, the population of the city grew rapidly throughout the 1970s and 1980s before starting to stabilise in the 1990s.

Comparison with the most recent (2001) census, contrasting data from Peterborough with the national averages, broadly indicates that there seems to be little that is extraordinary about the population composition of the city which might raise concerns over the specificity of the findings. It is notable, however, that the population of Peterborough tends to be somewhat more ethnically diverse with the 'Asian or Asian British – Pakistani' group being substantially over-represented at 4.5 per cent compared with 1.4 per cent nationally. The over-representation of the Asian population allowed for some specific analyses of young Asian people in the PYS and the same

Table 3.1 Detected offenders per 100 population 1999, and deprivation scores* by neighbourhood

Neighbourhood		Offenders per 100	Deprivation score*
Urban Area	Central	3.7	68.9
	Dogsthorpe	3.2	49.6
	Ravensthorpe	3.2	46.6
	East	4.5	41.0
	North	2.0	39.3
	Orton Longueville	3.3	34.8
	North Bretton	2.7	33.1
	Paston	2.8	32.1
	Fletton	1.8	28.2
	Walton	1.7	24.2
	Stanground	1.7	22.4
	South	1.8	21.5
	Park	1.4	18.9
	Orton Waterville	1.6	18.5
	South Bretton	1.9	18.3
	Werrington North	1.3	11.6
	Werrington South	0.5	7.1
	West	0.6	7.6
Nearby villages	Thorney and Eye**	1.0	19.8
	Farcet	n.a.	15.7
	Yaxley	n.a.	11.5
	Glinton	0.8	6.2

Notes:
 * The data from which the deprivation score is built refer mostly to the years 1998 and 1999.
** No separate figure for Eye was available, so the joint Thorney and Eye figures are used as an estimate of the Eye score.
 n.a. = not available.
Sources:
Offenders: Peterborough ward profiles, Policy and Communication Unit, Peterborough (2000). Deprivation scores: Supplement to the DETR IMD 2000 Report. IMD scores in Cambridgeshire and Peterborough, Cambridgeshire County Council Research Group (2000).

causal factors at work for the non-Asian population appeared to explain equally well the differential likelihood of offending among Asian youths. Therefore it seems there is little reason to believe that the ethnic composition of the city is likely to impinge on the extent to which the results of the study are applicable to other locations.

There is also considerable diversity among the neighbourhoods of Peterborough. The urban area is divided into 18 neighbourhoods (wards). Of these neighbourhoods, six were a result of the New Town development (North and South Bretton, North and South Werrington, Orton Longueville and Orton Waterville). According to the DETR Index of Multiple Deprivation 2000 (created for the Department of Environment, Trade and the Regions (DETR) by a team of researchers at Oxford University; see Cambridgeshire County Council 2001), Peterborough harbours some of the country's most disadvantaged neighbourhoods, but also includes some more affluent ones (Table 3.1). For example, the most disadvantaged neighbourhood in Peterborough (Central) was the third most deprived neighbourhood in the east of England (out of 1,192 wards), and the 99th most deprived in the country. There is, with one exception (Central), a close relationship between level of disadvantage and per cent local authority housing (Figure 3.1). Central has the highest disadvantage score but only around 10 per cent of its residents living in local authority housing.

We interpret our findings as being broadly concordant with extant criminological research from a wide range of other research locations. As Farrington (2002a: 659) has noted 'Many risk factors for offending

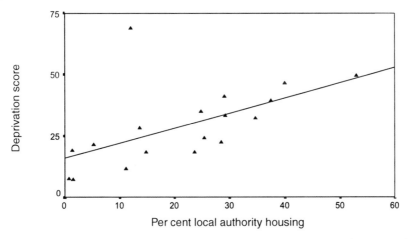

Figure 3.1. Scattergram of deprivation score by per cent living in local authority housing in Peterborough urban area

are well established and highly replicable' (see also Farrington, 2000: 4–6). The PYS utilises a number of variables (e.g. parental monitoring, family and school bonds, self-control, etc.) which have previously been shown to be associated with an increased risk of offending in a variety of other research locations. These findings have been replicated in Peterborough and, we hope, their theoretical consideration advanced. However, we see no reason why the model developed should be specific to Peterborough and indeed many of the relevant findings of this study have already been replicated in such diverse places as Reykjavik, Iceland (Olafsson 2004), Cardiff, Wales (Boxford 2003) and Macau, China (Ma 2006).

Classifying neighbourhood contexts

To analyse the role of the neighbourhood context two different measures were created, 1) one based on the neighbourhood IMD score and 2) one based on enumeration districts classified by a factor analysis of selected census variables. Both the measures were then also grouped into broader classes of neighbourhoods and enumeration districts.

It is acknowledged that the data available to classify neighbourhood contexts are far from ideal. In relation to psychometrics, the measurement of community contexts (what has been called ecometrics; see Raudenbush and Sampson 1999) is particularly underdeveloped. In the longer term, a primary aim of the research in Peterborough is to advance our ability to measure relevant aspects of the community context (currently being undertaken by the ongoing PADS study). For this study, however, we have had to settle for a summary measure of community context based on neighbourhood IMD scores or 1991 census data.

Neighbourhoods by IMD scores

The deprivation score (IMD; the Index of Multiple Deprivation 2000) is a summary measure of income deprivation, employment deprivation, health and disability, education, housing and geographical access to services (see Cambridgeshire City Council, 2000). These dimensions are differently weighted, with income and employment having the highest weights (each 25 per cent), and housing and geographical access to services having the lowest weights (each 10 per cent). For this study the IMD will be used as a measure of neighbourhood deprivation. The deprivation score strongly correlates with the neighbourhood rate of police-recorded offenders of all ages (Table 3.1; $r. = 0.86$).

In the IMD-based analysis of neighbourhood context we have included the Peterborough urban area and four nearby villages (Glinton, Yaxley, Farcet and Eye). In the questionnaire study, the subjects were asked to indicate the name of the street where they lived and the name of their neighbourhood. On the basis of this information each subject was located to an enumeration district (ED) in the Peterborough urban area, or to any of the four included villages or, if not living in any of these areas, to an 'other' category (Table 3.2). For the IMD-based neighbourhood context analysis the EDs were aggregated to neighbourhoods (IMD scores were not available at a lower level of aggregation than wards). Most subjects were living in the Peterborough urban area or one of the four nearby villages (91 per cent). Those living outside these areas have been excluded from the IMD-based analyses of neighbourhood context (Table 3.2).

For use in cross-tabular analysis, the neighbourhoods were divided into five classes of neighbourhood disadvantage (Table 3.2). It is acknowledged that the demarcation between the classes is somewhat arbitrary although they should reflect general differences in levels of disadvantage.

Enumeration districts by 1991 census data

In addition to the ward-level IMD scores, the Peterborough enumeration districts (EDs) were analysed using 1991 census data. The obvious advantage of the EDs is that they are a much smaller unit than wards (average population of about 500 inhabitants). The obvious disadvantage with the census data is that they are about ten years old (i.e. they refer to the point in time when the subjects were about 4–5 years old). The degree to which the census data will describe the current situation is dependent on how much change has taken place in the ED characteristics over the last ten years. Fortunately, the rapid population growth that took place in Peterborough in the 1970s and 1980s halted in the 1990s. Even so, it is likely that there have been some changes (for example, in demographic characteristics).

All in all, 286 enumeration districts were analysed. EDs with fewer than 100 inhabitants were excluded. Selected variables referring to household and tenure characteristics were included.

23

Table 3.2 Number of subjects in study by their neighbourhood of residence, disadvantage class, disadvantage score range and number of subjects in each disadvantage class

Neighbourhood	Number of subjects	Disadvantage class (score)	N
Central	119	4 (68.9)	119
Dogsthorpe	97	3 (39.3–49.6)	328
Ravensthorpe	84		
East	90		
North	57		
Orton Longueville	154	2 (28.2–34.8)	436
North Bretton	104		
Paston	102		
Fletton	76		
Walton	72	1 (15.7–24.2)	545
Stanground	113		
South	26		
Orton Waterville	125		
Park	80		
South Bretton	70		
Eye	36		
Farcet	23		
Werrington North	118	0 (6.2–11.6)	348
Werrington South	83		
West	68		
Yaxley	60		
Glinton	19		
Not included areas	181		
Total	1957		1,776

A factor analysis (oblique rotation) was performed. It resulted in three factors with an eigenvalue above 1 (Table 3.3). The first factor was labelled 'family disruption' with its highest loading for single parents followed by per cent households with children. The second factor was labelled 'ethnic minorities' with the highest loading on minority followed by crowded living conditions. The third factor was labelled 'high socio-economic status' with a high (positive) loading for per cent households with upper/upper middle class occupations and a high (negative) loading for per cent households with lower working-class occupations. The factor analysis also revealed close links between household characteristics and area dominating type of tenure. Family disruption tends to be highest in local authority (council) housing areas and lowest in owner-occupied housing areas, while ethnic minorities tend to live in rented accommodation. Not unexpectedly, high socioeconomic status tended to be found in areas of owner-occupied housing. Factor 3 (high socioeconomic status) was moderately negatively correlated to factor 1 (family disruption), while factor 2 (ethnic minorities) did not show any correlation to the other two factors.

Table 3.3 Factor analysis (oblique rotation) of selected key census variables: Peterborough enumeration districts (N = 286)

Variable	Factor 1 family disruption	Factor 2 ethnic minority	Factor 3 high socio-economic status	h^2
Per cent households				
Low SES occupations*	0.23	0.16	<u>–0.86</u>	0.75
High SES occupations**	–0.32	–0.15	<u>0.86</u>	0.75
Minority	0.24	<u>0.87</u>	–0.17	0.81
Single parents ***	<u>0.90</u>	0.04	<u>–0.40</u>	0.83
Children	<u>0.78</u>	0.37	–0.04	0.78
Crowded	0.24	<u>0.80</u>	–0.17	0.70
Tenure				
Rented	–0.24	<u>0.60</u>	–0.01	0.43
Owner-occupied	<u>–0.76</u>	0.15	<u>0.60</u>	0.77
Council	<u>0.81</u>	–0.30	<u>–0.59</u>	0.89
Eigenvalue	3.6	2.0	1.1	
Explained variance	39.6	22.3	12.7	

Notes:
Inter-factor correlations: F1 and F2 = 0.03; F2 and F3 = –0.04; F1 and F3 = –0.31.
Coefficients 0.40 and higher are underlined.
 * Unskilled and partly skilled occupations.
 ** Professional, managerial, etc., occupations.
*** Of all parents.

Factor scores were computed for each of the three factors. Enumeration districts were then grouped into classes by their factor scores for use in table analyses (see Chapter 7). Only EDs located in the Peterborough urban area were included in the classification (i.e. the four villages included in the IMD score classification were excluded).

Chapter 4

Involvement in crime and substance use

The main purpose of this chapter is to give a detailed account of Peterborough boys' and girls' involvement in crime (either as offenders or victims) and their substance use (i.e. alcohol use and use of controlled drugs). In subsequent chapters we will address how their offending and victimisation relate to their family social position, their individual characteristics (disposition and social situation), their community context (area of residence and school) and their lifestyles (routines). Substance use will be introduced as one dimension of life-style risk in Chapter 8.

Offending

More than one third have committed a crime

This study does not include all possible crimes that a juvenile may commit. Rather, we have focused the questions on some key property crimes, vandalism and assault (the specific wording of the offending questions can be found in Appendix A). We have predominantly included property crimes of a more serious nature: burglaries, thefts of and from cars and robberies (theft from persons including threats of violence). Only one type of minor property crime has been included, and that is shoplifting.

We have, for example, not included in the questionnaire questions on theft from a person (other than as a robbery), handling (of stolen goods) or crimes of fraud. Neither are questions on sexual or traffic crimes included. All questions refer to events that happened during the year 2000 (i.e. cover a one-year time period). With these restrictions in mind, we can turn to the findings (Table 4.1).

- More than one third have committed a crime.
- The majority of those who have offended have offended more than once.
- Almost one in ten has committed six or more crimes.
- One in fifteen has committed a serious crime of theft (burglary, theft from or of a car, or robbery).
- One in four has assaulted someone.

The offenders have on average committed four crimes (lambda), although this is likely to be an underestimate as we have only counted a maximum of six crimes for each crime type (see the notes to Table 4.1).

Table 4.1 Self-reported offending, prevalence and lambda

	Prevalence*	Prevalence by number of crimes**						Lambda***
		1	2	3	4	5	6+	
Shoplifting	13.9	5.8	2.3	1.5	0.6	0.8	3.0	2.8
Non-residential Burglary	3.1	2.0	0.5	0.3	0.2	0.1	0.1	1.7
Residential burglary	1.3	0.9	0.4	0.1	–	–	0.1	1.5
Thefts of or from cars	3.2	1.7	0.3	0.2	0.1	0.4	0.5	2.6
Robbery	1.4	0.8	0.3	0.1	0.1	0.1	0.1	1.9
Vandalism	17.0	7.0	3.4	1.6	1.3	1.0	2.6	2.6
Assault	24.0	11.4	5.8	2.8	1.2	0.9	1.9	2.1
Serious theft****	6.8	3.5	1.3	0.4	0.4	0.4	0.8	3.0
All crimes	37.7	12.1	7.2	4.4	1.8	2.6	9.4	4.1

Notes:
* Per cent of all juveniles who have committed the crime.
** Per cent of all juveniles who have committed the crime once, twice, etc.
*** Average crimes per offender. Lambda is underestimated. The maximum count for separate categories of crimes is 6 (i.e. reports of 6 or more crimes are all counted as 6). For 'all crimes' the maximum count of crime is 42 (i.e. 7 categories times 6).
**** Burglary, thefts of and from cars and robbery combined.

Many assaults take place at the offender's school

Follow-up questions to the assault, robbery and vandalism questions asked the subject to detail where the last crime was committed. A large number of assaults took place in the subjects' own school (40.3 per cent), followed by outdoor places in their own neighbourhood (19.9 per cent) or outdoor places elsewhere (10.7 per cent). Robbery is a quite uncommon crime (only 27 juveniles admitted to a robbery), so the figures for distribution by place have to be viewed with some caution. About one fifth of the robberies were committed outdoors in the offender's neighbourhood, another fifth outdoors elsewhere and yet another fifth in indoor public places like a shopping-mall, pub or disco. Cases of vandalism were predominantly committed outdoors in the offender's neighbourhood (36 per cent) or outdoors elsewhere (26.5 per cent).

A lot of crimes of serious theft are committed in the offenders' neighbourhoods

The follow-up questions on property crimes were less detailed. Basically, the subject was asked whether the crime took place in his or her neighbourhood or not. Quite a high proportion of the more serious crimes of theft took place in the offenders' neighbourhoods, and that is particularly so for residential burglaries. The proportion occurring in the offender's own neighbourhood was 73.1 per cent for residential burglary, 41.7 per cent for non-residential burglary, 37.1 per cent for thefts from or of cars and 15.0 per cent for shoplifting.

In every eighth crime, the offender was reported to or caught by the police

Another follow-up question concerned whether the offenders were caught by or reported to the police. The question again referred to the last event. With the exception of a somewhat higher proportion for residential burglary (35 per cent), the rate caught by or reported to the police varied between 7 and 15 per cent (see Figure 4.1).

On average, every eighth offender was reported to or caught by the police for his or her last committed crime, and therefore the overall detection risk can be conservatively estimated to about 10 per cent. This implies (assuming a uniform detection risk) that high-frequency offenders will sooner or later be reported to or caught by the police, and therefore the police are likely to have knowledge of most high-frequency adolescent offenders.

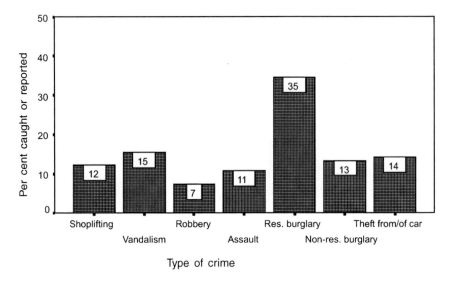

Figure 4.1 Per cent caught by or reported to the police by type of crime

Girls also commit a lot of crime

Boys commit more crimes than girls (44.8 per cent for boys v. 30.6 per cent for girls), with the exception of shoplifting (Table 4.2). Boys are clearly more involved in serious theft, assault and vandalism, roughly twice as much as girls. The average rates of offending are not that different for boys and girls who offend. The mean rate of crime for boys who offend was 4.5 compared with 3.6 for girls. However, of all boys there are about twice as many (12.3 per cent) as girls (6.7 per cent) who have committed six or more crimes, so boys make up a larger proportion than girls of the high-frequency offenders. Although boys tend to commit more crimes than girls, gender explains only 2 per cent of the variation in overall offending and just 1 per cent of the variation in serious theft.

Frequent juvenile offenders tend to commit many different types of crime

The findings presented in Tables 4.1 and 4.2 reveal that most of those who have committed a crime have committed more than one crime. This holds for both males and females. The findings presented in Table 4.3 show that there are significant relationships between committing one type of crime and committing other types of crime. A factor

Table 4.2 Self-reported offending, prevalence and lambda, by gender

	Prevalence*	Prevalence by number of crimes**						Lambda***
		1	2	3	4	5	6+	
Males								
Shoplifting	11.8	4.7	1.5	1.5	0.2	0.2	3.5	3.0
Non-residential burglary	4.8	2.9	0.7	0.6	0.4	–	0.1	1.8
Residential burglary	2.2	1.2	0.7	0.1	–	–	0.1	1.7
Thefts of and from cars	4.5	2.4	0.3	0.3	–	0.5	0.9	2.7
Robbery	2.5	1.4	0.5	0.1	0.1	0.1	0.2	6.0
Vandalism	22.7	9.4	3.7	2.1	1.5	1.4	4.5	2.8
Assault	32.2	14.2	8.3	4.0	1.7	1.2	2.9	2.3
Serious Theft****	9.8	4.8	1.7	0.6	0.6	0.5	1.6	3.0
All Crimes	44.8	14.0	8.7	4.7	2.0	3.1	12.3	4.5
Females								
Shoplifting	16.1	6.9	3.1	1.4	0.9	1.5	2.4	2.6
Non-residential burglary	1.5	1.0	0.3	–	–	0.1	–	1.5
Residential burglary	0.5	0.5	–	–	–	–	–	1.0
Thefts of and from cars	2.0	1.0	0.3	0.1	0.2	0.2	0.1	2.3
Robbery	0.3	0.2	0.1	–	–	–	–	1.3
Vandalism	11.3	4.7	3.0	1.1	1.1	0.6	0.7	2.3
Assault	15.7	8.6	3.3	1.6	0.7	0.5	0.9	2.0
Serious theft****	3.8	2.1	0.8	0.2	0.2	0.2	0.2	2.0
All crimes	30.6	10.2	5.8	4.0	1.7	2.2	6.7	3.6

Notes:
* Per cent of all juveniles who have committed the crime.
** Per cent of all juveniles who have committed the crime once, twice, etc.
*** Average crimes per offender. Lambda is underestimated. The maximum count of crimes reported by subjects is 6 (i.e. reports of 6 or more crimes are all counted as 6). For 'all crimes' the maximum count of crime is 42 (i.e. 7 categories times 6).
**** Burglary, thefts of and from cars and robbery combined.

analysis of the patterns of relationships between crime types resulted in two factors (Table 4.4), one that may be labelled 'common crime', defined by shoplifting, assault and vandalism (factor 1), and one that picks out crimes of serious theft (factor 2). As may be expected the two factors are correlated ($r. = 0.30$). What all this means is that not

Table 4.3 Zero-order correlations: frequencies of offending categories

	Shop-lifting	Burglary		Thefts of/from cars	Robbery	Vandalism	Assault
		Non-residential	Resi-dential				
Shoplifting	1.00						
Non-residential burglary	0.21	1.00					
Residential burglary	0.12	0.27	1.00				
Thefts of/from cars	0.24	0.31	0.39	1.00			
Robbery	0.09	0.15	0.37	0.26	1.00		
Vandalism	0.33	0.33	0.22	0.34	0.14	1.00	
Assault	0.25	0.18	0.18	0.26	0.18	0.40	1.00

Note:
All correlations significant on 0.01 level or better; n = 1,898; missing = 59.

Table 4.4 Factor analysis (oblique rotation): frequencies of offending categories

Crime categories	Factor 1 (common crimes)	Factor 2 (crimes of serious theft)	h^2
Shoplifting	<u>0.68</u>	0.07	0.49
Non-residential burglary	<u>0.53</u>	<u>0.41</u>	0.35
Residential burglary	0.26	<u>0.81</u>	0.66
Thefts of/from cars	<u>0.53</u>	<u>0.61</u>	0.50
Robbery	0.12	<u>0.76</u>	0.59
Vandalism	<u>0.78</u>	0.24	0.62
Assault	<u>0.66</u>	0.22	0.44
Eigenvalue	2.5	1.1	
Explained variance	35.9	16.2	
Inter-factor correlation: 0.30			

Note:
n = 1,898; missing = 59.

only do those who commit serious theft tend to commit different kinds of serious theft but also what here are called common crimes, while there is another group of offenders who tend to commit common crimes only. The findings also show that the latter group (common crimes only) is larger than the group that also commits serious crimes of theft. Cross-tabulating the two categories shows that 31 per cent of all juveniles have committed common crimes only (one or more of shoplifting, assault and vandalism), while 6 per cent have committed both (at least one) common crime and (at least one) serious theft. Fewer than 1 per cent of all juveniles have committed only serious thefts.

The more crimes a juvenile has committed the more likely his or her crimes will also involve serious crimes of theft (Figure 4.2). More generally, there is a clear tendency that the more crime a juvenile commits the more different types of crime he or she has committed (Figure 4.3). Obviously, if an offender has committed less than seven crimes there is a restriction in the possible number of types of crime committed. However, this fact does not alter the conclusion that, with an increasing number of crimes committed, there is also an increase in the number of different types of crime committed. The significance of this is that high-frequency offenders tend to be versatile rather than

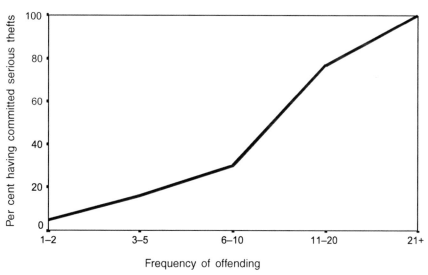

Figure 4.2 Per cent having committed serious thefts by frequency of offending

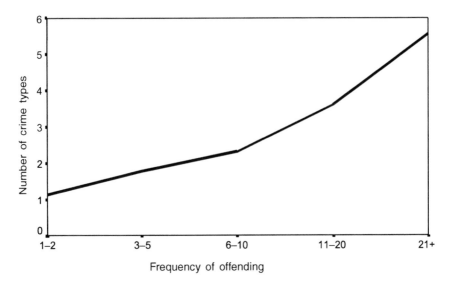

Figure 4.3 Mean number of different types of crime committed by frequency of offending

specialised, and that prevention policies targeting high-rate offenders rather than specific types of crime may be more effective.

Victimisation

Half of the juveniles have experienced victimisation

In contrast to the offending questions regarding theft, the victimisation questions only include one broad question on theft. It refers to theft directed against the subject's property only and has no restriction as to type of theft. This means, among other things, that it will include some minor types of theft not covered in the questions on offending. The questions regarding vandalism and violence are more directly comparable with the offending questions, although there are no separate questions for assault and robbery. As with the offending questions, not all types of crimes are covered in the victimisation questions. For example, no questions were asked about victimisation for sexual crimes. The follow-up questions to the victimisation questions, in particular for violence, were more detailed than the follow-up questions regarding offending. All questions refer to incidences of victimisation that took place in the year 2000. The findings show (Table 4.5):

- Half of the juveniles have been the victim of a crime.
- Of those victimised, most have been victimised more than once (65 per cent).
- Theft victimisation is the most prevalent (almost one third), followed by violence victimisation (one quarter) and vandalism victimisation (one tenth).

Table 4.5 Self-reported victimisation: prevalence and lambda

	Prevalence*	Prevalence by number of victimisations**						Lambda***
		1	2	3	4	5	6+	
Theft	31.9	15.1	8.0	3.1	0.9	1.5	1.4	1.9
Vandalism	10.7	5.6	2.5	1.2	0.3	0.2	0.2	1.6
Violence	25.7	11.9	5.1	2.0	1.3	0.7	2.8	2.1
All victimisations	48.8	16.9	10.5	5.9	1.8	3.7	2.9	2.7

Notes:
 * Per cent of all juveniles who have been victimised.
 ** Per cent of all juveniles who have been victimised once, twice, etc.
*** Average victimisation per victim. Lambda is underestimated. The maximum count for separate categories of victimisation is 6 (i.e. reports of 6 or more victimisations are all counted as 6). For 'all victimisations' the maximum count of victimisations is 18 (i.e. 3 categories times 6).

One in three boys has been assaulted

Boys have been victimised more often than girls (Table 4.6). The difference is particularly large for violence. Among those victimised the majority of boys (68 per cent) and girls (61 per cent) have suffered multiple victimisations. However, the boys make up almost twice as many as the girls among the small group with a larger number of victimisations (6 or more).

Four out of ten victims have been victimised in their school

The place where juveniles are most likely to suffer a victimisation is in their own school (Table 4.7). Four out of ten of the victims have been victimised, at least once, in their school. However, the chance of being victimised in one's own school varies by school. Depending

Table 4.6 Self-reported victimisation: prevalence and lambda by gender

	Prevalence*	Prevalence by number of crimes**						Lambda***
		1	2	3	4	5	6+	
Males								
Theft	38.2	17.1	10.1	3.9	0.8	1.6	1.9	1.9
Vandalism	12.1	6.0	3.1	1.1	0.1	0.3	0.3	2.1
Violence	33.8	15.2	6.8	2.7	1.4	1.0	3.9	2.1
All victimisations	58.9	18.8	12.7	7.2	4.8	3.5	8.1	2.8
Females								
Theft	25.5	13.1	5.9	2.4	0.9	1.4	0.9	1.9
Vandalism	9.3	5.1	1.8	1.2	0.5	0.1	–	2.0
Violence	17.5	8.5	3.3	1.3	1.1	0.4	1.6	2.0
All victimisations	38.5	15.0	8.2	4.6	2.7	2.3	4.4	2.6

Notes:

 * Per cent of all juveniles who have been victimised.

 ** Per cent of all juveniles who have been victimised once, twice, etc.

 *** Average victimisation per victim. Lambda is underestimated. The maximum count for separate categories of victimisation is 6 (i.e. reports of 6 or more victimisations are all counted as 6). For 'all victimisations' the maximum count of victimisations is 18 (i.e. 3 categories times 6).

on the school, between 7 and 33 per cent of the (Year 10) pupils have been victimised in their school (see further Table 7.11). Note that the percentages for the schools refer to 'out of all pupils', not only out of the victims.

The next two most likely places to be victimised are in the home or outdoors in their neighbourhood. A question to be raised here, given the relative high percentage of victims having been victims of theft (and vandalism) in their home, is to what degree this reflects general victimisation of their family (for instance, burglaries in which also some of the subject's property was stolen). Looking into what property they have reported being stolen from their home, bicycles rank first (26.3 per cent), followed by money (14 per cent), jewellery (12.3 per cent) computer games (10.5 per cent) and electronic equipment like PCs and CD-players (8.8 per cent). This makes it likely that theft victimisations at home are predominantly thefts of bicycles left outside their residence and burglaries of the family home where

Table 4.7 Where did the victimisation (last time) take place? (Percentages)

Place	Theft	Vandalism	Violence	Total*
In my home	21.2	30.6	10.3	14.3
In other's home	4.4	5.3	2.6	2.7
In my school	42.4	45.1	35.4	39.1
In a pub, disco or club	3.2	1.0	5.9	3.7
Shopping centre/mall	3.6	1.0	3.4	3.7
Other indoor place	2.0	0.5	1.8	1.6
Outdoors in my neighbourhood	6.1	8.3	17.0	11.8
Outdoors other place	5.9	4.4	11.7	9.7
Other	11.2	3.9	11.9	13.4
Total	100.0	100.0	100.0	100.0
n	590	206	495	1,032

Note:

* The same person may have been the victim of several types of crime and therefore the *n* in the total column is less than the *n*'s for the three crime categories summarised.

some of the subject's property may have been among that stolen. However, it cannot be excluded that some youths have reported theft victimisations at home directed more generally towards the subject's household rather than specifically at his or her property. It is also possible that some of the thefts at home represent thefts by visitors to the home. The theft victimisation question specifically asked the subjects not to report thefts by their siblings.

In one out of nine thefts the object stolen was a mobile telephone

Those victimised were asked to specify what objects they had stolen. In case they mentioned more than one object the one judged most valuable has been coded. Overall the most common objects stolen were bicycles, followed by money and school equipment. But also mobile telephones rank high on the list of stolen goods (Table 4.8). We have already listed the most stolen objects at the victim's home. In schools (the most common place to be victimised), the list of stolen objects, not surprisingly, is topped by school equipment like calculators and pencil cases (28.6 per cent). Although these may be regarded as minor acts of theft, most of the items stolen in school represent high values. For example, almost one quarter of the thefts involved money (23.7 per cent) followed by thefts of mobile telephones (10.4 per cent) and jewellery/watches (8.3 per cent).

Table 4.8 Main object stolen (last time) in rank order (per cent)

Object	%
Bicycle	17.7
Money	17.5
School equipment*	12.9
Mobile telephone	11.5
Jewellery/watch	7.4
Item of clothing/shoes	5.5
Wallet/purse	5.2
Electronics (e.g. PC, TV, CD)	5.0
Computer games/game sticks	3.4
Records, videos, books, etc.	2.7
Bag/handbag	2.6
Cigarettes/lighters	1.9
Sport equipment**	1.5
Motor vehicle (e.g. moped)	1.2
Alcohol/drugs	0.5
Keys	0.3
Other	0.9
	100.0

Notes:

$n = 582$; missing cases = 8.

When several objects have been stolen the estimated most valuable has been coded.

*For example, pencil case or calculator.

**For example, football or skateboard.

Theft outdoors in the subject's neighbourhood was dominated by theft of bicycles (52.8 per cent). The three most popular objects to steal in pubs, discos and clubs were mobile telephones (22 per cent), money (16.7 per cent) and handbags (11.1 per cent).

In one out of six cases of violence a weapon was used

The question on violence victimisations had a range of follow-up questions (Table 4.9). One concerned whether a weapon was used. Most violence involved only hands and fists, but a significant proportion also included a weapon (16.7 per cent), most commonly

Table 4.9 Selected key characteristics of violent victimisations: weapon use, injuries and offender characteristics

Incident characteristics	%	
Weapon use		
No weapon used	83.3	
Weapon used	16.7	
Thereof		
Knife	3.9	
Other sharp instrument *	1.8	
Blunt instrument **	5.5	
Other	5.5	
Total	100.0	*n* = 492, missing cases = 3
Injuries		
No injuries/pain	56.0	
Bruises, marks, etc., that did not require treatment by a doctor	37.4	
Serious injuries needing treatment***	6.6	
Total	100.0	*n* = 487, missing cases = 8
Offender characteristics		
Youth(s) from my school	47.2	
Youth(s) I know, but not from my school	15.2	
Youth(s) not from my school and not known to me	22.8	
An adult I know	9.7	
An adult I don't know	5.1	
Total	100.0	*n* = 487, missing cases = 8

Notes:
  * For example, broken bottle or razor.
 ** For example, a piece of wood or an iron bar.
*** For example, wounds or broken limbs needing hospital or doctor's treatment.

a blunt instrument (like a baseball bat or an iron bar). Most of the weapons used in the other category, as specified by the subject, could also be classified as blunt instruments (for example, belts and bricks). In no case has the use of firearms been reported.

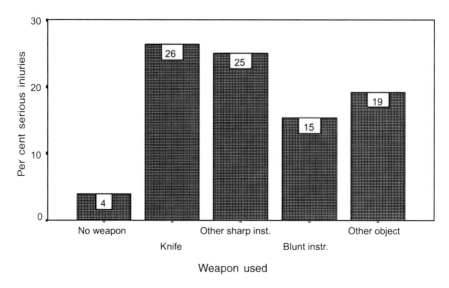

Figure 4.4 Per cent serious injuries by weapon use

In every fifteenth case the victim of violence received serious injuries

Most injuries were of a less serious nature, involving pain alone (Table 4.9). However, in a smaller number of cases (6.6 per cent) the victim needed medical treatment. There is, as expected, a relationship between weapon use and injury (gamma = 0.52). The percentage of serious injuries is highest when knives and other sharp instruments have been used (Figure 4.4).

Nearly half of the violent offenders were youths from the victim's school

Most of the juveniles who have been subjected to violence have been assaulted by other youths (85.2 per cent) and by someone they know, predominantly another youth from their school (Table 4.9). However, in a smaller number of cases the offender was an adult, predominantly an adult the subject knows (9.7 per cent). The question is whether or not this reflects parents using violence against their children. There is no way to know this for certain from the answers to the questionnaires. However, of the cases where an adult known to the subject was the offender, 70 per cent took place in the subject's home. In most of these cases the victim was female (76 per cent). Of the cases where the offender was a known adult and it occurred in the subject's home, almost all (boys and girls) reported to have been punished by their parents during the last year (96.9 per cent), in most cases many times (54.5 per cent, as compared with 16.9 per cent for all subjects). If these cases reflect parents' use of violence against their children, about 2 per cent of all juveniles have been subjected to parental violence. However, we can of course not exclude that some of these cases may have been committed by other adults (adult relatives or visitors to their home), so the figures must be treated with caution as an estimate of parental violence.

Offenders tend to be victimised more often than non-offenders

The risk of being a victim of crime is much higher for juveniles who offend themselves. The overall correlation between being an offender and being a victim is (phi) 0.32 for prevalence, and (r.) 0.35 for frequency (Table 4.10). The mean rate of victimisation appears to be particularly high for high-frequency offenders (Figure 4.5). Looking at particular categories of crime (Table 4.10), the strongest relationship is between having committed an act of violence and being a victim of violence (prevalence, phi = 0.37; frequency, r. = 0.34). The relationships between having committed a theft and being a victim of theft, and of having committed an act of vandalism and being a victim of vandalism, are significant but less strong (Table 4.10).

Substance use

In the study, questions were asked about alcohol use, use of cannabis and other drugs, and use of inhalants. All questions referred to the last year (i.e. the year 2000). The question referring to alcohol use concerned having been drunk. Therefore it is a question about heavier drinking rather than just having a glass of beer or wine. The question about cannabis use asked whether the subject had tried marijuana or hashish (grass, pot), while the question on other drugs (which will be referred to as hard drugs in this study) covered drugs like amphetamine (speed), LSD (acid), ecstasy, heroine, cocaine (coke) or crack. Finally, there was a question on the use of inhalants such as glue, gas or aerosol spray (see Appendix A). Given the nature of substance use, it was not deemed feasible to ask about the absolute number of times used; rather, we gave the subject categories of frequency ranges to choose from.

Table 4.10 Per cent offenders also victimised, by crime type and total

Combinations	%	Significance	Phi	r. *
Victimised by theft				
Shoplifters	46.5			
Others	29.6	0.000	0.13	0.09
Offenders of serious theft	56.2			
Others	29.9	0.000	0.14	0.16
Victimised by vandalism				
Vandalism offenders	19.5			
Others	8.8	0.000	0.13	0.11
Victimised by violence				
Violent offenders	54.7			
Others	16.5	0.000	0.37	0.34
All victimisations				
Offenders	69.2			
Non-offenders	36.2	0.000	0.32	0.35

Note:
*Calculated on frequency of offending and victimisation.

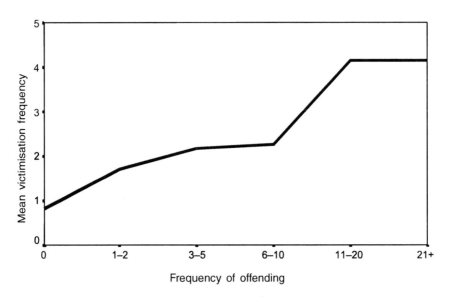

Figure 4.5 Mean frequency of overall victimisations by frequency of offending

One in eight has used inhalants

Being drunk on alcohol is a very common experience among the juveniles (63.7 per cent) and as many as over a fifth of them have been drunk six times or more (Table 4.11). Also, cannabis use is quite common (22 per cent), and it should be noted that as many as one in eight (11.8 per cent) has tried inhalants. The use of hard drugs is more restricted (6.7 per cent).

Table 4.11 Self-reported alcohol, drugs and inhalants use

	Prevalence*	Prevalence of number of times used**		
		1–2	3–5	6+
Alcohol (drunk)	63.7	24.1	18.4	21.2
Cannabis	22.0	10.2	4.5	7.3
Hard drugs	6.7	4.3	0.8	1.7
Inhalants (glue, etc.)	11.8	8.2	1.8	1.8
All substance use	66.8			

Notes:
 * Per cent of all juveniles who have used the substance.
 ** Per cent of all juveniles who have used once and twice, three to five times, etc.

Girls are drunk and use drugs as much as boys

Girls tend to use substances at the same rate as boys (Table 4.12). Considering different types of substances, girls have a marginally higher use of hard drugs and inhalants, while boys have a marginally higher use of alcohol (being drunk) and cannabis. The differences are, however, not very big. This also holds if one considers the groups of high frequency users (six or more times) in which the boys' rate is only 1 per cent or less higher than that for the girls. All gender differences in substance use were non-significant at the 10 per cent level.

Those who frequently use one substance also tend to use others

There are rather strong correlations between the frequency of use of different types of substances, particularly between the frequency of use of alcohol (being drunk) and cannabis, but also between the

Table 4.12 Self-reported alcohol, drugs and inhalants use by gender

	Prevalence*	Prevalence of number of times used**		
		1–2	3–5	6+
Males				
Alcohol (drunk)	65.0	26.1	17.2	21.7
Cannabis	23.9	11.1	5.2	7.7
Hard drugs	5.9	3.7	0.5	1.7
Inhalants (glue, etc.)	10.8	6.9	1.8	2.2
All substance use	69.7			
Females				
Alcohol (drunk)	62.3	22.0	19.6	20.7
Cannabis	20.1	9.4	3.7	6.9
Hard drugs	7.5	4.9	1.0	1.7
Inhalants (glue, etc.)	12.7	9.4	1.9	1.4
All substance use	63.9			

Notes:
* Per cent of all juveniles who have used the substance.
** Per cent of all juveniles who have used once and twice, three to five times, etc.

Table 4.13 Zero-order correlations: frequencies of substance use categories

	Alcohol (drunk)	Cannabis	Hard drugs	Inhalants
Alcohol (drunk)	1.00			
Cannabis	0.47	1.00		
Hard drugs	0.21	0.40	1.00	
Inhalants	0.28	0.42	0.45	1.00

Note:
All correlations significant at 0.01 level or better.

frequencies of use of cannabis, hard drugs and inhalants (Table 4.13). Of those who have been drunk six times or more, more than half have used cannabis, almost a third have used inhalants and one fifth have used hard drugs. Of those who have used cannabis six times or more, nearly half have used inhalants and more than a third have used hard drugs. Of those who have used inhalants six times or more, over half have also used hard drugs (Table 4.14).

High frequency substance users tend to be involved in crime more often than others

Those who have used any substance tend to be more often involved in crime than others, particularly as offenders (Figure 4.6). Looking into the relationship between frequency of use of different types of substances and offending by major types of crime shows an increase in offending by increased substance use (Figures 4.7–4.10).

Cannabis use has the strongest relationship to frequency of aggressive offending

Considering aggressive offending (assault and vandalism combined, the individual patterns for the two were very similar), there is a continuous increase for alcohol use; the more often the juvenile has been drunk the more likely he or she is to have been involved in an aggressive crime (Figure 4.7). For other substances (narcotics and inhalants) the main difference in aggressive offending is between those who never have used and those who have used (Figures 4.8–4.10). It is of particular interest to point out that the relationship between the frequency of aggressive offending and the *frequency* of cannabis use (eta^2 = 0.16) is even somewhat stronger that that of the frequency of having been drunk (eta^2 = 0.14), and much stronger than that of the use of hard drugs (eta^2 = 0.03) and inhalant use (eta^2 = 0.03). However, as already mentioned, the main dividing line for the cannabis users' frequency of aggressive offending is between those who have, and those who have not used, which is well illustrated by the relationship of the *prevalence* of substance use to frequency of aggressive offending (cannabis, eta^2 = 0.15; compared with the much less strong impact of alcohol, eta^2 = 0.05; and even less strong impact of hard drugs, eta^2 = 0.03; and inhalant use, eta^2 = 0.02).

In other words, having used cannabis is a much better predictor of the youths' frequency of aggressive offending than having been drunk, while high-frequent alcohol use (being drunk) is a predictor of aggressive offending in parity to that of frequent use of cannabis. However, these data do not say anything about whether cannabis use instigates aggressive offending, or whether it is just a marker of a lifestyle related to aggressive offending.

Table 4.14 Use of other drugs by high-frequency users (six or more times) of alcohol (being drunk), cannabis and inhalants

Combination	%
High-frequent drunkenness*	
Used cannabis	57
Used inhalants	30
Used hard drugs	20
High-frequent cannabis use*	
Used inhalants	45
Used hard drugs	37
High-frequent use of inhalants*	
Used hard drugs	59

Note:
* Six times or more.

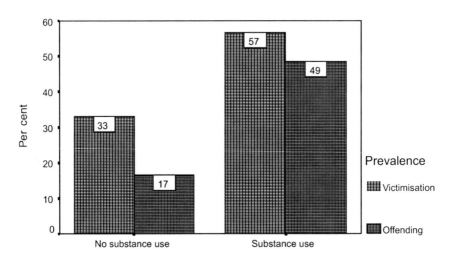

Figure 4.6 Overall prevalence of victimisation and offending by substance use

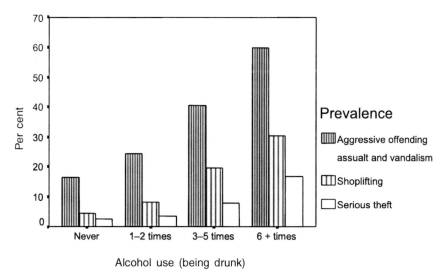

Figure 4.7 Main types of offending prevalence by frequency of alcohol use (being drunk)

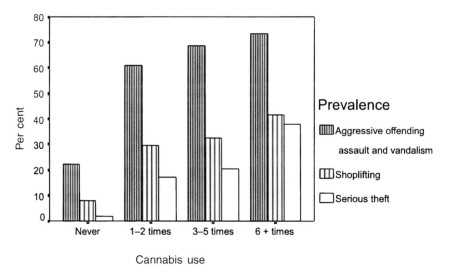

Figure 4.8 Main types of offending prevalence by frequency of cannabis use

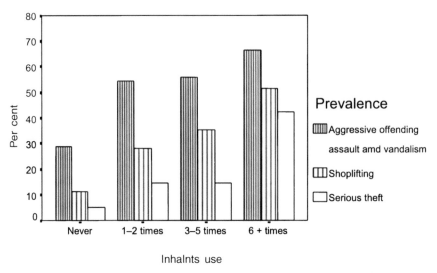

Figure 4.9 Main types of offending prevalence by frequency of inhalants use

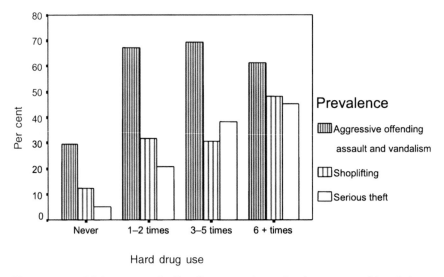

Figure 4.10 Main types of offending prevalence by frequency of hard drug use

Use of narcotic drugs is the strongest predictor of frequency of serious theft

The *frequency* of the use of narcotic drugs (hard drugs, eta² = 0.12; cannabis, eta² = 0.14) has a stronger influence on the frequency of serious theft than inhalant use (eta² = 0.09), and a much stronger influence than alcohol use (eta² = 0.03). As regards the frequency of shoplifting, the effects by different substances do not vary that much (hard drugs, eta² = 0.05; cannabis, eta² = 0.09; inhalants, eta² = 0.05; and alcohol use, eta² = 0.07). Considering *prevalence*, the relationship to frequency of shoplifting is stronger for use of narcotics (hard drugs, eta² = 0.04; cannabis, eta² = 0.08) and inhalants (eta² = 0.04) than alcohol (eta² = 0.03).

The same difference, but much stronger, holds for serious theft (hard drugs, eta² = 0.07; cannabis, eta² = 0.08; inhalants, eta² = 0.04; and alcohol, eta² = 0.01). These findings may, at least partly, reflect the need to get money to support, in particular, cannabis and hard drugs usage.

In this context, it should be recalled that there is an overlap between use of different substances, particularly for high-frequency users (of any kind of substance). For example, of the high-frequency users of alcohol (six times or more), one quarter (26 per cent) are also high frequency users of one or more of the three other studied substances (cannabis, inhalants and hard drugs).

Substance use is an equally important risk factor for offending for girls as for boys

Comparing the relationships between different types of substance use and offending by gender, the study shows that the relationships are as strong for girls as for boys (Table 4.15), although for a composite measure of substance use frequency the impact is stronger on boys' offending frequency (see Chapter 8). All in all, substance use, and in particular high-frequency use, is linked to a higher risk of offending both for boys and girls.

Substance use also increases the risk of victimisation

Generally, the risk of being a victim of crime is higher for those juveniles who use substances, particularly if they are frequent users. Alcohol use (being drunk) has the strongest relationship to the risk of being a victim of violence, but also the risk of vandalism victimisations and being subjected to theft increases with increasing frequency of having been drunk (Figure 4.11). It is no great surprise

Table 4.15 Substance use and offending by gender: probability value (chi-square), gamma coefficients and zero-order correlations

Combination	Males			Females		
	Prob-ability	Gamma	r.	Prob-ability	Gamma	r.
Aggressive offending *(assault and vandalism)*						
Alcohol use (drunk)	0.000	0.46	0.37	0.000	0.66	0.36
Cannabis use	0.000	0.63	0.35	0.000	0.80	0.48
Inhalants use	0.000	0.54	0.19	0.000	0.58	0.18
Hard drug use	0.000	0.49	0.09	0.000	0.77	0.31
Shoplifting						
Alcohol use (drunk)	0.000	0.52	0.23	0.000	0.62	0.28
Cannabis use	0.000	0.67	0.31	0.000	0.66	0.28
Inhalants use	0.000	0.57	0.25	0.000	0.57	0.19
Hard drug use	0.000	0.59	0.22	0.000	0.57	0.21
Serious theft						
Alcohol use (drunk)	0.000	0.48	0.16	0.000	0.78	0.18
Cannabis use	0.000	0.78	0.39	0.000	0.92	0.40
Inhalants use	0.000	0.62	0.34	0.000	0.61	0.19
Hard drug use	0.000	0.72	0.42	0.000	0.84	0.32

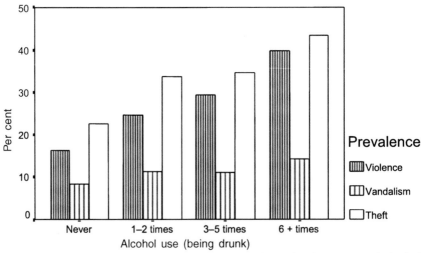

Figure 4.11 Main types of victimisation prevalence by frequency of alcohol use (being drunk)

that the link is strongest to violence victimisations since we already know that frequency of alcohol use is related to violent offending, and that being a violent offender also increases the risk of being a victim of violence.

For example, of those with a high frequency of having been drunk (six times or more), 28.1 per cent have been both a victim and an offender of violence, while 19.3 per cent have been a violent offender only, and 11.7 per cent a victim of violence only.

As was the case for violent offending, the strongest impact of cannabis use is on the risk of being a victim of violence. The vandalism risk shows no clear pattern, while the risk of being subjected to theft basically is somewhat higher for users (regardless of frequency) than for non-users (Figure 4.12). The relationship between inhalant use and victimisation shows a higher rate of violent and theft victimisations for high-frequency users (six times or more) and a somewhat lower risk for non-users. For vandalism there is an increase with frequency of use of inhalants (Figure 4.13). Finally, higher-frequency users of hard drugs (three to five times, and six or more times) have a higher risk of theft victimisations, the same holding for vandalism victimisations, while the pattern for violent victimisation is a bit more irregular (Figure 4.14). All in all, the main pattern is that high

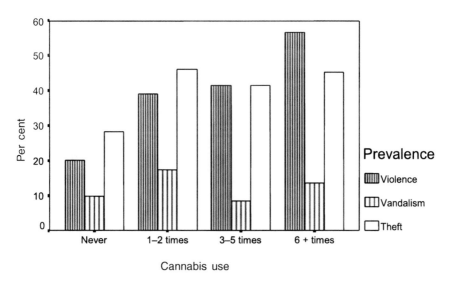

Figure 4.12 Main types of victimisation prevalence by frequency of cannabis use

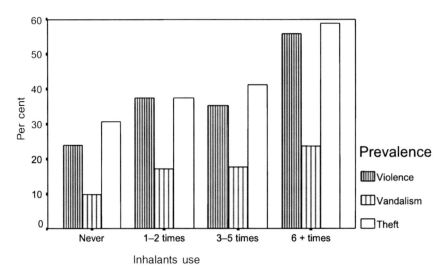

Figure 4.13 Main types of victimisation prevalence by frequency of inhalants use

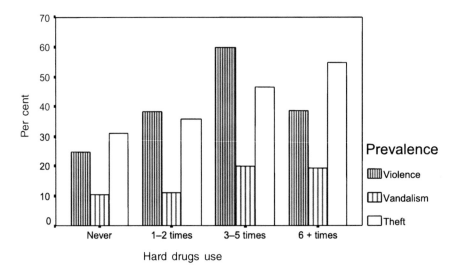

Figure 4.14 Main types of victimisation prevalence by frequency of hard drugs use

frequency substance users, just as they offend more than others, also tend to be more victimised than others.

This most likely reflects the inter-relationships between frequent substance use and the risk of getting involved in different types of crime, either as offender, victim or both. For example, of the substance users (any kind) 71.2 per cent have been either an offender or a victim of crime, while among those who haven't reported any substance use the corresponding figure is 39.1 per cent. Among the substance users, 34.1 per cent have been both an offender and a victim, while the corresponding figure among non-users was 10.5 per cent. These differences are even more significant if one considers high-frequency users compared with the rest.

Comparisons with the prevalence of offending in the 1992 and 1998–9 National Youth Studies

The question whether the prevalence of juvenile offending and substance use in Peterborough is high or low compared with other places in the UK is difficult, almost impossible, to answer. This is mainly due to the lack of comparable research on juvenile offending in UK cities (with some exceptions in the ongoing Edinburgh study from which some preliminary findings have been presented; see below). The first obvious points of comparison are the two national surveys from 1992 (Graham and Bowling 1995) and 1998–9 (Flood-Page et al. 2000). In making comparisons with these two studies, however, one has to be aware that:

- The national surveys cover a broader range of crimes than this study, particularly a broader range of more minor crimes (for example, handling of stolen goods and thefts from schools, phone boxes, etc.). Minor crimes are generally more prevalent than serious ones (all other things being equal, higher overall prevalence rates are therefore to be expected in the national surveys).

- The national surveys include both urban and rural areas. Comparing with an urban area like Peterborough, all other things being equal, one would therefore expect higher rates for Peterborough since crime is generally higher in urban areas.

- The 1992 national survey report does not give figures for directly comparable ages, the most comparable being that for the age group of 14–17-year-olds. Given that the overall prevalence rates for 16–17-years-olds are lower than that for 14–15-year-olds (as reported in the 1998–9 study), all other things being equal, one would expect some underestimation of the national rates when comparing the 1992 national figures for the ages of 14–17 with the Peterborough figures for the ages of 14–15.

- The national surveys have much lower response rates than this study. Both national surveys have a 69 per cent response rate,[1] compared with a 92 per cent response rate for the Peterborough study. Normally, non-responses tend to include a higher proportion of people with social problems of different kinds and, therefore, all other things equal, one would expect an underestimation of the national figures when compared with the Peterborough ones. However, this may be counteracted in the 1998–9 survey by the fact that a non-response weighting was applied (Flood-Page *et al.* 2000: 85), although the reliability of such non-response weighting is difficult to evaluate.

- The Peterborough study is more straightforward and, unlike the national surveys, does not include complex sampling and the related weighting of the data that may introduce biases to the findings. However, it is not possible to evaluate whether this fact has had any impact on the differences in findings.

- The Peterborough questionnaire study is self-completed and administered in a classroom setting (see Chapter 2), while the two national surveys were conducted as interviews during home visits (with self-completion on offending), and it is reported in both studies that the presence of others in some cases may have affected the responses (Graham and Bowling 1995: 107; Flood-Page *et al.* 2000: 83). For example, Flood-Page *et al.* (2000) report that as many as half of the interviews with subjects aged 12–15 were conducted in the presence of others, predominantly the mother (p. 83). This fact may very well have influenced the subjects and resulted in them reporting less crime than they otherwise would have done, although it is impossible to quantify the effect of this.

All in all, there are several differences between this study and the national studies that would make it likely that the rates are underestimated in the national survey in comparison with the Peterborough study (e.g. the national studies include rural areas they have high levels of non-response rates and, although an attempt

Table 4.16 Prevalence rates (annual) for overall offending and substance use, and some selected (roughly) comparable crime and substance use categories, for comparable age groups from the national surveys (ages 14–17) and 1998–9 (ages 14–15) (per cent)

Category	Males 92 (ages 14–17)	Males 98–9 (ages 14–15)	Females 92 (ages 14–17)	Females 98–9 (ages 14–15)
Crime				
Any offence	24.0	33	19.0	18
Shoplifting	3.2	4	5.3	6
Car theft	1.0		0.6	
Theft from car	0.9		0.7	
Burglary	5.0		0.3	
Threat for money	0.5		0.2	
Vandalism	3.3	18	3.9	7
Fighting	9.8	11	4.9	6
Other violence		7		1
Beat non-family members	2.8		1.8	
Beat family member	1.5		0.1	
Hurt with weapon	3.3		1.1	
Substance use*				
Any drug	17.0		17.0	
Cannabis	14.0		16.0	
Inhalants (glue, gas)	1.0		1.0	

Note:

* Questions about substance-use only asked in 1992 study. Alcohol use not included. What we have referred to as 'hard drugs' in this study is split up in greater detail in the national study and no overall measure for hard drugs is given.

Sources:

1992 – Graham and Bowling (1995: crime, Table C6, p. 116; substance use, Table 3.3, p. 26; 1998–9 – Flood-Page (2000: crime, Table 2.1, p. 12).

was made to correct for this in the 1998–9 study, others, often mothers, were present for a large part of the interviews). However, when considering the overall rate of offending the broader range of coverage in the national studies may be assumed partly to counteract the underestimating factors mentioned. The overall annual prevalence of offending in Peterborough is much higher, both for boys (45 per cent) and girls (31 per cent), than the national figures (see Table 4.16, and compare Tables 4.2 and 4.12). Even though it is difficult to make a direct comparison, on balance, it is likely that the Peterborough figures are higher than the national average. However, whether the Peterborough figures are higher than for comparable cities is difficult to say. The national rates for shoplifting and vandalism are surprisingly low compared with the Peterborough rate (and to what you would expect from the academic literature). The rate of shoplifting among males in Peterborough is three times higher, and the vandalism rate about seven times higher than the national rates. The corresponding figures for females are three times higher for shoplifting and four times for vandalism. A reasonable guess, given the problems of comparability listed above, is that the national figures are highly underestimated compared with the Peterborough data. The national violence rates are also low compared with those of the PYS. Again it is likely that the national figures are underestimations when compared with the Peterborough figures.

The overall rate of substance use is not comparable at all, since the Peterborough figure includes alcohol use (being drunk), which is by far the most prevalent type of substance use. The national survey estimate for cannabis use is lower, but not dramatically so, than the one for Peterborough, while the estimate for inhalant use is much lower in the national survey (inhalant use is more than ten times higher in Peterborough). The difference in cannabis use may to a large extent be due to methodological differences between the studies. However, it is unlikely that methodological differences alone would account for the big difference in use of inhalants.

Comparisons with the Edinburgh Study of Youth Transition and Crime

The Edinburgh study is part of a longitudinal study of all children who enrolled in secondary school in Edinburgh in 1998. Some preliminary findings have been reported (Smith *et al.* 2001). These findings concern, among other things, prevalence of crime among 12–13-year-olds. The prevalence of selected offending categories for the 'last 12 months' at the age of 13 in Edinburgh is compared with similar categories for Peterborough youths at the age of 14–15 (Table 4.17). The comparison shows that the Peterborough prevalence figures are about the same (vandalism, robbery) or substantially lower (shoplifting, assault). It is possible that the Peterborough assault question is more restrictive (beaten up or hit someone) than the Edinburgh question (fighting or injured someone) and therefore that the difference in prevalence

Table 4.17 Prevalence of selected crime categories in Edinburgh and Peterborough

	Edinburgh (aged 12–13)	Peterborough (aged 14–15)
Shoplifting	26.6	13.9
Vandalism	15.9	17.0
Assault (injure/fight*)	46.1	24.0
Robbery	1.7	1.4

Note:
* Category as labelled in Edinburgh study. The question may have a broader scope than the Peterborough assault questions.
Source:
Edinburgh data Smith *et al.* (2001: Table 33.3, p. 26).

may be highly overestimated (particularly given that the violence victimisation levels are close; see below). In making this comparison one also has to bear in mind that Edinburgh is a much bigger city than Peterborough (and that crime levels tend to increase with degree of urbanisation), and that the subjects in Edinburgh are younger than in Peterborough.

The Edinburgh study also contains information on victimisation (Smith *et al.* 2001: 66). At the age of 13, 27.9 per cent reported having had something stolen (compared with 31.9 per cent for Peterborough youth aged 14) and 27.1 per cent reported that someone deliberately hurt them (compared with 25.7 per cent of 14-year-olds in Peterborough who reported having been assaulted). However, the Edinburgh study also has a category of 'deliberately hurt by a weapon' (7.5 per cent), so the Edinburgh figure may be somewhat higher than the Peterborough one depending on how high the overlap is between the two assault categories. By and large, the level of victimisation is similar in Edinburgh and Peterborough.

Note

1 Actually, the response rate for the 1998–9 study appears to have been less than that reported since it is predominantly a sample from a sample (i.e. from the British Crime survey that had a 78 per cent response rate).

Chapter 5

Family social position

The question whether an individual's social position affects his or her criminality is one of the classic criminological questions. In the media and general debate it is sometimes taken for granted that this is one of the key factors, perhaps the key factor, explaining variation in offending among juveniles. However, academic research on the subject generally shows that the role of social position is more modest. The risk of being involved in crime may vary significantly by individual social position (i.e. increases the risk), but it is difficult to predict anyone's involvement in crime solely based on knowing his or her social position in society (i.e. the explained variance is low).

For juveniles their social position is largely determined by their family's social position. In this study we had three constructs referring to family social position: family social class, family structure (or composition) and family ethnicity/immigrant status. When talking about family social position we will regularly also refer to this as family structural characteristics.

Family social class

Of all the 'stable' independent variables of criminological research – age, sex, ethnicity, social class and size of community – the relationship between social class and offending behaviour has become peculiarly problematic (Kornhauser 1978; Wilson and Herrnstein 1985), in so far as the commonly accepted 'fact' that criminal behaviour is strongly and negatively correlated with social class has frequently refused to reveal itself in empirical studies.

Wootton's (1959) review of the state of criminological knowledge regarding social status gave an indication of the extent to which the class–crime association had been taken as a given, but also how sparse were the data available to support this view. She concluded:

> We thus reach the unsurprising conclusion that, on the definitions used by these investigators, those who find themselves in trouble with the criminal law on either side of the Atlantic are predominantly drawn from the lower social classes; but even so we are not able to say whether, or how far, this predominance exceeds that to be expected from the proportion which these classes contribute to the non-criminal population (1959: 107).

However, within ten years, as a result of the growing popularity of the self-report method, Hirschi (1969: 66), in discussing findings from the Richmond Youth Project, summarised research from the late 1950s and 1960s and highlighted the paradox that later provided the basis for the class–crime debate: 'While the prisons bulge with the socioeconomic dregs of society, careful quantitative research shows again and again that the relation between socioeconomic status and the commission of delinquent acts is small, or nonexistent.' Hirschi's own data led him to state: 'The findings in the present sample are consistent with previous research: we are dealing with what is, at most, a *very small* relation that could easily be upset by random disturbances of sampling or definition' (1969: 69).

The debate regarding the association, or lack thereof, between social class and offending reached its apogee in the late 1970s and early 1980's with the exchange between Tittle *et al.* (1978) and Braithwaite (1981). Tittle *et al.* (1978) conducted a review of a number of empirical studies on the association between social class and self-reported and official offending. They concluded that 'numerous theories developed on the assumption of class differences appear to be based on false premises' (1978: 654). Braithwaite (1981), in his response, suggested that a number of methodological issues (for instance, the range of studies included and also the dependent variables used) cast doubt on Tittle *et al.*'s claim and that, conversely to their argument, criminology needed to give a more central role to the study of class-based differences in offending. Similarly, Hindelang *et al.* (1979) and Elliott and Ageton (1980) have suggested that the reason for the small association between delinquency and social class in self-report studies, in comparison with studies that use official offending data, may well lie in the relative non-seriousness of offences frequently used in self-report studies. These authors thereby suggest that the association between social class and offending evident in official data relates to more serious and/or frequent offending than is typically caught by self-report studies.

Janson and Wikström (1995) have suggested that the class–crime debate may be seen as comprising three fundamental questions: first, the theoretical question of what definitions of class and crime should be employed and what form the association between social class and crime takes; secondly, the methodological question of what measures of social class and offending are appropriate to use; and, thirdly, the strength of the association between class and crime (the empirical question). Janson and Wikström (1995: 203) also differentiate between two different ways in which the class–crime association can be viewed. The first of these is seeing the relationship as relating to *differential life chances (risk differences)* and the second is the *predictive power (explained variance)* of the association.

Tittle *et al.*'s review of the empirical evidence suggested that the strength of the negative relationship between social class and crime has declined monotonically over time, resulting contemporaneously in 'essentially no relationship between class and crime/delinquency' (1978: 654). They argued: 'We also need to identify more generic processes. What these processes might be, we do not know, but we are confident that they will not be found as long as sociologists cling to the belief that almost everything ultimately can be reduced to a class variable' (1978: 653). In their review, Tittle *et al.* were primarily concerned with the predictive power of the class–crime relationship whereas, on the other hand, Braithwaite appears to have been concerned more broadly with the issue of how social class is associated with differential life chances and varying types of offending and suggested that there was a need for criminology to investigate more thoroughly the complex ways that class and offending are related.

Recent empirical work on the class–crime relationship has attempted to do this. Wright *et al.* (1999), for instance, suggested that there may be a causal relationship between class and crime, but no overall (linear) correlation due to the form of the relationship being 'U-shaped', with both low and high social class differentially influencing the levels of mediating variables that are associated with offending and hence acting, in aggregate, to cancel out one another.

The use of school samples, as in the Peterborough Youth Study, is a possible reason for the lack of a larger class–crime relationship in self-report studies. Kornhauser (1978: 98) noted:

> the nature of sample composition and sample attrition in self-report studies is likely to attenuate the relation between SES and delinquency. These studies are typically done on school populations. Dropouts and truants are not represented in such samples. Moreover, nonresponse is related to low achievement and to officially defined delinquency (Hirschi 1969). Dropout, truancy, and school success are thus related both to SES and delinquency. Hence, both sample composition and sample attrition should contribute to the diminution of the relation between SES and delinquency.

As discussed previously in the methodology section, steps were taken to minimise attrition from the response rate for the Peterborough Youth Study. Each school was revisited, after the original data collection, to try to secure the participation of young people who were absent during the original visit. Furthermore, subjects attending an alternative educational programme for young people who refused to go to, or are excluded from, ordinary schools were also included in the sample. On the other hand, at the higher levels of the class spectrum, there could be a slight danger of under-representation due to the exclusion of one, small, private, all-girl, day and boarding school. However, the number of young people omitted from the sample by this exclusion is so small it is implausible that this group could have meaningfully altered the findings from the data.

This is not to suggest that social class is irrelevant in the study of the aetiology of offending but that, rather, criminologists need to pay more attention to the mechanisms through which social class influences the differential likelihood of individuals committing criminal acts (Hagan 1992; Wright *et al.* 1999).

Overall, the results obtained here are generally in accordance with extant self-report study findings. In examining the linear relationship between class and crime, no great social class differences in overall offending were found, even at the 10 per cent significance level. Consistent with the view that social class differences may only reveal themselves when more serious crimes are considered, the composite serious thefts category did indicate a significant class difference, with young people from the highest socio-economic stratum displaying significantly less likelihood of being involved in this form of offending.

61

So far, we have said nothing regarding the issue of why (or why not), theoretically, there should be an association between social class and offending. This is an issue we shall return to in due course.

In the study the subjects were asked to specify their father's (or stepfather's) and their mother's (or stepmother's) occupation. We asked them to give a specified account of their parents' occupations, for example, primary schoolteacher or salesman at B&Q. On the basis of this information (we used the highest-ranking occupation of their parents), the subjects were classified according to main type of (occupational) social class. We used a broad division of social class in four categories: 1) lower working class, unskilled workers; 2) working class, skilled workers and low-rank white-collar employees; 3) lower middle class, officials and small-scale entrepreneurs; 4) upper middle and upper class, large-scale entrepreneurs, high-rank officials and high-rank white-collar employees. We also asked whether their parents were unemployed or not. The final classification combined occupational social class and employment status. All unemployed were referred to as a specific category, the rest classified by their occupational social class (Figure 5.1). Among the unemployed, the previous employment had for the majority (81.5 per cent) been a working or lower-working class occupation (assuming that the stated occupation for parents reported to be unemployed was their occupation before being unemployed).

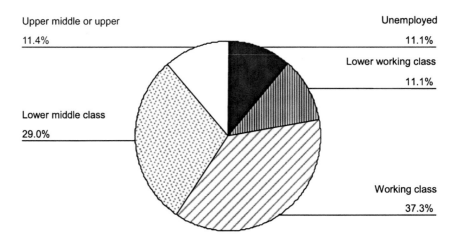

Figure 5.1 Family social class distribution (per cent)

It is acknowledged that classifying family social class on the basis of the child's information about their parents' work may have some problems of reliability and therefore it should be viewed as a rough classification.[1] However, some attempts were made to validate the family social class scale by studying its relationship to reported car ownership and holidays abroad (Figures 5.2 and 5.3). The findings

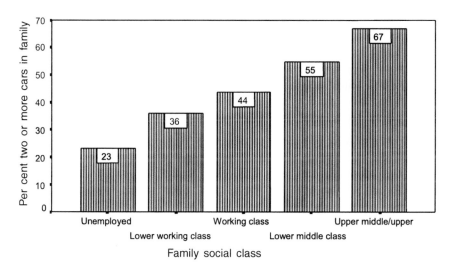

Figure 5.2 Per cent families with two or more cars by family social class

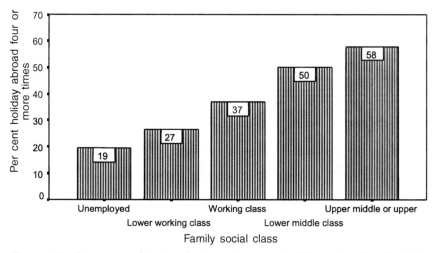

Figure 5.3 Per cent subjects who have been on holiday abroad with their parents four times or more

show clearly that the higher the social class, the more often the subjects' families have two or more cars, and the more often they have been on holiday abroad four times or more (in their lifetime).

These findings reassure us that the social class scale is likely to pick up some main differences in the subjects' families' social position. Key alternative ways to determine family social class would have been to ask about parents' educational level and income. However, it is unlikely that any greater number of juveniles would be able to give reliable information, particularly about parents' income. Therefore, we did not include these measures in the study. Although far from a one-to-one relationship, education and income generally have strong correlations with occupational class.

There are no great social class differences in overall offending

Family social class is a poor predictor for the overall rate of offending. In fact, the differences are not even statistically significant at the 10 per cent level (Figure 5.4). This also holds when the relationship is analysed separately for boys and girls (both non-significant). Considering serious thefts only (Figure 5.5), the main finding is that subjects from upper-middle/upper-class backgrounds tend significantly less to be involved in crimes of serious theft than others (the differences between other social classes are non-significant). Tested separately for boys and girls, the pattern of difference is the

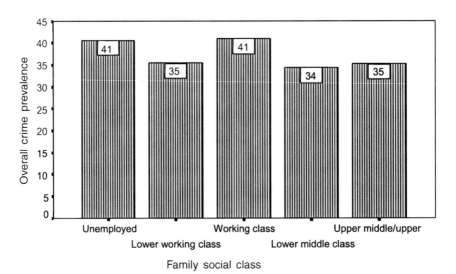

Figure 5.4 Overall offending prevalence by family social class

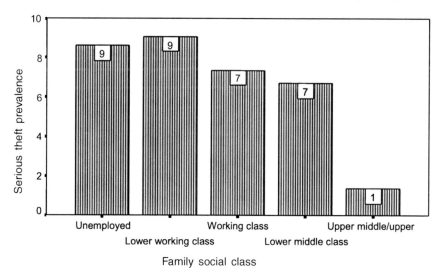

Figure 5.5 Serious theft (burglaries, theft of or from cars, robbery) prevalence by family social class

same for both boys and girls (i.e. a markedly lower rate for upper-middle/upper-class subjects) but only for the boys does this difference reach significance ($p = 0.024$).

Looking into specific crime categories (Table 5.1), of the three more frequent types of crime (previously referred to as 'common crimes' – see earlier in this chapter), only shoplifting shows a significant (but in no way dramatic) variation by subject's family social class. It is worthwhile to note that neither vandalism nor assault shows any significant variation by family social class. Of the smaller crime categories (all crimes of serious theft as defined here), none reached statistical significance. However, as reported above, if one combines the categories of serious theft, subjects coming from an upper-middle/upper-class background will be significantly less involved in these types of crime (Figure 5.5).

There are no social class differences in victimisation

The level of overall victimisation varies only marginally by the subjects' family social class and all inter-class differences are non-significant (Figure 5.6). The same also holds for the three main types of victimisations: theft, vandalism and violence victimisations (Figure 5.7), and for boys and girls analysed separately (no significant differences by social class for overall victimisation or for the three main types of victimisation).

Table 5.1 Self-reported offending prevalence by family social class

Crime type	Un-employed	Lower working	Working	Lower middle	Upper middle	Signifi-cance
Shoplifting	14.1	14.5	16.6	12.2	9.0	0.038
Non-residential Burglary	0.9	4.7	3.6	3.5	0.9	n.s.
Residential Burglary	2.4	0.5	1.1	1.8	0.9	n.s.
Thefts of/from cars	5.2	3.3	3.2	3.2	1.4	n.s.
Robbery	1.4	0.9	1.8	1.2	0.9	n.s.
Vandalism	18.3	18.3	19.4	14.3	14.0	n.s.
Assault	24.4	21.7	26.4	22.4	22.3	n.s.

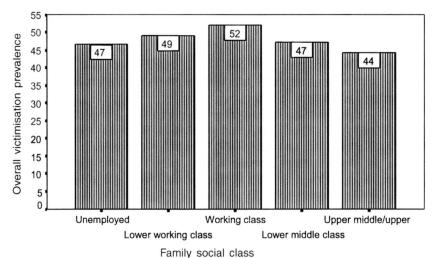

Figure 5.6 Overall victimisation prevalence by family social class

Family structure

A key feature of youths' social position that often figures in discussions of potential causes of youth involvement in crime is their family composition (or structure). In particular, the role of living in a split family, either with a single parent or with step-parents, has been highlighted as a potential risk factor (e.g. Loeber and Stouthamer-Loeber 1986).

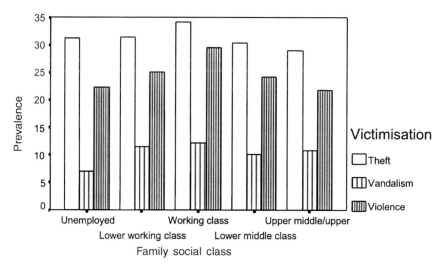

Figure 5.7 Theft, vandalism and violence victimisation prevalence by family social class

In this study we asked whether the subjects lived with their parents, either one or both, or with somebody else, or whether they moved between parents. We also asked whether any of the parents they were living with was a step-parent. On the basis of these two questions, the subjects' family compositions were classified into five groups: 1) living with both (biological) parents; 2) living with two parents, of which one was a step-parent; 3) living with a single parent; 4) moving between parents (living parts of the time at different locations); and 5) living with foster-parents (including grandparents) or in care. The findings show that almost four out of ten adolescents do not live with both of their biological parents (Figure 5.8). Most of them live with a single parent, or in a two-parent family in which one of the parents is a step-parent.

Family disruption is only linked to an increased offending risk for girls

Those subjects who live with both of their (biological) parents tend to be involved in offending somewhat less than those who live in split families (with a step-parent, a single parent or those who move between parents), who, in turn, tend to offend less than those who live with foster parents or in care (Figure 5.9). All differences between the three groups are statistically significant at the 5 per cent level or better. The same basic pattern also holds for crimes of serious theft (Figure 5.10).

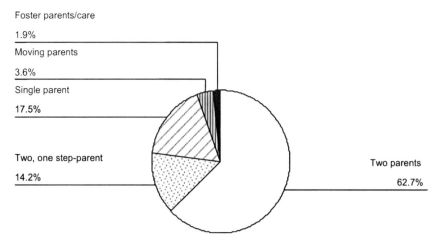

Figure 5.8 Family structure (composition) (per cent)

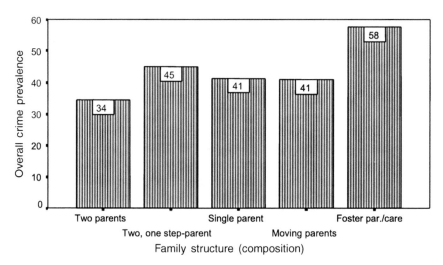

Figure 5.9 Overall offending prevalence by subjects' family structure (composition)

However, comparing boys and girls, the difference in overall crime involvement between subjects living in two (biological) parent families and subjects living in split families almost vanishes for boys (and is non-significant), but remains and is stronger for girls (25.7 per cent of the girls in two (biological) parent families have offended compared with 37.9 per cent of the girls in split families, $p = 0.000$). A similar comparison for serious theft shows the same pattern – i.e. a

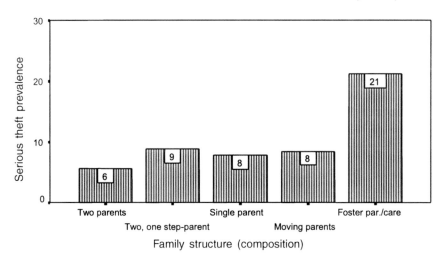

Figure 5.10 Serious theft (burglaries, theft of or from cars, robbery) prevalence by family structure (composition)

greater difference for girls (1.8 times) than boys (1.4 times) – although in both instances the difference is non-significant (but rather close to reaching significance at the 5 per cent level for girls, $p = 0.062$).

All in all, it appears that family disruption is only linked to crime involvement for girls, although the difference between those living in 'complete' and split families cannot be described as dramatic. However, for both boys and girls, the highest levels of offending are among those living with foster parents or in care (53.3 per cent of the girls and 61.1 per cent of the boys with foster parents/in care have offended). The patterns for special types of crime are, by and large, the same as for the hitherto reported more inclusive categories of overall offending and serious theft (Table 5.2). In all cases except assault, those living with foster parents/in care have the highest rates, while in most cases those living with a step-parent rank second. It should be noted that the 'moving parents' ($n = 71$) and 'foster parents/in care' ($n = 37$) categories are comparatively small in numbers and therefore the estimates for these groups may be somewhat less reliable.

Females in split families tend to be somewhat more victimised than other females

Overall there is a tendency that those from split families tend to be somewhat more often victimised than others (Figure 5.11). However,

Table 5.2 Self-reported offending prevalence by family composition

Crime type	Two-parent (biological) family	Two-parent (one step-parent) family	Single-parent family	Moving between parents	Foster parents or in care	Signifi-cance
Shoplifting	11.8	19.0	15.1	16.9	32.4	0.000
Non-residential burglary	2.6	5.5	1.8	2.8	8.8	0.028
Residential burglary	1.1	1.1	1.8	2.8	6.1	n.s.
Thefts of/ from cars	2.5	4.4	2.4	8.5	17.6	0.000
Robbery	1.2	0.4	2.1	4.2	5.9	0.012
Vandalism	15.0	22.6	18.7	14.1	35.3	0.000
Assault	21.8	30.8	25.7	26.8	27.0	0.024

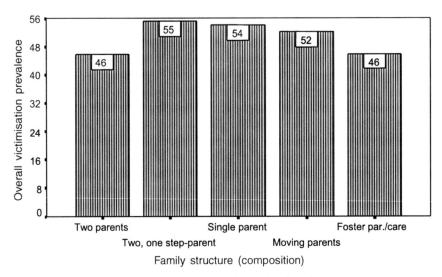

Figure 5.11 Overall victimisation prevalence by family structure

this difference is only significant ($p = 0.001$) for females. Looking at different victimisation categories, there are no significant differences in vandalism by family structure (Figure 5.12). However, some modest (and significant) differences are found for theft and violence victimisations. In both cases these are only significant for females ($p = 0.000$ for theft; $p = 0.011$ for violence). The main difference among females is there being on average about a 10 per cent lower rate of

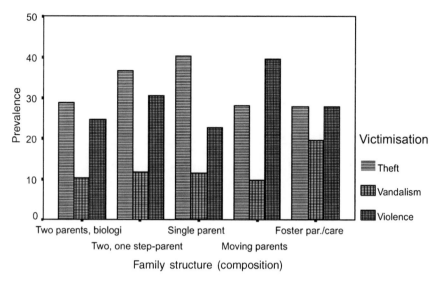

Figure 5.12 Theft, vandalism and violence victimisation prevalence by family structure (composition)

theft victimisation for females in families with two (biological) parents compared with other family categories (20.1 per cent as compared with rates varying between 27.8 per cent and 34.9 per cent for other family categories). For violent victimisation, females living with step-parents or moving between parents have a significantly higher rate of violent victimisation (25.9 per cent and 27 per cent respectively) compared with other family categories (varying between 14.5 per cent and 17.6 per cent).

A further analysis showed that the higher rate of violent victimisation for females in families with step-parents or those moving between parents was not explained by a higher rate of violent victimisations taking place in their home or by an adult the victim knows (i.e. no indication that the higher rate of female violent victimisations were caused by a higher rate of parental violence in those families). All in all, compared with females living in a complete family of origin, females in a split family tend to have a somewhat higher involvement in crime (both as offenders and victims).

Family ethnicity/immigrant status

Perhaps one of the most controversial topics in the media and general debate relating to individual social position and crime is the question of the relationship between ethnic background and involvement in crime. In general, research shows that immigrants overall tend to have higher rates of crime involvement compared with native populations, although this varies a great deal, for example, between different immigrant groups and according to the circumstances under which a specific group have immigrated (see Tonry 1997b; Junger-Tas 2001).

Ethnic/race differences in offending have long been a focus for criminological research. However, there remain a number of issues that have yet to be addressed in a systematic fashion. First, while criminologists have frequently identified the presence of substantial differences in the participation in offending between members of different ethnic groups (see e.g. Wilson and Herrnstein 1985; Gottfredson and Hirschi 1990; Tonry 1997b), there remains something of a void in bringing these findings into extant criminological theory (Hawkins *et al*. 2000), particularly in addressing the social mechanisms by which differences in ethnicity become instantiated into differences in actual behaviour.

Indeed, it appears to have frequently been the case that empirical findings of ethnic differences in offending are addressed methodologically rather than theoretically. For instance, it has been suggested that for ethnic differences in arrest figures, the cause may lie within systematic bias operating within the criminal justice system (see the discussion in Bowling 1990; cf. Junger 1990b). On the other hand, ethnic differences found via the self-report methodology have frequently been attributed to there being a differential validity of responses obtained by respondents from different ethnic groups (e.g. Junger 1989; cf. Bowling 1990). Secondly, some group differences have received greater attention than others (Hawkins *et al*. 2000). Differences between Caucasians and Afro-Caribbean/Afro-Americans have proved a fertile area of research, especially in the USA, whereas the relatively low rate of offending by those of Asian ancestry (see Rutter and Giller 1983) has received rather less attention (Smith 1997). Finally, interactions between gender and ethnicity have been largely ignored but may prove to enhance attempts at explanation (Hawkins *et al*. 2000).

Smith (1997: 111) noted that, in England and Wales, while those of Southern Asian ancestry have rates of imprisonment no higher than those of the white population, this fact has generally been overlooked by those commenting on ethnic differences in involvement with the criminal justice system. Rutter and Giller (1983: 160), in their review of juvenile delinquency in the UK, did, however, note: 'the delinquency rate for Asians has been equal to or lower than that for the white population at all times when it has been studied.' Wilson and Herrnstein (1985) suggested that a similar situation had been found among Oriental-Asians in America. They also note an apparent paradox when juxtaposing involvement in crime among Oriental-Asians with African-Americans, in so far that, while living in similarly poor housing conditions and both experiencing discriminatory practices from the ethnic majority population, for Oriental-Asians the separation from the majority has been suggested to lead to lower offending rates (as they live in isolated but more cohesive communities), whereas, for African-Americans, separation from the majority has been suggested to lead to higher rates of offending (see also Tonry 1997b).

Most studies of ethnicity and crime have been more concerned with establishing the existence of differences in the prevalence of offending between ethnic groups than they are in finding the social mechanisms by which they come about. Talking about the higher rate of arrests for Afro-Caribbeans, Rutter and Giller (1983: 161) suggested that:

> There is, of course, every reason to suppose that the major factors associated with crime in white people apply also to black people. One of the features of criminological research in different cultures is the relative consistency with which the same associations appear. But we know next to nothing of why crime rates should be lower in Asian youths and higher in West Indian Youths.

Despite the fact that Rutter and Giller's comment was made 20 years ago, the situation has not improved a great deal, with Powis and Walmsley (2002) suggesting that it is unclear whether the risk factors explaining individuals' involvement in crime differ by ethnic group.

In this study, information was collected both about the subjects' immigrant status and their family ethnicity (based on their parents' country of origin). The first construct classified subjects by whether they were natives (both parents and the subject born in the UK), first-generation immigrant (the subject is born abroad) or second-generation immigrant (at least one of the parents was born abroad, while the subject was born in the UK – see Figure 5.13). A second construct classified subjects as natives, Asians and non-Asian foreigners (Figure 5.14). Being Asian is by far the most common ethnic background among the subjects with an immigrant

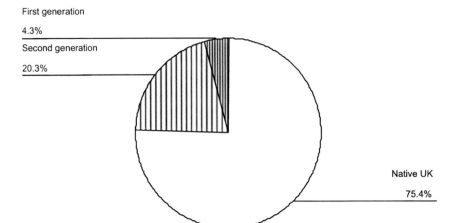

First generation

4.3%

Second generation

20.3%

Native UK

75.4%

Figure 5.13 Immigrant status (per cent)

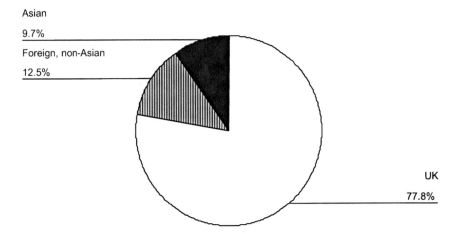

Asian

9.7%

Foreign, non-Asian

12.5%

UK

77.8%

Figure 5.14 Ethnic background (per cent)

background in Peterborough. Since many of the other immigrant groups are comparatively small, it was not judged appropriate (and in most cases also not statistically reliable) to present findings in more detail for non-Asian ethnic minority groups. In the non-Asian group of foreigners the great majority come from three regions, in rank order: continental Europe, Africa and the Middle East. Given this group's heterogeneous background, it is difficult to talk about the non-Asian foreign group as an ethnic group. The only thing they have in common is a foreign background.

The main reason that the proportion of UK natives is somewhat higher in the ethnic background classification (Figure 5.14) than in the immigrant status classification (Figure 5.13) is that there is a small group of the subjects who have been born abroad to two UK nationals (parents) on a temporary visit abroad (typically armed forces personnel). It should be noted that most subjects in the study with a foreign background are second-generation immigrants (i.e. they have been born and brought up in the UK).

The differences in offending by immigrant status were marginal and non-significant (Figures 5.15 and 5.16). Therefore, the presented findings will focus on ethnicity, where the analysis shows some interesting findings, particularly for girls.

Asian girls commit very few crimes

The analyses of variation in crime involvement by ethnicity revealed, with one exception, only small and non-significant overall variations between the compared groups. The exception was a lower rate for those with an Asian background. However, further analyses showed that this was due only to a much lower rate of crime involvement among Asian girls (Figure 5.17). Asian boys have rates in parity with other boys. This overall finding also holds if one considers aggressive crimes (assault and vandalism combined – see Figure 5.18) and

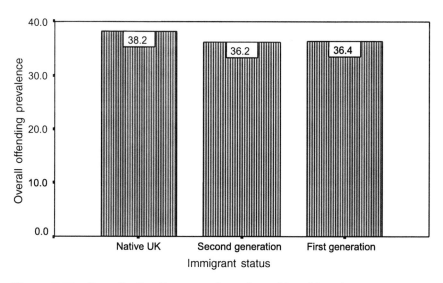

Figure 5.15 Overall offending prevalence by subjects' immigrant status

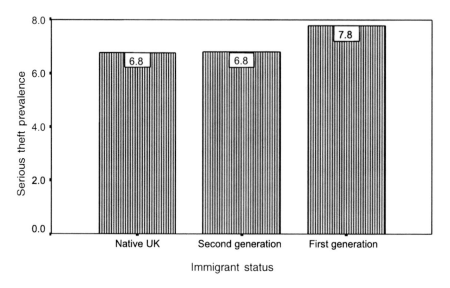

Figure 5.16 Serious theft prevalence by subjects' immigrant status

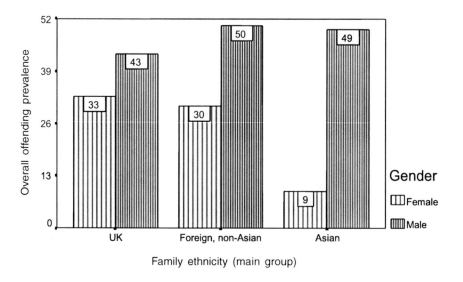

Figure 5.17 Overall offending prevalence by subjects' ethnic background and gender

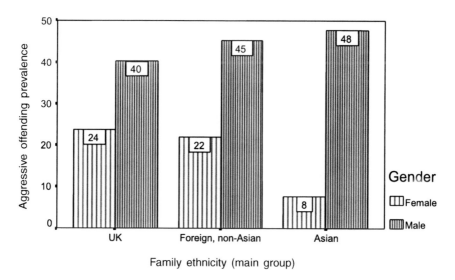

Figure 5.18 Aggressive offending prevalence by subjects' ethnic background and gender

shoplifting (where, however, the Asian boys also have lower rates compared to others – see Figure 5.19). For serious theft, hardly any Asian girls are involved, but here also very few girls from other backgrounds are involved. For boys, those of a foreign non-Asian background have the highest level of crime involvement and the Asian boys the lowest level of crime involvement (Figure 5.20). All in all, the main finding appears to be the low rate of crime involvement among Asian girls.

Asian girls also have low rates of victimisation

Asian girls, just as they had low rates of crime involvement, also have a low level of victimisation (Figure 5.21). This holds for all three main types of victimisation (Table 5.3). In addition, compared to other males, Asian males also have a lower rate of vandalism and violence victimisation, but not of theft victimisation.

Asians, and particularly Asian girls, have low rates of substance use

One factor that may be of relevance in explaining Asian girls' low offending and victimisation risk is their alcohol and drug use patterns (which we know are closely linked to, in particular, offending but also victimisation risk). Asians, and especially Asian girls, have much

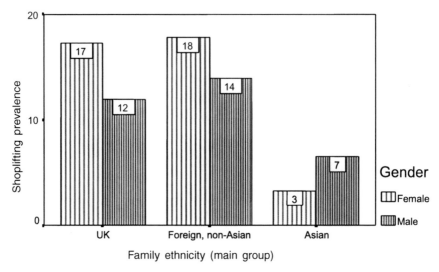

Figure 5.19 Shoplifting prevalence by subjects' ethnic background and gender

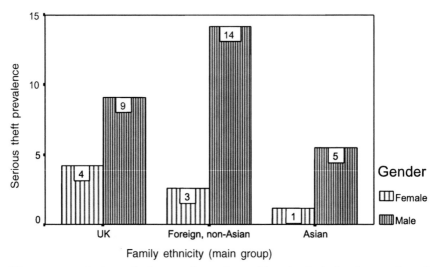

Figure 5.20 Serious theft prevalence by subjects' ethnic background and gender

lower rates of substance use. For example, if we consider overall substance use (that is heavily influenced by prevalence of alcohol use (being drunk)), Asian males have a lower prevalence (45.1 per cent) than non-Asian foreigners (69.0 per cent) and native youths (72.6 per cent). The same, but more extreme, pattern holds for Asian females

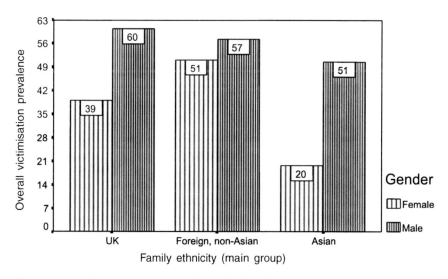

Figure 5.21 Victimisation prevalence by family ethnicity and gender

Table 5.3 Theft, vandalism and violence victimisations by family ethnicity and gender: per cent victimised

	Males			Females		
	Native	Non-Asian	Asian	Native	Non-Asian	Asian
Theft	39.0	34.2	35.2	25.0	38.8	13.0
Vandalism	12.5	11.1	7.5	9.7	10.0	5.4
Violence	34.5	38.5	22.6	18.3	20.0	9.7

who have a substance use prevalence of 18.3 per cent, compared with 63.6 per cent for non-Asian foreign females, and 69.8 per cent for native females. Looking at specific drugs, Asians have lower usage of alcohol (being drunk) and cannabis, while their levels of inhalants use and hard drug use are in parity with other youths.

Explaining Asian girls' low rates of crime involvement and substance use

Although one may suggest theoretically plausible and empirically supportable mechanisms which translate the interaction between gender and ethnicity into differential likelihood of offending, through the influence of factors relating to youths' structural position on their development of more protective individual characteristics and less risky lifestyles, a number of questions remain. First, precisely what factors have influenced this – that is, what mechanisms explain the impact of structural characteristics on adolescents' individual characteristics and lifestyles? Sampson and Laub (1993: 97) noted, 'it is troubling that many sociological explanations of crime ignore the family' and, in their reanalysis of the Gluecks' data, 'family processes mediated approximately 75 percent of the effect of structural background on delinquency' (p. 96), so family processes clearly suggest themselves as a profitable field of research in attempting to explain Asian females' lower rate of involvement in offending.

Following this line of thought, research on immigration and socialisation suggests a number of factors that could plausibly be implicated as causal mechanisms linking ethnic groups' structural position and individual differences in the outcome of the socialisation processes. Dion and Dion (2001) have suggested that in immigrant families there exist 'greater socialization expectations for daughters to embody traditional ideals of behaviour compared to those for sons', that greater restriction and monitoring are afforded to daughters' behaviour in their relationships with their peers and especially with opposite sex peers, and that these factors may be particularly strong for second-generation daughters (as were 90 per cent of the Asian females in our sample) due to their parents feeling that the values of the receiving society are threatening their own cultural values. Bhopal (1997) has suggested that a general characteristic of Southern Asian families is the elevation of family over the individual – a gender differential in the goals and emphasis of child rearing, pronounced family values among females and the placing of responsibility for the honour of the family on the female family members. Wardak (2000) adds that, in the general Punjabi family culture, daughters are expected to display even greater obedience than sons, their behaviour is subject to 'scrutiny and gossip among kin and neighbours' (p. 64), with disobedience adversely affecting their chances of marriage (see also Merry 1984 on 'gossip' operating as a form of social control). As such it is unsurprising to see behavioural differences between males and females among the second-generation children of Southern Asian immigrants, especially a lower rate of participation in offending by Asian female youths, who, as a group, appear to have the highest expectations of conformity placed upon them during socialisation.

Smith (1997) has offered a slightly different thesis, proposing that the difference may be due to Southern Asians having adopted a more 'inward-looking' survival strategy, relying more upon their own social networks for support and consequently leading them to experience less discrimination and rejection from the native community. This appears to be consistent with the literature on Southern Asian socialisation patterns and furthermore raises the interesting question of how networks of relationships, which Coleman has termed 'social capital' (Coleman 1988), impact upon individual likelihood of offending, whether directly or indirectly, through its influence on individuals' contexts of socialisation and development (see Coleman 1988; Furstenberg *et al.* 1999). However, it does seem that Smith's notion of a Southern Asian protective culture needs to be amended to take into account the apparent gender-specific nature of this protection.

The data from the Peterborough Youth Study suggest that the same risk and protective factors predict likelihood of involvement in offending for both the predominantly Southern Asian group in our sample as well as for the other youths. Furthermore, the difference in the distribution of these scores across the youths' social positions accounts for the lower prevalence of offending by the Asian females in our sample (see Chapters 6, 8 and 9). It seems plausible to suggest that the difference in the distribution of risk and protective factors comes about due to processes operating within Southern Asian families particularly and the wider communities in which they are more generally embedded. To increase our understanding of the whole range of social mechanisms involved in producing differences between ethnic groups in their prevalence of offending, it seems likely that multi-level studies which examine youths' individual characteristics, the socialisation behaviour of their parents, as well as the community processes and resources in the areas in which they live, may be necessary (see also Hawkins *et al.* 1998; Wikström and Sampson 2003).

Multivariate analyses

Family social class is a significant risk factor for serious theft among native youths

So far we have considered only one dimension of the subjects' social position at a time. From the joint analyses of several dimensions, some interesting patterns become clear. The first is that the relationship between family social class and the prevalence of serious theft only holds for native youths. The relationship for native youths (gamma = –0.33, signf. = 0.000) is clearer and stronger than for all youths (gamma = –0.20, signf. = 0.010) (see Figure 5.22 and compare Figure

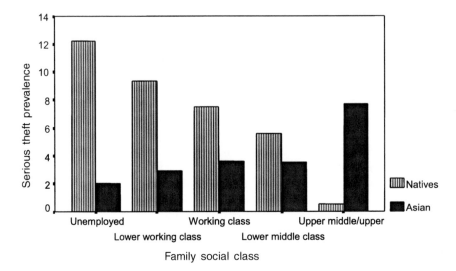

Figure 5.22 Comparison of serious theft prevalence between natives and Asians by family social class

5.5). The social class–serious theft offending relationship holds for both native boys and girls (Figure 5.23). However, for youths with a foreign background (Asians and non-Asians), the relationship between social class and serious theft offending is non-significant.

In the case of Asian youths it almost appears that the relationship between offending and social class is the reverse (Figure 5.22). The higher the family's social class, the higher the level of offending (although the level of serious theft offending in each social class, with the exception of the upper middle/upper class, is significantly lower for Asian youths). Given that relatively few Asian subjects belong to the highest social class, and that serious theft is a relatively uncommon crime, these figures should be treated with caution. However, the same pattern also holds for overall offending prevalence: Asian youths from unemployed and lower working-class families have the lowest rates of overall offending (in both cases a prevalence of 24 per cent), while Asian youths from upper middle/upper class families have the highest rate of overall offending (a prevalence of 42 per cent).

One can only speculate about the reason for this apparently reverse relationship. It should be recalled that Asian girls have very low rates of offending and therefore this pattern is predominantly an Asian male pattern. One possibility may be that Asian youths (males) from higher social class families are more 'Westernised' than those from lower social classes and therefore have a lifestyle (more like

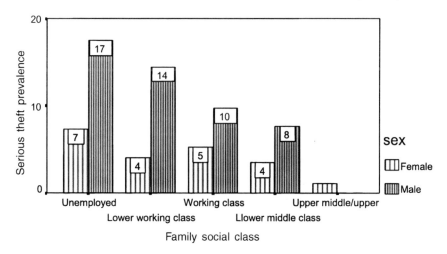

Figure 5.23 Serious theft prevalence by family social class and gender: natives only

natives) that may bring them more into contact with risky situations and opportunities to offend. Another possible, but speculative, contributory reason may be that family social class does not have the same significance in determining social position for those of a foreign background as for native youths. One factor that should be mentioned in this context is that Asian youths to a much higher degree than others live in a complete family of origin (i.e. live with both their biological parents). As many as 86.1 per cent of Asian youths live in a complete family of origin, while the corresponding rate for UK natives is 61.4 per cent and for non-Asian foreigners is 56.3 per cent.

It is also the case that the overwhelming majority of Asian youths live in a complete family of origin regardless of their family social class (proportions vary between 83 and 100 per cent), while, for UK natives, the proportion living in a complete family of origin, although lower than for the Asians in each social class, is much larger in higher social classes (e.g. 73 per cent in the upper middle/upper class) than in the lower social classes (e.g. 27 per cent among the youth with unemployed parents).

For all social classes the male overall offending prevalence is not significantly different between those who live in complete and split families (Figure 5.24). In contrast, in all social classes (except the working class) the difference in offending between females living in a complete family of origin and a split family is significant (Figure

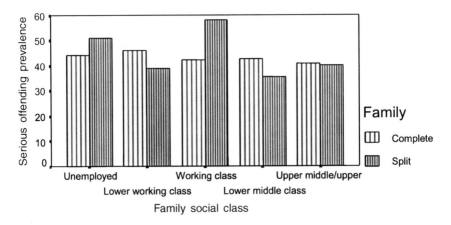

Figure 5.24 Overall offending prevalence by family structure and family social class: males only

5.25). This finding reinforces the more general finding reported earlier that it is only for females that family disruption is related to offending levels.

Family structural risk score

Family social class and family composition were used to create a composite *family structure risk score*. Family ethnicity was not included in the index. Subjects whose families belonged to the lower working class or were unemployed received a value of 1, those whose families belonged to the working class or lower middle class received a value of 0 and those whole families belonged to the upper middle/upper class received a value of –1. For family structure, those living in a complete family of origin (with two biological parents) received a score of –1, and those living with foster parents or in care a score of 1. All other family types received a score of 0. Summing the values for the two created variables developed an index of structural risk. This index can vary between –2 and 2, where –2 is assumed to measure the most protective side (high family social class and complete family) and 2 the most high-risk side (low family social class and living with foster parents or in care). Only 12 subjects scored 2. Therefore, when considering rates shown for this particular group, these rates need to be treated with utmost caution.

Looking into the overall prevalence of offending (Figure 5.26), shows that there are no significant differences by family structural

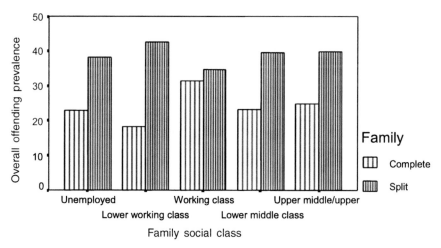

Figure 5.25 Overall offending prevalence by family structure and family social class: females only

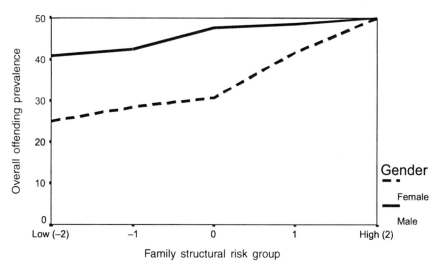

Figure 5.26 Overall offending prevalence by family structural risk score

risk group for boys, while for girls there is a significant (signf. = 0.053) but not very strong difference (gamma = 0.14).

Multiple regression analyses

The analyses of family structural variables (social position) and gender have shown that family social class is not a strong predictor of juvenile offending, nor of juvenile victimisation, although it does have an impact on the risk for more serious offending (serious theft), particularly for native youths (but not youths with a foreign background). It has also been shown that family structure has somewhat of an impact on females' involvement in offending and risk of victimisation, but not on males. In general the ethnicity of juveniles does not have much of an impact on offending. However, the interaction between being of an Asian background and being female does have a highly significant impact on offending risk.

Asian girls have much lower offending rates than others. Asian boys have lower rates than other boys of violent and vandalism victimisations, and Asian girls have the lowest rates of all kinds of victimisations. This chapter will conclude with a test of whether the identified structural predictors of offending hold up in multivariate regression analyses.

A multiple logistic regression analysis carried out on prevalence of offending for four major categories of crime, by and large, supports the observations already made (Table 5.4). The logistic regression analysis shows that being female, especially an Asian female, and living in a complete family of origin entails a lower overall risk of involvement in offending. For serious theft, being female again lowers the risk of offending, while having unemployed or lower working-class parents increases the risk of offending. The reason why being an Asian girl is not significant for serious theft is simply that all girls, regardless of ethnicity, have a very low involvement in serious theft.

For shoplifting, and in contrast to the other crime categories, being female increases the risk of being involved in crime, while, as for other crimes, coming from a complete family of origin decreases the risk. The fact that being from a working-class family has a significant effect on shoplifting, while coming from any other class does not have any significant effect, is not easily explained and may just be an artefact. Finally, being female, and in particular an Asian female, and coming from a complete family lower the risk of involvement in aggressive offending (assault and vandalism combined).

A multiple ordinary least squares (OLS) regression with overall *frequency* of offending as the dependent variable showed, just as the logistic regression analysis, that being female, particularly an Asian female, and living in a complete family of origin reduce the risk of offending (Table 5.5). In contrast to the (logistic regression) analysis of overall offending prevalence, low family social class was a significant predictor of overall offending frequency – i.e. social class does not influence whether a juvenile commits crime or not,

Table 5.4 Logistic regression: gender and key structural variables, main groups of offending, prevalence, odds ratios (exp.(B)) and significance levels

Variable	Overall offending		Serious theft		Shoplifting		Aggressive crimes	
	Exp. (B)	Signif.	Exp. (B)	Signif.	Exp. (B)	Signif.	Exp. (B)	Signif.
Female	0.60	0.000	0.39	0.000	1.52	0.002	0.44	0.000
Asian	1.30	n.s.	0.53	n.s.	0.54	n.s.	1.41	n.s.
Asian female (interaction term)	0.17	0.000	0.47	n.s.	0.31	n.s.	0.20	0.000
Complete family	0.73	0.002	0.73	n.s.	0.69	0.009	0.72	0.003
Family social class*								
Unemployed	1.16	n.s.	1.65	0.043	1.14	n.s.	1.08	n.s.
Lower working	0.94	n.s.	1.72	0.025	1.16	n.s.	0.95	n.s.
Working	1.15	n.s	1.28	n.s.	1.30	0.022	1.14	n.s.
Lower middle	0.87	n.s.	1.11	n.s.	0.90	n.s.	0.85	n.s.
Chi-square (prob.)	86.7 (0.000)		50.9 (0.000)		46.6 (0.000)		118.1 (0.000)	
−2 Log	2,385		857		1,482		2,257	

Note:
* Upper middle/upper class is the reference category.

Table 5.5 OLS Regression: gender and key structural variables, overall frequency of offending, beta coefficients and significance levels

Variable	Overall offending		Serious theft		Shoplifting		Aggressive crimes	
	Beta	Signif.	Beta	Signif.	Beta	Signif.	Beta	Signif.
Female	−0.12	0.000	−0.10	0.000	0.04	n.s.	−0.18	0.000
Asian	0.00	n.s.	0.02	n.s.	−0.03	n.s.	0.01	n.s.
Asian female	−0.07	0.038	−0.03	n.s.	−0.05	n.s.	−0.06	0.055
Complete family	−0.06	0.013	−0.04	n.s.	−0.02	n.s.	−0.05	0.033
Family social class	−0.04	0.055	0.01	n.s.	−0.03	n.s.	−0.05	0.024
Multiple $R^2 \times 100$	3		1		1		5	

but has some impact on the frequency with which he or she commits crimes. Offenders from the lower social classes tend to be somewhat more active than those from the higher social classes. Considering specific types of crimes, this holds only for aggressive crimes. The total variance explained by gender and structural characteristics was modest (3 per cent for overall offending, and varying by 1–5 per cent for the different categories of crime).

Overall, gender and some structural characteristics are significant predictors of offending and, to a lesser degree, victimisation risks. However, taken together they do not explain much of the variation between juveniles in their offending. This perhaps should not have been expected anyway since there is no obvious reason why social position in society should have a direct impact on adolescent offending. It is probably more likely that the youths' social position has more of an indirect effect on offending through its influence on their immediate social situation (e.g. school bonds), and perhaps also (the development of) their dispositions (e.g. level of self-control). This issue is addressed in the next chapter.

Note

1   Preliminary analyses of the ongoing Peterborough Adolescent Development Study (PADS) data, utilising *parents'* reports of their occupational social class, education and income as a basis for creating an index of social position, show a somewhat stronger relationship to their children's offending, although the fundamental picture of a rather weak association between family social position and children's offending did not change.

Chapter 6

Individual characteristics: social situation and dispositions

Although crime and victimisation do vary significantly by some aspects of the youths' social position, their direct impact on adolescent offending (as shown in the previous chapter) is quite modest. However, another major strand of thought in criminology is the importance for criminality of social integration (e.g. Hirschi 1969). The basic idea is that those who are poorly integrated into conventional society will offend more than those who are well integrated, because the social costs of offending (i.e. social disapproval from significant others if detected) are lower for less well integrated individuals. For adolescents, two basic aspects of social integration are family and school integration. Consequently, it may be hypothesised that the risk of offending is greater for those with weak family bonds and weak school bonds.

While social bonds primarily refer to an individual's (current) relationship to others, an important related idea in criminology is that the person's morality and self-control (when developed, as more stable characteristics of the individual) are related to his or her risk of offending (e.g. Wilson and Herrnstein 1985; Gottfredson and Hirschi 1990). It may be hypothesised that a person with weak morality (cares less about others) and low ability to exercise self-control (more likely to act on the spur of the moment) may be more likely to offend than others. Although the relationship between an individual's social bonds and his or her morality and self-control is not well addressed in the theoretical literature, it seems reasonable to assume a link. It is likely that individuals' social bonds and their degree of self-control and morality develop in a mutually reinforcing and complex way.

However, the nature of the development of this relationship cannot be addressed in a cross-sectional study like this one.

In this chapter the focus will be primarily on the role of key aspects of the youths' social situations (i.e. social bonds, parental control) and dispositions (i.e. self-control and morality) for his or her offending. Six different scales (representing four constructs) were created to measure a youth's individual social situation and disposition. The constructs and scales are summarised in Table 6.1 and will be presented in more detail in subsequent sections.

Social bonds

The constructs for family bonds and school bonds were created by adding responses to selected questions regarding the subject's family and school situations. The constructs were made so that a high score indicates weak family/school bonds and a low score indicates strong family/school bonds.

Creation of constructs

The questions used to create the *weak family bonds* scale are presented in Table 6.2. The four selected questions each have a range from 0 to 2 and the resulting scale therefore a variation between 0 and 8. At

Table 6.1 Key individual constructs

Domain	Constructs	Scales	No. of items	Alpha
Social situation	Social bonds	Weak family bonds*	4	0.64
		Weak school bonds*	4	0.70
	Parental control	Parental monitoring*	3	0.82
Dispositions	Self-control	Low self-control**	13	0.79
	Morality	Pro-social values***	14	0.92
		High shaming*	6	0.85

Notes:
 * Scale created by Wikström.
 ** Modified version of the Grasmick *et al.* (1993) self-control scale.
 *** Taken from a scale used in the Pittsburgh Youth Study.

Table 6.2 Variables used to create the weak family bonds construct

Variable	Code	*n*	%
How well he or she gets along with parents			
Very well	0	999	51.5
Quite well	1	778	40.1
Not very well/not at all	2	162	8.4
Total		1,939	100.0
Missing cases		18	
How often have evening meals with parents			
All or most days (5–7 days a week)	0	1,117	57.8
Some days (2–4 days a week)	1	578	29.9
Never/almost never	2	237	12.3
Total		1,932	100.0
Missing		25	
How often do something fun with parents			
Often (at least once every week)	0	482	24.7
Sometimes (at least once every month)	1	1,110	56.5
Never/almost never	2	366	18.8
Total		1,948	100.0
Missing		9	
Talks to parents if having a problem			
Always/almost always	0	404	20.9
Sometimes	1	972	50.1
Never/almost never	2	562	29.0
Total		1,939	100.0
Missing		18	

one extreme we have those with a score of 0 who get along very well with their parents, have an evening meal with their parents every day or most days, often do something fun with their parents and can always or almost always talk to their parents if they have a problem. The reverse holds for those at the other extreme, with a score of 8, who do not get along very well or at all with their parents, never or almost never have an evening meal with their parents, never or almost never do something fun with their parents and never or almost never talk to their parents if they have a problem. The distribution of scores for the weak family bonds construct is shown in Figure 6.1.

The questions used to create the *weak school bonds* scale are presented in Table 6.3. The four selected questions each have a range from 0 to 3 and the resulting scale therefore a variation between 0 and 12. Those with a score of 12 don't like school at all, don't get

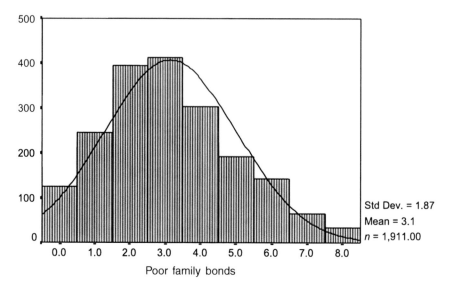

Figure 6.1 Distribution of weak family bonds scores

along at all with their teachers, do poorly in school and never do any homework. The reverse holds for those with a score of 0: they like school very much, get along with their teachers very well, do very well in school and spend two hours or more per day on homework. The distribution of the scores for the weak school bonds construct is shown in Figure 6.2.

Youths with weak family bonds more often get punished by their parents and more often run away from home

Partly because it is interesting in itself, and partly to check how well the weak family bonds construct was working in capturing family conditions, its relationship to two selected aspects of family life and relationships was studied.

First, the weaker the youth's family bond, the more often he or she had received repeated punishments by his or her parents (Figure 6.3). This may indicate that higher levels of punishment weaken the family bonds, or that weak family bonds and high levels of parental punishment reflect family dysfunction more generally. That the latter may be the case is indicated by the fact that the weaker the family bond, the more often the youths had run away from home at least once during the studied year (Figure 6.4).

Table 6.3 Variables used to create the school bonds construct

Variable	Code	n	%
Like school?			
Like school very much	0	139	7.1
Like school	1	1,165	59.7
Don't like school	2	454	23.3
Don't like school at all	3	192	9.8
Total		1,950	99.9
Missing		7	
Get along with teachers?			
Very well	0	298	15.3
Quite well	1	1,322	67.9
Not very well	2	255	13.1
Not at all	3	72	3.7
Total		1,947	100.0
Missing		10	
Do well in school?			
Very well	0	292	15.0
Rather well	1	1,431	73.5
Not very well	2	195	10.0
Poorly	3	30	1.5
Total		1,948	100.0
Missing		9	
How often do homework?			
2 hours or more per day	0	172	8.8
1–2 hours per day	1	843	43.4
Less than 1 hour per day	2	808	41.6
Never do homework	3	121	6.2
Total		1,944	100.0
Missing		13	

Parental monitoring is poorer in families with weak family bonds

Poor parental monitoring is generally reported as a key risk factor for involvement in crime (e.g. Martens 1997; Loeber *et al.* 1998). To study the relationship between family bonds and parental monitoring, a parental monitoring construct was created from three questions asking the subjects whether their parents had knowledge of their whereabouts when they were out by themselves or with friends in the evenings. The three questions ask whether their parents know where

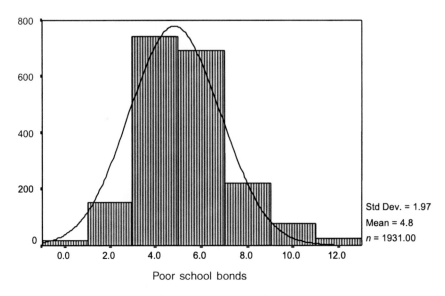

Figure 6.2 Distribution of weak school bonds scores

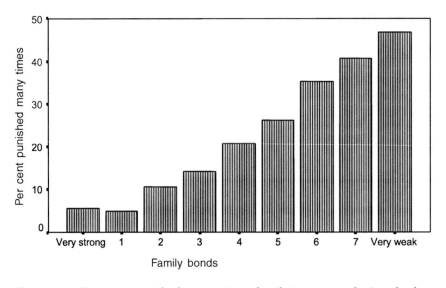

Figure 6.3 Per cent punished many times by their parents during the last year by strength of family bond

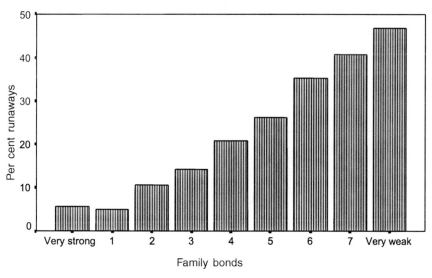

Figure 6.4 Per cent who had run away from home at least once during the last year by strength of family bond

they are, what they are doing and with whom they are hanging out. Each question had four alternatives ('yes, always', 'yes, most of the time', 'yes, sometimes', and 'no, never') and they were each scored 0 to 3 (see Appendix C). The resulting scale varied between 0 and 9, where 0 indicates very strong parental monitoring and 9 very poor parental monitoring. The analysis showed clearly that the weaker the family bonds, the poorer the parental monitoring (Figure 6.5). The zero-order correlation between weak family bonds and poor parental monitoring is 0.46. It should come as no great surprise that parents who have poor relationships (bonds) with their child also know much less about what their child is doing when outside the home. As might be expected from the results presented so far, there was also a relationship between poor parental monitoring and frequent punishments: in families with poorer parental monitoring frequent punishment was more common (Figure 6.6).

Youths with weak family bonds offend more than others

The weaker the bond to the family, the higher the risk the youth has offended. This holds both for boys and girls, although the boys' prevalence of offending at each level of family bond is higher (Figure 6.7). Considering the main groups of crime (Table 6.4), the findings

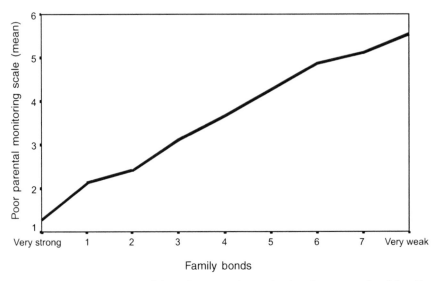

Figure 6.5 Mean score of (poor) parental monitoring by strength of family bond

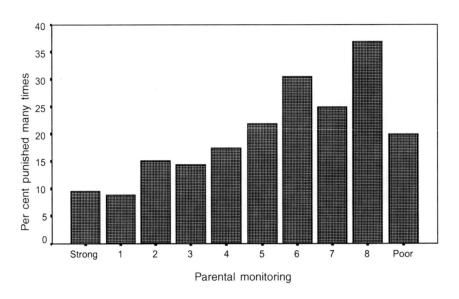

Figure 6.6 Per cent frequently punished by their parents by level of (poor) parental monitoring

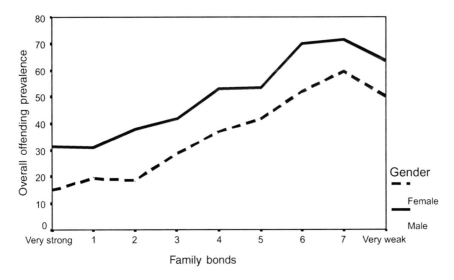

Figure 6.7   Overall offending prevalence by (poor) family bonds

Table 6.4   Offending prevalence by family bonds and gender

Family bonds*	Overall offending	Shoplifting	Aggressive crimes**	Serious theft
Males				
Strong	35	6	32	6
Medium	48	14	44	10
Weak	70	23	66	23
Signif.	0.000	0.000	0.000	0.000
Females				
Strong	18	8	13	1
Medium	34	18	24	4
Weak	54	32	43	11
Signif.	0.000	0.000	0.000	0.000

Notes:
  * Family bond scale grouped into strong (scores 0–2), medium (scores 3–6) and weak (scores 7–9).
** Assault and vandalism combined.

are the same with the exception that the prevalence of shoplifting at each level of family bond is higher for girls than boys.

Youths with weak school bonds are more often truant than others and would like to leave school if they could

The construct of school bonds was related to selected other aspects of school life to see how well the construct performed in picking up relevant variation among the subjects. First, the rate of frequent truancy by school bond was studied, and the result showed that the weaker the bond to the school the more often the pupil was frequently truant (Figure 6.8). Secondly, as might be expected, the pupils with poor bonds to their school stated to a much higher degree than others that they would quit school right away if they could (Figure 6.9). All in all, weak school bonds go together with higher rates of truancy and a more frequent wish to quit school.

Youths with weak school bonds offend more than others

The weaker the bond to the school, the higher the risk that the youth has offended. This holds both for boys and girls. However, in contrast to family bonds, there is no systematic gender difference in prevalence by level of (poor) school bonds. The effect of the school

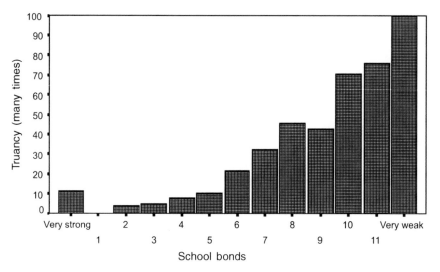

Figure 6.8 Per cent frequently truant from school by level of (weak) school bonds

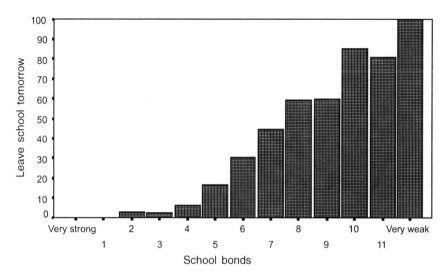

Figure 6.9 Per cent stating that they would like to leave school tomorrow if they could by level of (weak) school bonds

bond on offending is also stronger than that of the family bond (see Figure 6.10 and compare Figure 6.9). Considering overall crime and the different main groups of crime (Table 6.5), for overall offending the boys' prevalence is slightly higher in the strong-to-medium groups of school bonds but the females' prevalence is higher in the group with the weakest school bonds. Just as for the family bond, and reflecting the overall gender difference (see Table 4.2), shoplifting is more prevalent at each level of (poor) school bonds for girls, while the reverse holds true for aggressive crimes and serious thefts.

Many youths with weak family bonds also tend to have weak school bonds

There is a clear, but far from perfect, relationship between having a poor family bond and a poor school bond ($r. = 0.38$, $p = 0.000$). The weaker the family bond, the higher the percentage of subjects who belong to the group with a weak school bond (Figure 6.11). The most common combination among the youths is to have strong family bonds and medium-strength school bonds or strong school bonds and medium-strength family bonds (45 per cent), followed by those who have a medium-strength of both family and school bonds (36 per cent). Some 14 per cent of all subjects had both strong family and strong school bonds. An extreme group of subjects that have

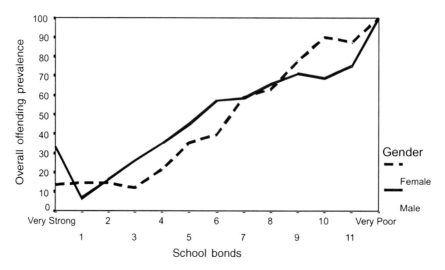

Figure 6.10 Overall offending prevalence by level of (weak) school bonds

Table 6.5 Offending prevalence by school bonds and gender

School bonds*	Overall offending	Shoplifting	Aggressive crimes**	Serious theft
Males				
Strong	22	3	19	3
Medium	46	11	43	9
Weak	69	31	65	27
Signif.	0.000	0.000	0.000	0.000
Females				
Strong	13	6	8	0
Medium	33	17	23	3
Weak	75	46	62	20
Signif.	0.000	0.000	0.000	0.000

Notes:
* School bond scale grouped into strong (scores 0–3), medium (scores 4–7) and weak (scores 8–12).
** Assault and vandalism combined.

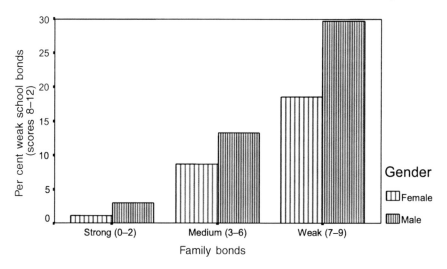

Figure 6.11 Per cent with weak school bonds (scores 8–12) by main group of family bond

both a poor family and a poor school bond constitutes 3 per cent of all subjects. However, a small extreme group of subjects have very poor family bonds but very strong school bonds, or the reverse. They make up 2 per cent of all subjects. All in all, the group with very weak social bonds (both family and school) is rather small.

Family social position affects school bonds more than family bonds, although the effect is not very strong

To explore whether the subjects' variation in social bonds was related to their families' social position the mean scores of family and school bonds were calculated for the categories of family social class, family structure and family ethnicity (see Chapter 5). The findings showed overall that the school bond varies more with family social position than the family bond (Table 6.6). In the latter case it was only for family structure that there was a significant difference: youths living in a complete family of origin tended to have a somewhat stronger family bond than others. This makes sense since as it is likely that family disruptions may negatively affect the family bond. There were no significant differences in family bond by family social class or family ethnicity. As regards the school bond, there was a family social class difference in that the lower the social class, the weaker the school bond. This difference may reflect social class-based differences

Table 6.6 Mean scores of family and school bonds by family social position variables, mean, significance and eta^2

Family social position	Weak family bonds	Weak school bonds
Family social class		
Unemployed	3.3	5.2
Lower working	3.3	5.1
Working	3.2	5.0
Lower middle	3.0	4.5
Upper middle/upper	3.0	4.4
Signif.	n.s.	0.000
Eta^2	–	0.02
Family structure		
Two parents (biological)	2.9	4.6
Two parents (one step-parent)	3.5	5.2
Single parent	3.5	5.3
Moving between parents	3.2	4.8
Foster parents/in care	3.4	5.1
Signif.	0.000	0.000
Eta^2	0.02	0.02
Family ethnicity		
Native	3.2	4.9
Foreign, non-Asian	3.2	4.8
Asian	2.9	4.4
Signif.	n.s.	0.003
Eta^2	–	0.01

in educational cultures. The school bond was somewhat stronger for those living in complete families and for those of Asian origin. None of the effects (as shown by eta^2) was very strong, explaining only 1–2 per cent of the variance.

Self-control

The construct used to measure self-control is based on that developed by Grasmick *et al.* (see Bursik and Grasmick 1993). This was an attempt to measure the concept of self-control as applied by Gottfredson and Hirschi (1990). Self-control refers to the ability to resist temptation and provocation when facing a particular circumstance (Wikström 2006). Individuals with a low ability to exercise self-control will act more on the spur of the moment and hence may be more likely to act upon temptation. Therefore the risk of offending may be assumed to be higher for those with a low degree of self-control than those with a high degree of self-control.

The Construct

A self-control scale was created by summing the subjects' responses to 13 statements about themselves to which they could 'strongly agree', 'mostly agree', 'mostly disagree' and 'strongly disagree'. For example: 'Sometimes I will take a risk just for the fun of it' or 'I never think about what will happen to me in the future.' Each statement was coded 0–3, where 3 was the score for the answer indicating the lowest degree of self-control and 0 for the answer indicating the highest degree of self-control. The scores for the 13 items were summed to form the overall measure of low self-control ranging from 0 to 39, where 0 is the highest and 39 the lowest level of self-control. The distribution of the scores is shown in Figure 6.12. The 13 statements are listed in Appendix D.

Youths with low self-control more often feel tempted to steal, more often get angry with other youths and would more often rather have £50 today than wait a year to get £200

To validate the low self-control scale as a measure capturing variation in temper, impulsivity and discounting behaviour the scale was

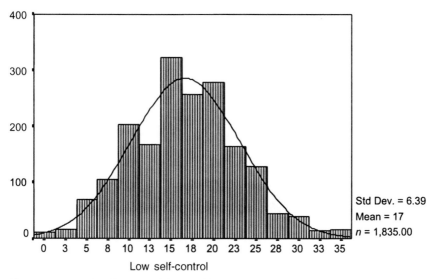

Figure 6.12 Distribution of low self-control scores

related to selected other questions. For ease of presentation the 39-point scale has been grouped into 13 classes (0–2, 3–5, etc.). First, individuals with low self-control more often stated that they got angry with other youths on a daily basis (Figure 6.13) and that they were tempted to steal at least once every week (Figure 6.14).

It should be noted that this predominantly applies to those at the far end of the distribution (i.e. having very low self-control). A classic question about discounting (i.e. take £50 today or wait a year and get £200) showed that the lower the subject's level of self-control, the more likely he or she is to take £50 today rather than wait a year for £200 (Figure 6.15). All in all, subjects with low self-control reported that they were tempted (to steal), provoked by others (angry with other youths) and tended to prefer immediate gratification (£50 today) more often than subjects with higher self-control.

Youths with low self-control offend more than others

Youths with low self-control offend far more frequently than those with high self-control (Figure 6.16). At most levels of self-control (with the exception of some of the highest levels of low self-control) boys have a slightly higher criminal prevalence than girls. Examining overall criminal prevalence, and prevalence for main groups of crime by self-control divided in three main classes (Table 6.7), there is no gender difference in overall criminal prevalence for those with the

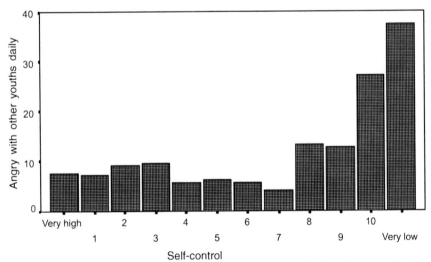

Figure 6.13 Per cent angry with other youths daily by degree of self-control

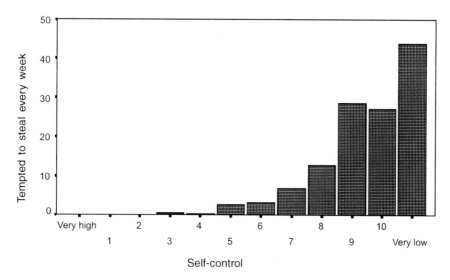

Figure 6.14 Per cent tempted to steal at least weekly by degree of self-control

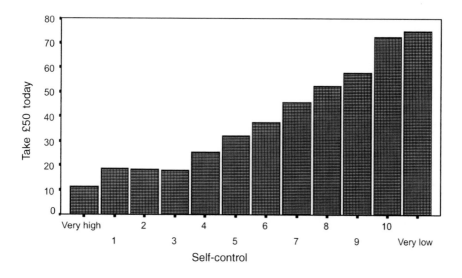

Figure 6.15 Per cent who prefer £50 today over £200 in one year's time by degree of self-control

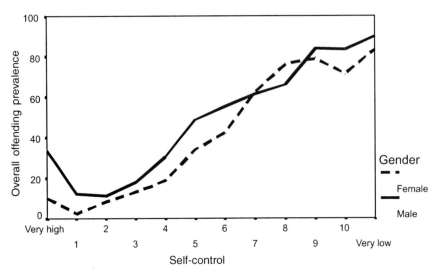

Figure 6.16   Overall offending prevalence by (low) self-control

Table 6.7   Offending prevalence by self-control and gender

Self-control*	Overall offending	Shoplifting	Aggressive crimes**	Serious theft
Males				
High	15	2	14	1
Medium	49	11	45	8
Low	76	35	70	34
Signif.	0.000	0.000	0.000	0.000
Females				
High	9	5	5	0
Medium	36	19	25	3
Low	77	42	70	22
Signif.	0.000	0.000	0.000	0.000

Notes:
* Self-control scale grouped into high (scores 0–12), medium (scores 13–24) and low (scores 25–39).
** Assault and vandalism combined.

lowest self-control, while there is a significant gender difference in overall criminal prevalence for those with high-to-medium levels of self-control. The same holds for aggressive crimes, while for serious thefts the male criminal prevalence is higher at all levels. As regards shoplifting the pattern is the reverse: girls have a higher prevalence at all levels.

Youths from the middle classes tend to have slightly higher self-control than others

The level of (low) self-control is significantly related to family social class and family structure but not to family ethnicity (Table 6.8). Subjects in lower social classes, on average, have somewhat lower self-control than those in higher social classes. The main difference lies between the middle and other classes, which may reflect general class differences in child-rearing methods. Youths living with foster parents/in care or living with a step-parent, on average, have somewhat lower levels of self-control than those living in other types of families.

Table 6.8 Mean scores of (low) self-control by family social position variables, mean, significance and eta^2

Family social position	Low self-control
Family social class	
Unemployed	17.9
Lower working	17.5
Working	17.4
Lower middle	15.5
Upper middle/upper	15.0
Signif.	0.000
Eta^2	0.03
Family structure	
Two parents (biological)	16.1
Two parents (one step-parent)	18.3
Single parent	17.0
Moving between parents	16.1
Foster parents/in care	20.1
Signif.	0.000
Eta^2	0.02
Family ethnicity	
Native	16.5
Foreign, non-Asian	16.7
Asian	17.2
Signif.	n.s.
Eta^2	–

It is possible that this reflects some general influence of family disruption on the level of self-control. However, the differences in self-control by family social position are not great and the explained variance is low (between 2 and 3 per cent). The role of family social position can probably best be described as having weak general influences on the subjects' levels of self-control.

Morality

Two constructs believed to measure aspects of the youths' morality were created, one regarding pro-social values and the other regarding shaming. Both primarily focused on criminal behaviour and not on morals in general. The measure of pro-social values was taken from a scale used in the Pittsburgh Youth Study (directed by Professor Rolf Loeber, University of Pittsburgh), while the measure of shaming was one created by one of the authors and previously used in Swedish studies of youth crime. Pro-social values refers to the youths' evaluation of whether it was wrong for someone of his or her age to engage in a number of specific behaviours, ranging from 'skipping school without an excuse' to 'attack[ing] someone with a weapon with the idea of seriously hurting that person'. Shaming refers to the stated degree of shame the subject would feel in relation to parents, teachers and peers if it became known to them that the subject had engaged in shoplifting or breaking into a car. The hypothesis is that subjects with a high degree of pro-social values and a high potential for shaming would offend less frequently than others.

The construct of pro-social values

The *pro-social values* construct was created by summing the scores for 14 statements regarding potential wrongdoings (see Appendix E). For each statement the subject could state it was 'very wrong', 'wrong', 'a little wrong' or 'not wrong at all'. The answers were coded from 3 (very wrong) to 0 (not wrong at all). The resulting scale therefore varied between 0 and 42, where 0 indicates high anti-social values and 42 high pro-social values. The distribution of the scores is shown in Figure 6.17.

Most youths have strong pro-social values

The distribution of pro-social values is highly skewed (mean 33); the overwhelming majority of the youths scored high on pro-social values.

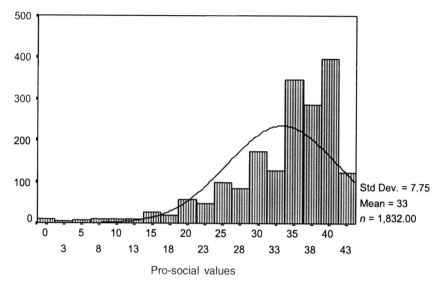

Figure 6.17 Distribution of pro-social values scores

This is something that challenges the idea sometimes put forward of the existence of 'a criminal subculture' among adolescents, if that is taken to mean the existence of large groups of youths who hold positive views regarding breaking the law.

The construct of shaming

The six questions used to create the *shaming* construct are presented in Table 6.9. Each question was coded 0–2, where 2 indicated the highest level of shame. The final construct was made by summing the scores for the six questions giving a score that could vary from 0 to 12, where 12 indicates the highest level of shame. The distribution of scores is shown in Figure 6.18. Just as for pro-social values, the distribution is highly skewed, most youths tend to report high levels of shame in front of significant others (parents, teachers and peers) if caught having committed a crime. However, the importance of parents, teachers and peers as a source of shame varies significantly, as illustrated by the frequencies presented in Table 6.9.

Parents are the most important, and peers (best friend) the least important, source of shame. For example, 79 per cent would feel very much ashamed if their parents knew they had shoplifted, while the corresponding figure for 'best friend' is 36 per cent.

Table 6.9 Variable used to create the shaming construct

Variable	Code	*n*	%
If you were caught shoplifting would you feel ashamed if:			
a. Your *best friend* found out about it?			
No, not at all	0	522	26.9
Yes, a little	1	719	37.1
Yes, very much	2	696	35.9
Total		1,937	99.9
Missing		20	
b. Your *teachers* found out about it?			
No, not at all	0	375	19.4
Yes, a little	1	630	32.6
Yes, very much	2	927	48.0
Total		1,932	100.0
Missing		25	
c. Your *parents* found out about it?			
No, not at all	0	101	5.2
Yes, a little	1	313	16.2
Yes, very much	2	1,522	78.6
Total		1,936	100.0
Missing		21	
If you were caught *breaking into a car* would you feel ashamed if:			
a. Your *best friend* found out about it?			
No, not at all	0	454	23.4
Yes, a little	1	631	32.6
Yes, very much	2	853	44.0
Total		1,938	100.0
Missing		19	
b. Your *teachers* found out about it?			
No, not at all	0	337	17.4
Yes, a little	1	538	27.8
Yes, very much	2	1,061	54.8
Total		1,936	100.0
Missing		21	
c. Your *parents* found out about it?			
No, not at all	0	83	4.3
Yes, a little	1	260	13.4
Yes, very much	2	1,593	82.3
Total		1,936	100.0
Missing		21	

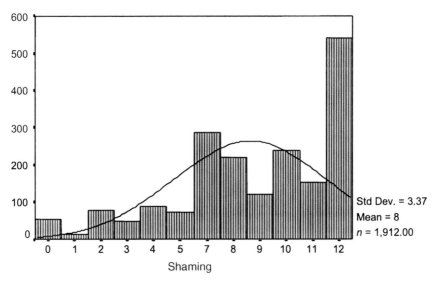

Figure 6.18 Distribution of shaming scores

Youths with strong pro-social values tend to have stronger social bonds than others

Social bonds theory predicts that those with stronger social bonds should also have more pro-social values since they are better integrated in conventional society. This also holds true for the Peterborough youths. High pro-social values go together with stronger family and school bonds. This is illustrated by the negative zero-order correlations between pro-social values and weak family bonds ($r. = -0.35$, $p = 0.000$), and pro-social values and weak school bonds ($r = -0.43$, $p = 0.000$). These relationships are also portrayed in Figure 6.19 (please note that the two curves refer to the mean scores for *weak* family and *weak* school bonds respectively by level of pro-social values).

Youths with high levels of shaming also evaluate the risk of getting caught and being in trouble if caught as higher than do others

To study the relationship between levels of shaming and (perceived) deterrence a construct was made based on two questions about the subjects' perceived risk of getting caught if committing a crime (shoplifting and breaking into a car) and two questions on the perceived consequences of getting caught (being in a lot of trouble or not). The four alternatives for the 'risk of being detected' questions

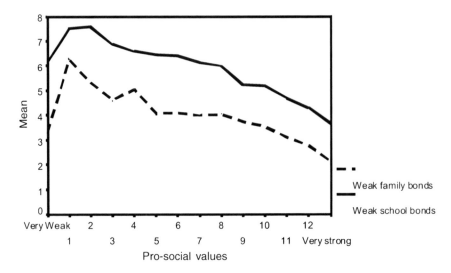

Figure 6.19 Mean scores of weak family bonds and weak school bonds by level of pro-social values

ranked from 'no risk at all' to 'a very great risk' and were coded 0–3, where 3 indicates a very great risk. The four alternatives for the 'being in trouble if caught' questions ranked from 'no, nothing would happen' to 'yes, serious problems' and were coded 0–3, where 3 represents serious problems (see Appendix F). The resulting construct of perceived deterrence ranged from 0 to 12, where 12 indicates a high-perceived deterrence.

The higher the level of shaming, the higher the perceived risk of getting caught and being in trouble if caught ($r. = 0.56$, $p = 0.000$). The effect is the same both for boys and girls (Figure 6.20): the percentage with high scores for perceived deterrence is essentially the same for boys and girls (i.e., non-significant gender differences) for each main level of shaming.

Youths with strong pro-social values offend less than others

Youths with strong pro-social values offend much less than those with anti-social values – i.e. those having low scores on pro-social values (Figure 6.21). There is a tendency that girls with low levels of pro-social values tend to offend equally to or more than boys, while girls with high levels of pro-social values tend to offend somewhat less than boys. Considering the main groups of crime (Table 6.10), it

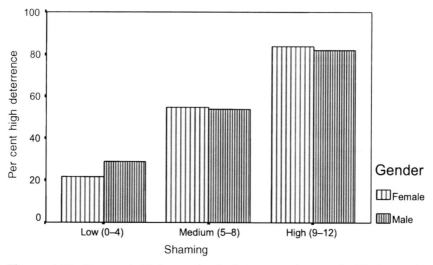

Figure 6.20 Per cent high-perceived deterrence (scores 9–12) by main groups of shaming

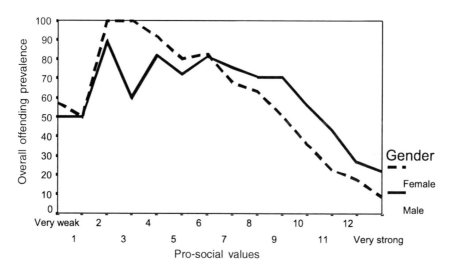

Figure 6.21 Overall offending prevalence by pro-social values

is clear that for all types of crime the main dividing line is between those in the high pro-social value category and the rest. In this context, it should be remembered that the overwhelming majority of the youths are in the highest categories (see Figure 6.17).

Table 6.10 Offending prevalence by pro-social values and gender

Pro-social values*	Overall offending	Shoplifting	Aggressive crimes**	Serious theft
Males				
High	37	7	34	5
Medium	74	26	69	25
Low	68	35	53	26
Signif.	0.000	0.000	0.000	0.000
Females				
High	22	10	15	1
Medium	67	42	51	17
Low	78	52	70	18
Signif.	0.000	0.000	0.000	0.000

Notes:
 * Pro-social values scale grouped into high (scores 29–42), medium (scores 15–28) and low (scores 0–14).
** Assault and vandalism combined.

Youths with a high degree of perceived shaming offend less than others

Youths who perceive that they would have a high degree of shame if caught committing a crime offend much less than others (Figure 6.22). Just as for pro-social values, girls tend to have higher levels of offending prevalence than boys among those having the lowest level of shame, while the reverse is true for the higher levels of shame. Considering specific categories of crime (Table 6.11), this only applies to overall offending and, particularly, to shoplifting, but not to aggressive crimes and serious thefts where boys' prevalence is somewhat higher in the groups of low shaming.

There are no social class differences in pro-social values

Exploring the mean levels of pro-social values and shaming by the three studied aspects of family social position shows that there are no social class differences in the level of pro-social values, a fact that speaks against the idea of the existence of a 'lower class' subculture of delinquency (Table 6.12). However, there are some slightly higher levels of shaming for the middle classes, which may reflect general class differences in child-rearing techniques.

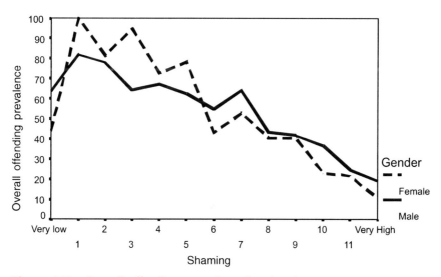

Figure 6.22 Overall offending prevalence by shaming

Table 6.11 Offending prevalence by shaming and gender

Shaming*	Overall offending	Shoplifting	Aggressive crimes**	Serious theft
Males				
High	28	2	26	2
Medium	53	14	48	10
Low	70	30	65	27
Signif.	0.000	0.000	0.000	0.000
Females				
High	18	8	12	0
Medium	48	27	35	6
Low	76	44	59	23
Signif.	0.000	0.000	0.000	0.000

Notes:
 * Shaming scale grouped into high (scores 9–12), medium (scores 5–8) and low (scores 0–4).
** Assault and vandalism combined.

Table 6.12 Mean scores of pro-social values and shaming by family social position variables, mean, significance and eta^2

Family social position	Pro-social values	Shaming
Family social class		
Unemployed	32.8	8.3
Lower working	33.8	8.2
Working	32.8	8.2
Lower middle	33.9	8.9
Upper/upper middle	34.0	8.9
Signif.	n.s.	0.001
Eta^2	–	0.01
Family structure		
Two parents (biological)	33.8	8.8
Two parents, one step-parent	32.6	8.1
Single parent	32.9	8.2
Moving between parents	31.9	7.7
Foster parents/in care	29.0	7.1
Signif.	0.000	0.000
Eta^2	0.01	0.01
Family ethnicity		
Native	33.3	8.4
Foreign, non-Asian	32.8	8.5
Asian	35.1	9.4
Signif.	0.007	0.001
Eta^2	0.01	0.01

Considering family structure, those living with foster parents or in care tend to have somewhat lower levels of pro-social values and shaming, but again the differences are not very great. This difference may possibly reflect that some youths living with foster parents or in care may do so because of their criminality, and we know from previous analyses that there is a relationship between involvement in crime and having weaker pro-social values (see Figure 6.21).

Youths of Asian origin tend to have slightly higher pro-social values and shaming compared with other groups. However, as will be shown in a subsequent section, this is predominantly due to higher levels of pro-social values and shaming among Asian females (see Table 6.17 below).

Individual characteristics and victimisation

While individual variations in offending are often assumed to reflect variation in individual characteristics, research into individual variation in victimisation has mainly focused on its link to different lifestyles, and sometimes to the concept of ecological risk (i.e. risk determined by where one lives and spends ones time, which is obviously related to lifestyle). This is probably because victimisation is often regarded as something more passive (happens to you) and offending as something more active (something you do), although we know that the distinction between victimisation and offending is not always that clear cut (for example, in a fight) and that some people may be offenders at one time and victims at another (see Chapter 4). When individual characteristics have been included in victimisation studies they have predominantly been used as predictors of lifestyle variation, and the focus has been on demographic characteristics such as gender, age and social position (e.g. Hindelang *et al.* 1978).

While the rates of offending vary greatly with the youths' social situations and dispositions, rates of victimisation do not vary as much, or sometimes not at all (Table 6.13). Considering overall victimisation, those with weak family and school bonds and low self-control have higher levels of victimisation, while for pro-social values those in the middle group have higher levels of victimisation, as do those with higher levels of shaming. However, it may be noticed that, when considering the main types of victimisation, the most consistent relationship to the youths' social situation and dispositions is for violence victimisations. However, for vandalism victimisation the differences are mostly non-significant and for theft victimisation most of the differences are rather small or non-significant. Given that having property stolen or vandalised does not necessarily involve any direct contact between victim and offender it makes sense that individual characteristics, if having any direct influence, should predominantly influence victimisation for crimes of direct contact such as assault. For example, it cannot be excluded that an individual's personality may have some effect on the risk of being assaulted.

The composite risk-protective score

Until now we have considered a number of different dimensions of the youths' social situations and dispositions. It has been shown that

Table 6.13 Victimisation prevalence by key constructs of youths' social situation and dispositions

Construct	Overall		Violent		Vandalism		Theft	
	Male	Female	Male	Female	Male	Female	Male	Female
Family bonds								
Strong	56	33	30	13	12	9	33	21
Medium	59	37	34	16	11	8	40	26
Weak	72	59	45	35	15	16	53	37
Signif.	0.017	0.000	0.022	0.000	n.s.	0.019	0.001	0.001
School bonds								
Strong	52	32	28	12	10	9	32	22
Medium	59	39	33	17	12	10	37	26
Weak	70	58	46	37	18	9	51	37
Signif.	0.015	0.000	0.008	0.000	n.s.	n.s.	0.005	n.s.
Self-control								
High	55	30	27	9	12	9	34	21
Medium	59	39	34	19	12	9	39	26
Low	67	56	48	34	13	7	43	31
Signif.	n.s.	0.000	0.000	0.000	n.s.	n.s.	n.s.	n.s.
Pro-social values								
Weak	56	48	23	37	18	4	47	26
Medium	69	54	44	34	13	13	45	33
Strong	56	35	32	13	11	9	36	24
Signif.	0.004	0.000	0.004	0.000	n.s.	n.s.	0.050	n.s.
Shaming								
Low	66	54	40	31	18	9	45	31
Medium	61	43	36	21	11	12	40	30
High	54	35	30	14	11	9	34	23
Signif.	0.010	0.001	0.027	0.000	0.023	n.s.	0.028	0.050

most youths have what can be described as adequate (i.e. medium strength) social bonds and levels of self-control, and strong pro-social values and a high degree of (perceived) shaming if caught committing a crime. It is also clear from the analyses carried out that all the studied individual characteristics were important predictors of offending. Juveniles with weak social bonds, low self-control, anti-social values and a low degree of shaming tend to offend, while juveniles with the reverse characteristics tend not to offend. All in all, a youth's involvement in crime is closely related to aspects of his or her social situation and disposition.

In this section we shall first address how all these aspects (constructs) hang together, and then create a summary measure of the subjects' overall risk-protective characteristics. People act as individuals and, in so doing, may draw upon many of their characteristics in complex interactions; therefore a composite measure may better (and more realistically) portray them as individuals.

The zero-order correlations show that all aspects of the youths' social situations and their dispositions are quite strongly correlated (Table 6.14). A factor analysis (principal component) resulted in one factor with an eigenvalue above 1, explaining 55 per cent of the variance (Table 6.15). This factor can be thought of as a risk-protective dimension, where different aspects of the youths' social situations and their dispositions contribute to their overall risk-protective score.

The overall risk-protective score

Two composite measures of the overall risk-protective score were created. First, factor scores for the factor presented in Table 6.14 were calculated. Secondly, a score was calculated based on risk and protective points for each of the six constructs. Each construct was divided into the third of scores at the protective end of the distribution (given the value of –1), the third of scores in the middle

Table 6.14 Zero-order correlations between constructs measuring youths' social bonds, parental control, self-control and morality

	Weak family bonds	Weak school bonds	Poor parental monitoring	Low self-control	Strong pro-social values	High shaming
Weak family bonds	1.00					
Weak school bonds	0.38	1.00				
Poor parental monitoring	0.46	0.44	1.00			
Low self-control	0.41	0.56	0.51	1.00		
Strong pro-social values	–0.35	–0.43	–0.47	–0.52	1.00	
High shaming	–0.34	–0.47	–0.49	–0.54	0.55	1.00

Note:
All correlations significant at the 1 per cent level or better.

Table 6.15 Factor analysis: individual characteristics, principal component

Constructs	Factor loadings	Communalities
Weak family bonds	0.64	0.41
Weak school bonds	0.75	0.56
Poor parental monitoring	0.75	0.57
Low self-control	0.80	0.64
Strong pro-social values	−0.75	0.56
High shaming	−0.77	0.60
Eigenvalue	3.3	
Explained variance	55.7	

(given the value of 0) and the third of scores at the risk end of the distribution (given the value of 1). For example, subjects having a score among the highest third of scores of low self-control were given the value of 1, those belonging to the lowest third of scores for low self-control were given a value of –1, and the rest a score of 0. The risk and protective points were then added for all the six constructs resulting in an overall score ranging from –6 (most protective) to 6 (most risk).

The zero-order correlation between the factor score and the risk and protective points score measures was almost perfect ($r. = 0.97$). Therefore it was decided to use the risk and protective points score as the overall risk-protective score measure, because the interpretation of these values is more intuitive than that of the factor scores. The distribution of the risk-protective score is shown in Figure 6.23. Most youths are on the protective side (the mean score is –2).

Girls tend to have more protective factors than boys

A comparison between the distributions for boys' and girls' scores is shown in Figure 6.24. It is clear that girls, on average, have more protective characteristics than boys. The mean score for boys is –1.5 (SD = 2.5) and the mean score for girls is –2.5 (SD = 2.5), a difference that is significant ($p = 0.000$, eta^2 = 0.03).

Considering the gender differences in the individual constructs that makes up the overall risk-protective score reveals some interesting variation (Table 6.16). Shaming shows by far the greatest gender difference, followed by self-control. Also parental monitoring, school bonds and pro-social values show significant, but less strong, gender differences, with pro-social values being the weakest. In the case of

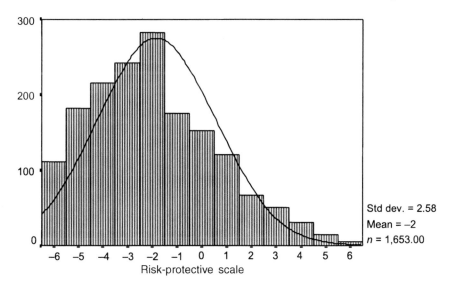

Figure 6.23   Distribution of scores for overall risk-protective measure

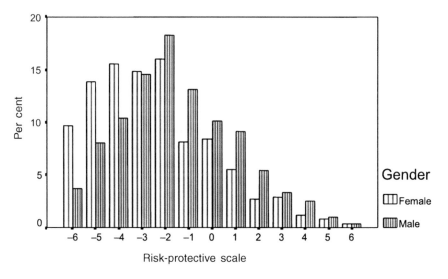

Figure 6.24   Distribution of scores for overall risk-protective measure by gender

Table 6.16 Gender differences in social situation and disposition constructs in rank order, mean, significance and eta^2

Construct	Male	Female	Signif.	Eta^2
High shaming	7.7	9.3	0.000	0.05
Low self-control	17.6	15.6	0.000	0.03
Poor parental monitoring	3.5	2.8	0.000	0.02
Weak school bonds	5.1	4.5	0.000	0.02
Strong pro-social values	32.8	33.9	0.001	0.01
Weak family bonds	3.1	3.1	n.s.	–

family bonds, there are no significant gender differences. What this all means is that the most important gender differences in the risk-protective score refer to aspects of the youths' dispositions (shame and self-control) rather than to their social situations. A significant reason, then, why girls, on average, tend to have higher protective scores than boys is that they tend to have higher levels of shame and stronger self-control.[1]

Asian girls have the highest average of protective scores

Adding the ethnicity dimension (Asian v. non-Asian) to the gender comparison shows that Asian girls have the highest protective scores for all six constructs and for the overall risk-protective score. Asian females have the highest level of shaming and pro-social values, and the lowest level of poor parental monitoring, low self-control, weak school bonds and weak family bonds, although the family bonding is not significantly different among the compared groups (Table 6.17). In contrast, Asian males have scores similar to, or higher than, non-Asian males, with the exceptions of shaming (higher) and weak school bonds (lower). Considering the overall risk-protective score, the main differences are between males and females, and between non-Asian females and Asian females. These differences mirror very well the differences between these groups in offending prevalence (see Figure 5.17).

Youths in more advantageous social positions tend to have more protective factors than others

To answer the question whether youths' risk-protective scores, in addition to their variation by gender and ethnicity, also varied by their family social position the index of *family structural risk*, combining

Table 6.17 Mean scores of social situation and disposition constructs by Asian or non-Asian background and gender (in rank order), mean, significance and eta^2

Construct	Males		Females		Signif.	Eta^2
	Non-Asian	Asian	Non-Asian	Asian		
Shaming	7.6	8.5	9.2	10.3	0.000	0.06
Poor parental control	3.5	3.8	2.9	1.7	0.000	0.04
Low self-control	17.4	19.5	15.7	14.8	0.000	0.03
Weak school bonds	5.4	4.9	4.6	3.8	0.000	0.03
Pro-social values	32.8	33.0	33.7	37.4	0.000	0.02
Weak family bonds	3.1	3.1	3.2	2.7	n.s.	–
Risk-protective score*	–1.5	–1.2	–2.4	–3.5	0.000	0.04

Note:
* The higher the negative value, the higher the protective score.

family social class and family structure, was used (see Chapter 5). Since there were only 12 subjects in the category of highest risk (scoring 2), these subjects were combined into one category with those scoring 1. The category of high risk therefore contains those who either have parents who are unemployed or have a lower working-class occupation, those who live with foster parents or in care, or those to whom both criteria apply.

The findings show that those young people with more favourable structural characteristics tend to have more protective factors (Figure 6.25). The relationship holds both for males (p = 0.000, eta^2 = 0.03) and females (p = 0.000, eta^2 = 0.03). However, at all levels of structural risk females have a lower (more protective) score. The difference for boys between the two most favourable scores of structural risk was marginal.

Structural risk has a greater importance for non-Asians than for Asians

Finally, bringing together all aspects of structural position, structural risk evidently has a greater importance for the non-Asian risk-protective score than for the Asians risk-protective score (Figure 6.26). In fact, while the differences are significant for non-Asians they are not for Asians. In this analysis the categories of structural risk have been combined into two (low risk = scores of –2 and –1, high risk = scores of 0 and 1) because the number of Asians in some categories was far too small to justify making any calculations.

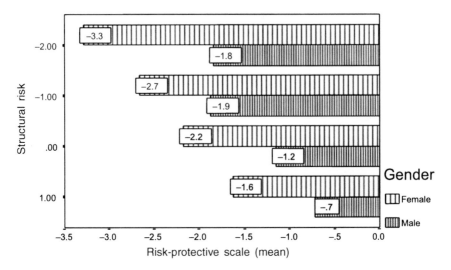

Figure 6.25 Risk-protective scores by structural risk and gender

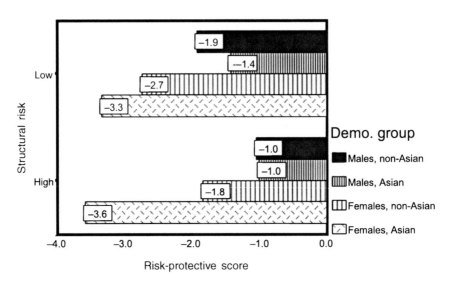

Figure 6.26 Risk-protective scores by structural risk, gender and ethnicity

Gender and structural risk are important factors accounting for variation in youths' social situations and dispositions (i.e. their risk-protective scores)

A multiple regression, predicting the risk-protective score, showed, that being female, being Asian and particularly being an Asian female, coming from a higher social class and living in a complete family were all significant factors. The total variance explained was 8 per cent (Table 6.18). Roughly, gender and family social position each account for half the explained variance. All in all, the joint effect of the youths' gender and social position does have an important impact on their individual social situations and dispositions.

Table 6.18 Risk-protective score by gender and family social position: OLS multiple regression

Variable	Beta	T-value	Probability
Female	−0.19	−7.8	0.000
Asian	−0.05	−2.1	0.032
Asian female	−0.09	−3.5	0.004
Complete family	−0.11	−4.5	0.000
Family social class	−0.13	−5.2	0.000
Multiple $R^2 \times 100 = 8$			

Almost all youths with a high risk score offend, while almost none with a high protective score offend

There is a strong relationship between the youths' score on the risk-protective scale and their offending. The higher the score, the more they have offended (Figure 6.27). However, a careful look at the graph shows that the curve tends to reach its near maximum of prevalence and level off before reaching the maximum level of risk.[2] The same pattern basically holds when comparing the curves for males and females (Figure 6.28). The male prevalence increases steadily with increasing risk until about score 3, where it levels off at its near maximum. For females the corresponding pattern is a steady increase in prevalence to score 0, then a sharp increase in prevalence between scores 0 and 2 (from about 40 to about 90 per cent), and thereafter the female curve levels off at its near maximum.

Offenders with high-risk scores, and particularly male offenders with high-risk scores, tend to commit more crimes per capita than other offenders

The number of crimes per offender (sometimes referred to as lambda) is a measure of offender activity. Comparing offenders' crime frequency by risk-protective score shows that, while initially (score −6 and onwards) the average number of crimes committed only increases at a very modest rate, around score 0 the average shows a much faster increase, particularly for boys (Figure 6.29). What this

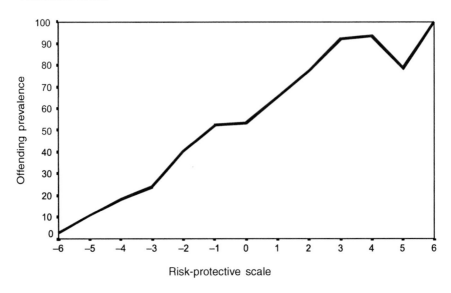

Figure 6.27   Offending prevalence by risk-protective score

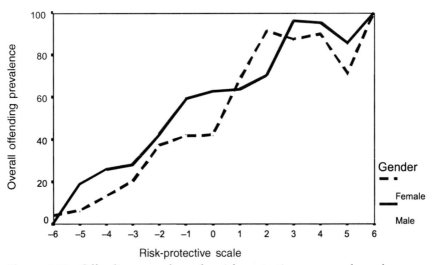

Figure 6.28   Offending prevalence by risk-protective score and gender

means is that offenders, and particularly male offenders, with higher values on the risk-protective score tend to be much more active than offenders with lower risk-protective scores. So, not only do more youths at the risk end of the distribution offend more, but also, of

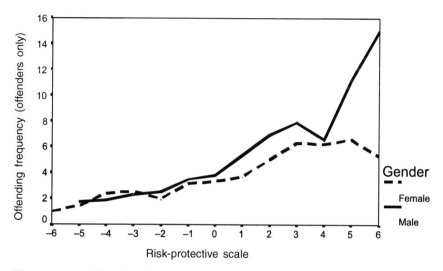

Figure 6.29 Offenders' frequency of offending by risk-protective score and gender

those who offend, they tend to be much more active (i.e. commit more crimes per capita).

Offenders with high-risk scores tend to be more versatile than other offenders

Youths with high-risk scores do not only commit more offences at a greater frequency, but also commit a wider range of offences (Figure 6.30). This was partly to be expected, since we know from previous analyses that the higher the frequency of offending the more versatile the offender (see Figure 4.3), and high-risk scoring youths offend more frequently (as shown in Figure 6.29).

Multiple regression analyses

To study the joint influence of family social position and individual characteristics on youth offending, a series of multiple regression analyses were carried out. An analysis of a model adding only the social situation constructs (i.e. family bond, school bonds, parental monitoring) to the social position variables was created (Table 6.19, Model 1). Including the social situation constructs meant that all family social position variables lost significance. Only gender still had an impact, though very modest, on offending. The strongest impact of gender was for aggressive crimes (less offending by females) and

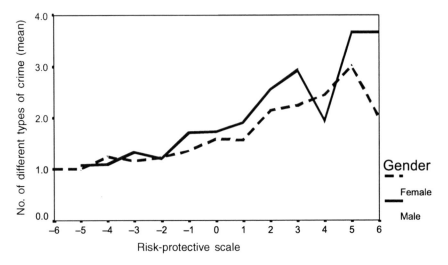

Figure 6.30 Versatility in offending by risk-protective score and gender (offenders only)

shoplifting (more offending by females). Parental monitoring and school bonds were the strongest predictors, while family bonds were quite weak predictors (and non-significant as regards serious thefts and aggressive crimes).

In Model 2 (Table 6.19), the three disposition constructs were added. Including low self-control, pro-social values and shaming resulted in gender losing significance as a predictor for overall offending and serious theft (while remaining significant for aggressive crimes and shoplifting). Also the two social bonds constructs lost significance for all types of crimes. Of the social situation constructs only parental monitoring kept its significance as a predictor for overall offending, and for all types of crime except serious theft. Interestingly, the self-control construct lost significance as a predictor for the only crime type where females dominate: shoplifting.

A possible interpretation of these results is that, as one includes constructs closer to social action, the more distant determining factors fade in importance (as illustrated in Figure 6.31). Self-control, pro-social values and shaming can all be regarded as aspects of the individual close to his or her decision-making processes and perception of action alternatives. Conversely, the individual's social bonds and, in particular, social position, have a more distant and indirect influence on behaviour, mediated through their impact on

Table 6.19 Main types of offending (frequency), social position, social situation and dispositions: OLS multiple regression

Variable	Overall offending		Serious theft		Shoplifting		Aggressive crimes	
	Beta	Prob.	Beta	Prob.	Beta	Prob.	Beta	Prob.
Model 1								
Female	−0.06	0.005	−0.06	0.013	0.08	0.001	−0.13	0.000
Asian	0.00	n.s.	0.03	n.s.	−0.04	n.s.	0.00	n.s.
Asian female	0.00	n.s.	0.03	n.s.	−0.04	n.s.	0.00	n.s.
Complete family	−0.01	n.s.	−0.02	n.s.	0.01	n.s.	−0.00	n.s.
Family social class	−0.01	n.s.	0.02	n.s.	−0.01	n.s.	−0.02	n.s.
Weak family social bonds	0.05	0.028	0.03	n.s.	0.06	0.026	0.03	n.s.
Weak school bonds	0.20	0.000	0.12	0.000	0.15	0.000	0.17	0.000
Poor parental monitoring	0.25	0.000	0.12	0.000	0.17	0.000	0.26	0.000
Multiple $R^2 \times 100 =$	19		5		9		18	
Model 2								
Female	−0.04	n.s.	−0.04	n.s.	0.11	0.000	−0.10	0.000
Asian	0.02	n.s.	0.04	n.s.	−0.02	n.s.	0.02	n.s.
Asian female	−0.01	n.s.	−0.00	n.s.	−0.02	n.s.	−0.01	n.s.
Complete family	−0.01	n.s.	−0.01	n.s.	−0.00	n.s.	−0.01	n.s.
Family social class	0.00	n.s.	0.03	n.s.	0.01	n.s.	−0.00	n.s.
Weak family social bonds	0.00	n.s.	−0.02	n.s.	0.03	n.s.	−0.01	n.s.
Weak school bonds	0.02	n.s.	−0.02	n.s.	0.03	n.s.	0.03	n.s.
Poor parental monitoring	0.12	0.000	0.01	0.001	0.07	0.019	0.15	0.000
Low self-control	0.15	0.000	0.11	0.000	0.03	n.s.	0.17	0.000
Pro-social values	−0.17	0.000	−0.16	0.000	−0.15	0.000	−0.10	0.000
Shaming	−0.19	0.000	−0.13	0.000	−0.17	0.000	−0.14	0.000
Multiple $R^2 \times 100 =$	28		11		14		25	

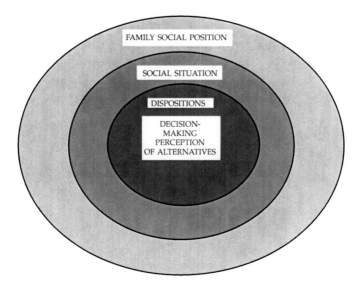

Figure 6.31 A model of individual factors' influence on decision-making and perception of alternatives for action

factors closer to actual behaviour. Another way to put it is that youths' dispositions are embedded in their social situation which, in turn, is embedded in the youths' wider social position. The fact that parental monitoring still keeps its significance for most types of offending may be because (in a cross-sectional snapshot in time) it is more directly related to the youths' contexts of action rather than their offending propensities (i.e. strong parental control may mean that a child is less often exposed to risky situations for offending, a topic we shall return to and explore further in Chapter 8).

When including the social situation variables (Model 1), the explained variance for overall offending reaches 19 per cent (compared with 3 per cent when only including the social position variables – see Table 5.5). Moreover, when the disposition variables are added (model 2) the explained variance further increases to a respectable 28 per cent. Looking at specific types of crime, the models explain most variance for aggressive crimes, followed by shoplifting and, lastly, serious theft.

The final question to be raised in this chapter is whether the composite overall risk-protective score does equally well in explaining the variance in offending frequency. To test this, the risk-protective score variable was included in a model with the social position variables, while the social situation and disposition constructs that

Table 6.20 Main types of offending (frequency), social position and risk-protective score: OLS multiple regression

Variable	Overall offending		Serious theft		Shoplifting		Aggressive crimes	
	Beta	Prob.	Beta	Prob.	Beta	Prob.	Beta	Prob.
Female	−0.05	0.018	−0.06	0.024	0.10	0.000	−0.12	0.000
Asian	0.02	n.s.	0.04	n.s.	−0.03	n.s.	0.02	n.s.
Asian female	−0.02	n.s.	−0.01	n.s.	−0.01	n.s.	−0.02	n.s.
Complete family	0.01	n.s.	−0.01	n.s.	0.00	n.s.	0.01	n.s.
Family social class	0.01	n.s.	0.03	n.s.	0.01	n.s.	0.00	n.s.
Risk-protective score	0.49	0.000	0.28	0.000	0.37	0.000	0.43	0.000
Multiple $R^2 \times 100$ =	26		8		13		23	

make up the overall risk-protective score were excluded (Table 6.20). By and large, the overall risk-protective score does as well in predicting offending as a model including each of the single constructs (the risk-protective score explains a couple of per cent less variance). When using the composite measure, gender returned as a significant (but very weak) predictor for overall offending and serious theft. Using the index of family structural risk (see Chapter 5) instead of the single family social position predictors in the model did not affect the result.

Notes

1 An illustration of this is the fact that, if one excludes shaming and self-control from the calculation of the overall risk-protective score, the importance of gender, although still significant, reduces from explaining 3 per cent to 1 per cent of the variance in the overall risk-protective score.
2 The fact that there is a marked dip at risk score level 5 should not concern us too much in this context, since the numbers in each category at this level are relatively small, and therefore the dip most likely reflects this fact rather than reflecting any substantial reason.

Chapter 7

The community context: neighbourhoods and schools

Criminological theory and research point to the community context as an important factor influencing individuals' offending and risk of victimisation (e.g. Kornhauser 1978; Sampson and Groves 1989; Bottoms and Wiles 1997; Wikström 1998). The basic idea is that community structural characteristics (e.g. population mix) affect the conditions for social life and control (e.g. through levels of social cohesion and residents' social and economic resources) and that this, in turn, has some bearing on people's behaviour, including offending.

There are two main ways in which community context can influence offending behaviour. First, by being the *context of development* that contributes to shaping and forming the growing individual (see, e.g. Bronfenbrenner 1979; Martens 1993). This aspect cannot be addressed in a cross-sectional study such as this, though it should be examined as it may be the most important aspect of community influence on offending behaviour (i.e. by its potential influence on the development of individual characteristics – social situation and dispositions – linked to offending propensity).

Secondly, the community context may influence offending, and victimisation risk, by providing *contexts of action* (behaviour settings). For example, communities may vary in the extent to which the individual is confronted with situations entailing risk (e.g. temptations or provocations) or being exposed to networks (peer groups) that promote offending behaviour. This is the aspect of community context influence that is the focus of this study (i.e. situational influences).

A particularly difficult problem when studying the situational influence of community context on offending behaviour is that of disentangling which effects are due to community characteristics and which are due to individual characteristics. For example, community contexts are likely to vary in the composition of youths by their individual risk-protective characteristics. The key question, then, is to what extent community variation in offending is due to variation in youths' individual characteristics (compositional effects) and to what extent it is due to variation in social life and informal social control as a result of structural and organisational features of the community. In addition, the relationship between individual characteristics and offending behaviour may also have *context-specific* elements. For example, certain individual characteristics (e.g. low self-control) may be reinforced or moderated by (risk or protective) community characteristics. If so, one would expect interaction effects between individual and community characteristics. Finally, as noted, in a cross-sectional study like this one (a snapshot in time) we have had to ignore the developmental aspects of community influences (i.e. the degree to which individual characteristics related to offending propensity may be the result of the type of community in which the individual has grown up).

Another important problem is the lack of well developed measures of relevant aspects of community context (as discussed in Chapter 3). Most studies, including this one, rely upon structural characteristics and, generally, only residential population characteristics when classifying community contexts. Residential population characteristics are only part of an area's structural characteristics. The characteristics of the non-residential population (visitors to the area) and the land-use-related type of activities that take place in the neighbourhood (for example, the presence of commercial and entertainment activities) are perhaps equally, or even more, important as a cause of environmental risk (Wikström 1991). No such data were available for this study.

Pursuing the same line of argument as we did discussing the influence of individual characteristics (see Chapter 6), it may be assumed that the impact of structural characteristics on the production of 'criminogenic' behaviour settings is distant and indirect. Therefore one should not expect too strong a relationship with offending behaviour, particularly when only covering residential population characteristics (Figure 7.1). Advancing the knowledge on the role of community context will also require the development of measurements more proximate to offending behaviour – for example, techniques to map out the prevalence and frequency of 'criminogenic' behaviour

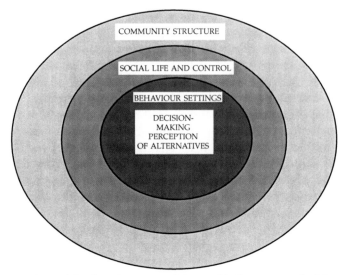

Figure 7.1 A model of environmental factors' influence on decision-making and perception of alternatives

settings in a community (in studies where the developmental aspect of community influence is the focus of investigation other types of community measurement may be relevant).

When considering a specific age group like adolescents, one has to bear in mind that the role of the community is likely to vary by age. For the newborn the home may be the most important context, but as a child grows older his or her context of action expands into the wider environment of the area of residence (and the environments of kindergartens and schools), and then further into the area in which the neighbourhood is located (e.g. a city). Perhaps the two most important aspects of urban youths' community context are their neighbourhood and their school.

Finally, and perhaps the most troublesome when using neighbourhoods as a measure of exposure to environmental conditions, adolescents (as adults) will, to varying degrees, spend time outside their neighbourhood and many of the risk situations they face (and crimes they commit) may not be located in their neighbourhood environment. This implies that using neighbourhood context as a measure of the adolescents' environment will prove to be a biased measure. This fact should be kept in mind when evaluating the findings about the relationship between community context and offending (victimisation). What is really needed is a measure of exposure to environments, rather than a measure based on the surrounding area of the place of residence. (In the ongoing PADS study, we are experimenting with developing such a measure of environmental exposure based on data from space-time budgets.)

The space-time budget study (see further Chapter 9) shows that, if one discounts sleeping time, Peterborough adolescents spend on average 58 per cent of their time in the ward in which their home is located (48 per cent in their home ED; 38 per cent in their home), 28 per cent of their time in school and the remaining 14 per cent of their time in other places outside their neighbourhood or school (e.g. visiting the city centre, visiting friends or participating in leisure and other activities in other parts of the city or outside Peterborough). In this context it should be recalled that the subjects' neighbourhood is defined and measured as their home ED and that they spend less than half of their waking time in that ED. In this chapter we will explore the link between structural aspects of the community context and youths' offending and victimisation risk focusing on neighbourhoods and schools.

The neighbourhood context

The area of residence structural risk measure

A general presentation of Peterborough and its neighbourhoods was carried out in Chapter 3. Two basic sources of data were used to describe variation in area of residence structural characteristics: the IMD deprivation scores for neighbourhoods ($n = 22$) and factor scores for enumeration districts ($n = 286$) based on a factor analysis of the 1991 census data (see Table 3.3). The latter analysis produced three factors: family disruption, ethnic minorities and high socioeconomic status. Based on two of the factors (the family disruption factor and the (high) socioeconomic status factor), a composite measure of *area of residence structural risk* was created to summarise key enumeration district structural characteristics. The measure was created using the following procedure:

1 The factor scores for each of the two factors were re-scaled to include only positive values while keeping the relative distance between each score.[1]

2 The score for high socioeconomic status was then subtracted from the family disruption score to give the composite measure of area structural risk.[2]

The resulting measure combines risk aspects of area of residence (ED), socioeconomic status and level of family disruption. The areas with high family disruption and low socioeconomic status will have high positive scores while, at the other extreme, areas with low family disruption and high socioeconomic status will have high negative scores. As pointed out earlier, this measure ignores structural aspects of the non-residential population and activities located in the area.

The mean values of ED area structural risk scores were calculated for the five neighbourhood disadvantage classes as defined by the IMD scores (see Table 3.2). The result showed a sharp increase in average ED area structural risk by neighbourhood IMD disadvantage score group, except for the two most disadvantaged neighbourhood groups where the mean ED structural risk score was roughly the same (Figure 7.2). This shows that there is an overall correspondence between the two measures.

However, a closer analysis of ED structural risk variations shows that in some cases there are significant variations in structural risk between enumeration districts within a given neighbourhood. Although there is an increase by neighbourhood disadvantage class in the percentage EDs above the overall area structural risk mean (mean = −0.87), even in the most disadvantaged neighbourhood group there

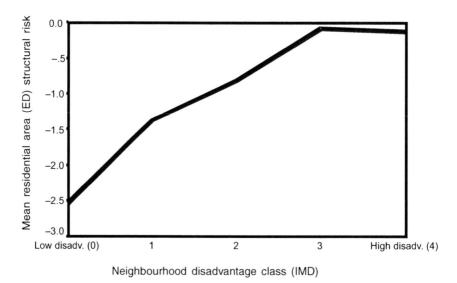

Figure 7.2 Mean ED structural risk score by neighbourhood disadvantage class (IMD)
Note: The data in figure refer to ED-level data ($n = 286$).

are EDs that have structural risk scores that are among the lowest of all EDs (Table 7.1). It was therefore decided to use the ED level as the basic unit of analysis for the area of residence context (bearing in mind the potential problems with the ED data referring to 1991).

Each subject was assigned the factor score value for the enumeration district of his or her area of residence as a measure of his or her *area structural risk*. The distribution of the number of youths by their area structural risk score is shown in Figure 7.3. There is a concentration of youths living in areas towards the protective side of the scale (i.e. having negative values).

A first classification of the ED level variable into ten groups was made for use in table analysis and graphs. This classification was made by dividing the ED structural risk scores into ten equal groups. Based on their home ED, the subjects were then assigned to one of the ten groups. Looking at the frequency distribution of this variable showed that some of the classes with the highest structural risk had fewer than 60 subjects. To avoid having groups with fewer than 100 subjects, the four groups with the highest risk scores were grouped into two, resulting in a final classification of *eight groups of area structural risk*. This means that, instead of representing a 10 per cent score interval, the two groups of highest risk each represent 20 per cent of the scores. The distribution of the studied youths by main group of area structural risk is shown in Table 7.2.

Table 7.1 Area of residence (ED) structural risk score for main classes of neighbourhood disadvantage (IMD): minimum and maximum value, mean, median, standard deviation, number of EDs in class, number and per cent EDs over the overall neighbourhood risk score mean

Neighbourhood EDs disadvantage mean class (IMD)						No. of EDs above the mean		
	Min.	Max.	Mean	MD	SD	n	n	%
0 low disadvantage	−3.7	−0.1	−2.5	−2.6	0.86	43	2	5
1	−3.7	3.1	−1.4	−1.6	1.47	74	24	32
2	−3.4	2.3	−0.8	−0.7	1.47	65	36	55
3	−2.8	3.2	−0.1	−0.3	1.58	58	41	71
4 high disadvantage	−3.1	2.0	−0.1	−0.2	1.35	16	13	81

Note:
Analysis made on ED-level data, including only EDs ($n = 235$) where at least one subject resides.

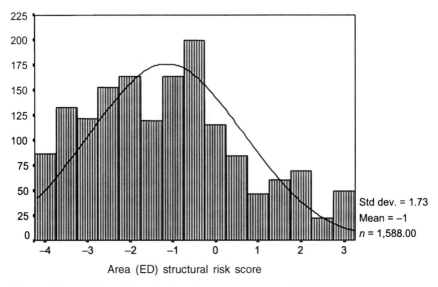

Figure 7.3 Subjects' distribution by area structural risk scores

Table 7.2 Number of boys and girls by main group of ED structural risk

ED structural risk group	Boys (*n*)	Girls (*n*)	Total (*n*)	%
0 (Lowest)	101	101	202	12.7
1	77	94	171	10.8
2	94	94	188	11.8
3	103	114	217	13.7
4	106	123	229	14.4
5	131	118	249	15.7
6	83	79	162	10.2
7 (Highest)	83	87	170	10.7
Total	778	810	1,588	100.0
Missing data: 369*				

Note:
*Predominantly youths living outside the Peterborough urban area.

The wards of Peterborough, with the EDs shaded according to their area structural risk, are shown in Figure 7.4. The dark areas are more disadvantaged (area structural risk groups 5–7), while the light areas are more advantaged (area groups 0–2) and the rest (i.e. the striped areas) are areas in the middle range (area groups 3–4). Studying the

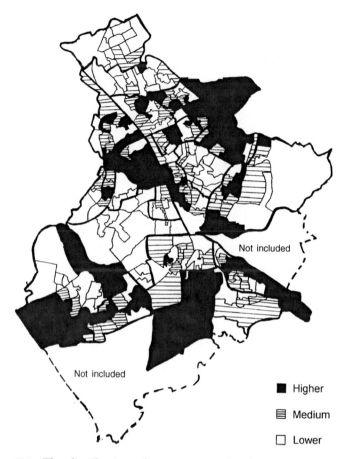

Figure 7.4 The distribution of area structural risk groups by Peterborough urban enumeration districts

map, one can identify one cluster of EDs with higher structural risks covering the eastern part of Paston, the eastern (and middle) part of North, most parts of Dogsthorpe and some of the west parts of East ward. Another cluster of EDs with higher structural risk scores can be found in the middle part of Central extending into and covering most of Ravensthorpe but also some of the North Bretton EDs bordering Ravensthorpe. A third high structural risk cluster of EDs covers the southern parts of Orton Waterville and most of the parts of Orton Longueville where it borders Orton Waterville but also extending into central parts and some north parts of Orton Longueville. Finally, we have some clustering in the South ward and in most of the north part and the west part of Stanground.

Clusters of the more advantaged EDs can be found covering 1) most areas of Park; 2) West ward, extending into the south part of Ravensthorpe and Central, but also into the south and east parts of South Bretton; 3) the northern parts of Orton Waterville; and, finally, 4) most areas of Werrington South and Werrington North.

The map gives some indication of the areas to which we refer when analysing areas of different structural risk. By and large, the pattern of variation of ED area structural risk is consistent with that of the more recent (1998–9) pattern of neighbourhood disadvantage scores (see Table 3.1). However, it is also evident that there is some major within-neighbourhood variation, for example, in Orton Waterville and Ravensthorpe. However, it should again be stressed that the ED-level analysis is based on 1991 census data. Any processes of gentrification or decline which have taken place in the EDs since 1991 (and it is likely that some changes have taken place) will introduce bias into the analysis of the impact of area structural risk on offending behaviour and victimisation.

Youths in high structural risk families, and youths with higher individual risk scores, more often live in disadvantaged areas

A scatterplot (Figure 7.5) of the mean youth risk-protective score by the mean family social position risk score for the eight groups of area of residence structural risk, and indicating the ED structural risk group by the number next to the marker (see Table 7.2), shows, on average, that the youths living in families of higher structural risk, and youths with higher scores on the risk-protective scale, tend to live in more disadvantaged areas (i.e. areas of higher structural risk).

The reverse is true for more advantaged areas (i.e. fewer families with higher structural risks and fewer youths with high-risk scores). Another way to put this is that areas of different levels of disadvantage (structural risk) also vary in their composition of adolescent youths' family social position and in the composition of adolescent youths' individual risk-protective scores. In the next two sections we will explore these relationships in somewhat more depth: first, the relationship between family social position and area of residence structural risk; and, secondly, the relationship between youth risk-protective scores and area of residence structural risk.

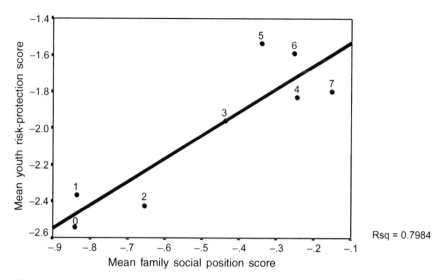

Figure 7.5 Mean youth risk-protective score by mean family social position risk score for groups of ED area of residence structural risk
Note: Numbers next to the marker show group of area of residence structural risk, where 0 indicates lowest and 7 highest risk (see Table 7.2)

Families in less advantaged social positions tend to live in less advantaged areas

Analyses of the relationship between family social position and area of residence structural risk show that less advantaged families tend to live in less advantaged areas. The fact that the adolescents in families in less advantaged social positions more often than others tend to live in less advantaged areas is, of course, to be expected. However, it is far from a one-to-one relationship. Some advantaged families live in disadvantaged areas, and some disadvantaged families live in advantaged areas.

Family social class has the strongest impact on area of residence structural risk, and the main dividing line is between the middle classes and the rest (Table 7.3). Area structural risk also varies by family structure. There is a tendency that youths living in a complete family of origin (i.e. with both biological parents) and those who move between (split up) parents tend to live in more advantaged areas than others (Table 7.3). However, the impact on area structural risk is not as strong as that of family social class. As regards family ethnicity, there is a small difference in area structural risk in that

Table 7.3 Area of residence mean structural risk score by family social position variables, significance and eta^2

	Area of residence mean structural risk score
Family social class	
Unemployed	4.5
Lower working	4.2
Working	3.8
Lower middle	2.7
Upper middle/upper	2.4
Signif. 0.000	
Eta^2 0.11	
Family structure	
Two parents (biological)	3.2
Two parents, one step-parent	3.9
Single parents	4.1
Moving parents	3.3
Foster parents/in care	3.9
Signif. 0.000	
Eta^2 0.03	
Family ethnicity	
Native	3.4
Foreign, non-Asian	3.5
Asian	4.0
Signif. 0.007	
Eta^2 0.01	

youths in Asian families, on average, tend to live in somewhat less advantaged areas (Table 7.3).

These findings were reinforced by a multiple regression analysis of the influence of family social position on area structural risk score (Table 7.4). This analysis showed that family social class was the strongest predictor of the youths' area of residence structural risk (higher social classes tend to live in areas with less structural risk), followed by living in a complete family (complete families tend to live in areas with lower structural risk), while being of Asian origin did not significantly predict area structural risk when taking into account (controlling for) family social class and family structure. Gender was not included as a predictor because there is no reason to expect that

Table 7.4 OLS regression: area of residence structural risk score by family structural risk characteristics (n = 1,566)

Variable	Beta	T-value	Significance
Asian	0.03	1.1	n.s.
Complete family	−0.13	−5.4	0.000
Family social class	−0.27	−11.0	0.000
Multiple R^2 × 100 = 11			

gender would have any influence on the residential segregation of an adolescent's family. If gender is included in the model, its effect was, as expected, highly non-significant: T-value = 0.43.

Youths with higher individual risk scores tend more often to live in less advantaged areas, although this relationship is weaker than that between individual risk and family social position

The analyses of the relationship between area of residence structural risk and individual risk-protective scores show that, although the youths' mean risk-protective scores vary significantly by area of residence structural risk, one cannot very well predict a youth's risk-protective score from knowledge of his or her area of residence structural risk score.

As already illustrated in Figure 7.5, on the aggregate level, there are important area of residence variations in the youths' mean risk-protective score. Another way to illustrate this is with the fact that the proportion of youths with positive scores on the risk-protective scale (i.e. in the range 1–6 – see Figure 6.23) who live in areas with a higher-than-average structural risk is about twice as large as the proportion of such youths living in areas of lower-than-average structural risk (Figure 7.6).

The relationship between area of residence structural risk and the youths' individual risk-protective scores is significant but not as strong as for the relationship with family social position. Just about 1 per cent of the variance in the youths' risk-protective score is explained by their area of residence structural risk score (see zero-order correlations, Table 7.5). The main reason for this is that EDs are more homogeneous as regards the social position (particularly the social class) of the adolescent's family than as regards the youths' individual risk-protective scores.

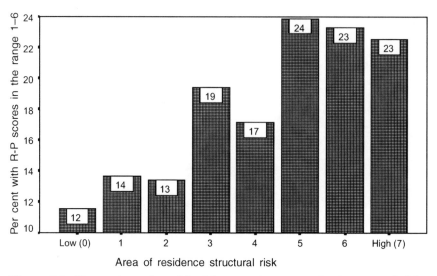

Figure 7.6 Per cent youths with risk-protective scores in the range 1–6 by area of residence structural risk group

Table 7.5 Mean social situation and disposition scores and overall risk-protective score by ED structural risk group, ANOVA and zero-order correlations

Construct	ANOVA*		Zero-order correlations**	
	Eta²	Signif.	r.	Signif.
Social situation				
Weak family bonds	–	n.s.	0.04	n.s.
Weak school bonds	0.01	0.003	0.11	0.000
Poor parental monitoring	0.01	0.039	0.06	0.015
Dispositions				
Low self-control	0.02	0.000	0.10	0.000
Pro-social values	–	n.s.	−0.04	n.s.
Shaming	0.02	0.001	−0.07	0.005
Overall risk-protective score	0.02	0.000	0.12	0.000

Notes:

* ANOVA test of mean differences between the 8 classes of area structural risk.

** *r.* refers to correlations calculated on non-grouped data.

Considering the different constructs that make up the overall risk-protective score (Table 7.5), all but weak family bonds and pro-social values are significantly different by area of residence structural risk score. There are somewhat more youths living in areas of higher structural risk that have weaker school bonds, poorer parental monitoring, lower self-control and who are less prone than their peers to feel ashamed if they commit a crime. The fact that pro-social values did not show any significant variation by area of residence structural risk is of particular interest, especially as pro-social values did not vary by family social class either (see Chapter 6). These findings undermine the idea that any delinquent subculture flourishes among 'lower class' youths living in more disadvantaged areas.

There are no area differences in the prevalence of youth offending, but youth offenders living in more disadvantaged areas tend to offend more frequently than youth offenders living in more advantaged areas

The analyses of offending prevalence and frequency show that the prevalence of youth offending is about the same in all types of areas of residence, but that the offenders living in more disadvantaged areas tended to be more active in their criminality than offenders living in more advantaged areas.

There is no significant variation in overall offending *prevalence* by area of residence structural risk. The same also holds true when males and females are considered separately (see Figure 7.7). However, there is a significant difference by area of residence structural risk in offenders' *frequency* of crime. Offenders living in areas of higher structural risk tend to offend more frequently than offenders in other areas (eta^2 = 0.03, signf. = 0.029). No separate analyses by gender were carried out.[3]

Considering main groups of offending, there is no area of residence variation in the prevalence of shoplifting (this holds for both boys and girls), but shoplifters living in more disadvantaged areas tend to shoplift much more often than others (eta^2 = 0.09, signf. = 0.019). The same pattern holds for aggressive offending (assault and vandalism combined). There is no significant difference in prevalence (this holds for both boys and girls) but offenders of aggressive acts of crime tend to offend somewhat more if they live in disadvantaged areas (eta^2 = 0.01, signf. = 0.036). Finally, as regards serious theft, there are no significant differences in either prevalence or offender frequency of crime. However, when analysing prevalence separately for the two sexes, the area differences are significant for the girls (signf. = 0.044).

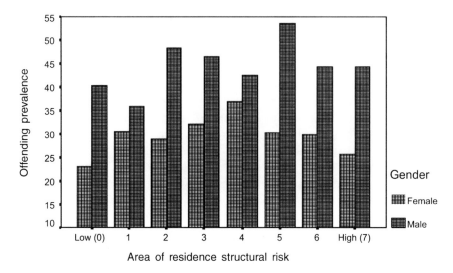

Figure 7.7 Overall offending prevalence by area of residence structural risk group

In this context it is important to bear in mind that serious theft is a rather uncommon crime among this group of adolescents.

Youths in disadvantaged areas commit more crimes locally than others

Although there is no strong (significant) variation in overall prevalence of offending by area of residence structural risk, analyses of the prevalence of locally committed crimes show that youths living in disadvantaged areas (higher structural risk) tended to commit crimes in their neighbourhood more often than youths living in other areas.

The data on crimes committed locally refer to information given by the subject about his or her last committed crimes. The subject defines what is meant by 'his or her neighbourhood' and therefore there is no necessary correspondence to official neighbourhood boundaries. However, these data show the variation in the prevalence of crime committed in and around the youths' place of residence.

Youths in more disadvantaged areas of residence tend to have a higher prevalence of crimes committed locally (Figure 7.8). This holds both for males (gamma = 0.20, signf. = 0.009) and females (gamma = 0.29, signf. = 0.035). This finding is consistent with the assumption that the area of residence structural risk measure captures some of the area variations in environmental risk and hence situational factors

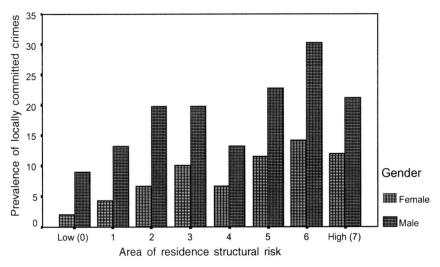

Figure 7.8 Prevalence of locally committed crimes by area of residence structural risk group

that may influence offending. No data on offenders' frequency of locally committed crimes were collected.

Multivariate analyses

To explore further the role of area of residence for the youths' criminality, a series of multivariate analyses were performed. First, the prevalence of overall offending and prevalence of locally committed crimes were analysed by logistic regression in relation to the youths' gender, family social position risk score (using the family index of structural risk), area of residence structural risk score and the individual risk-protective score. To make the odds ratios (i.e. Exp. (B)) comparable, all variables except gender have been standardised (Z-scores). Analyses were performed for 1) the overall prevalence of offending; and 2) the prevalence of locally committed crimes. Two models were tried: one without interactions (Model 1), and one allowing for interactions between independent variables excluding gender (Model 2).

The findings (Table 7.6) show that area of residence structural risk does not have any independent influence on *overall prevalence* of offending, nor does it have any effect interacting with any other of the predictors. The individual risk-protective score is the strongest predictor of overall offending prevalence (youths with higher risk scores offend more) followed by the much weaker predictor of

Table 7.6 Multiple logistic regression: overall prevalence of offending and local prevalence of offending by gender, area of residence structural risk score, family social position risk score and individual risk-protective score

	Overall offending		Local offending	
	Exp. (B)	Signif.	Exp. (B)	Signif.
Model 1				
Female	0.60	0.000	0.46	0.000
Family social position risk	1.05	n.s.	1.23	0.026
Area of residence risk	0.91	n.s.	1.28	0.007
Individual risk-protective score	3.69	0.000	2.84	0.000
Model 2 (including interactions)				
Female	0.60	0.000	0.47	0.000
Family social position risk	1.06	n.s.	1.32	0.022
Area of residence risk	0.91	n.s.	1.38	0.003
Individual risk-protective score	3.71	0.000	3.04	0.000
Family risk*area risk	1.01	n.s.	0.99	n.s.
Family risk*individual risk	0.98	n.s.	0.90	n.s.
Area risk*individual risk	0.97	n.s.	0.88	n.s.

Note:
All variables, except gender, standardised (Z-scores).

gender (females offend less). The rest of the predictors failed to reach significance (see Model 1) and there were no significant interaction effects (see Model 2).

However, considering the prevalence of *locally committed crimes*, area of residence does have a significant impact when controlling for the other predictors (see Model 1).[4] None of the interaction effects reached significance, although the interaction between area of residence risk and individual risk-protective score came close. Because interaction effects are sometimes difficult to detect by regression analysis, it was decided to explore this potential interaction a bit further. An exploration into this pattern of potential interaction did show that youths with higher protective scores tended to be more influenced by their area of residence structural risk than youths with higher risk scores.

A cross-tabulation (Table 7.7) of the prevalence of locally committed crimes by area of structural risk in three classes, and individual risk-protective score in three classes, shows that while there is a significant variation by area of residence structural risk for youths with protective scores (risk-protective scores in the range −6 to −3)

Table 7.7 Prevalence of locally committed crimes by main groups of area of residence structural risk and individual risk-protective scores

Individual risk-protective score	Area of residence structural risk			Significance	Gamma
	Low	Medium	High		
Protective	0.8	2.5	7.1	0.001	0.66
Balanced	12.8	16.7	23.5	0.012	0.25
Risk	45.5	47.8	51.4	n.s.	–
Significance	0.000	0.000	0.000		
Gamma	0.88	0.77	0.64		

Note:
The percentages in the table refer to the percentage who have committed crimes locally. For example, less than 1 per cent (0.8 per cent) of those living in an area of low structural risk and that have a protective score on the individual risk-protective scale have committed a local crime.

and balanced scores (risk-protective scores in the range –2 to 2), there is no significant variation for those with high-risk scores (risk-protective scores in the range 3 to 6). Moreover the analysis also shows that the area of residence structural risk influence is strongest for those with the most protective scores.

What this all means is that not only (when controlling for their gender, family social position risk and individual risk-protective score) have youths living in areas of higher structural risk committed crimes in their neighbourhood more often than youths living in areas of lower structural risk, but also that the area of residence effect is somewhat stronger for more well adjusted youths than for other youths. This finding is consistent with those reported by Wikström and Loeber (2000) in a study in Pittsburgh in which they showed that the youths whose adolescent crime involvement was most influenced by community context were the most well adjusted.

Data on *frequency of crime* were not available for local offending. An analysis of the overall frequency of crime showed that the individual risk-protective score was the strongest predictor, while gender was also a significant but much weaker predictor. Neither family social position nor area of residence risk reached significance (Table 7.8 – model 1). However, by introducing interaction effects the interaction between area of residence risk and individual risk-protective score reached significance (Model 2).

Table 7.8 OLS multiple regression: overall frequency of crime by gender, area of residence structural risk score, family social position risk score and individual risk-protective score

	Beta	Significance
Model 1		
Female	−0.06	0.009
Family social position risk	−0.00	n.s.
Area of residence risk	0.03	n.s.
Individual risk-protective score	0.50	0.000
Multiple $R^2 \times 100 = 27$		
Model 2 (including interactions)		
Female	−0.06	0.006
Family social position risk	−0.00	n.s.
Area of residence risk	0.03	n.s.
Individual risk-protective score	0.49	0.000
Family risk*area risk	0.00	n.s.
Family risk*individual risk	0.02	n.s.
Area risk*individual risk	0.05	0.038
Multiple $R^2 \times 100 = 28$		

A special exploration of this interaction effect (Table 7.9) showed that there was a tendency for the frequency of offending by youths with higher risk scores to be more affected by their area of residence structural risk than other youths. For the youths in the high individual risk group the main difference in frequency of offending was between those in the low area of residence risk group and the other two groups (a difference that was significant when tested as such). However, only for those in the middle group of individual-risk protective scores was the area of residence structural risk difference significant.[5]

All in all, the exploration into the relationship between neighbourhood context, as represented by ED area of residence structural risk score, showed that, although there was no significant variation in overall offending prevalence, there was significant variation in the overall frequency of crime and the prevalence of locally committed crimes (no data of frequency of local and non-local crimes were available because these data only referred to the last crime committed). The fact that the overall frequency of crime and the prevalence of locally

Table 7.9 Overall frequency of offending by main groups of area of residence structural risk and individual risk-protective scores, all youths and offenders only, respectively

Individual risk-protective score	Area of residence structural risk			Significance
	Low	Medium	High	
Protective				
All	0.3	0.4	0.3	n.s.
Offenders	2.2	2.0	2.3	n.s.
Balanced				
All	1.6	2.0	2.4	0.044
Offenders	3.1	3.7	4.7	0.006
Risk*				
All	5.8	7.7	7.2	n.s.
Offenders	6.7	8.0	7.8	n.s.
Significance				
All	0.000	0.000	0.000	
Offenders	0.000	0.000	0.000	

*Difference between low and other two categories significant

committed (last) crimes varied by area of residence risk suggests that frequent offenders are more likely to have committed crime locally than non-frequent offenders. A further indication that this is true is a comparison of the prevalence of locally committed crimes (last crimes) by frequency of offending (Figure 7.9). This comparison shows that, with an increasing frequency of crime there is an increasing likelihood that at least one of the last crimes was committed in the offender's own neighbourhood. This further suggests that the main impact of area of residence structural risk may be on the frequency of locally committed crimes. This makes sense if, as assumed, the measure of area structural risk basically reflects the area of residence production of 'criminogenic' behaviour-settings (or situations).

The analyses in this section also indicated that there were some interactions between area of residence risk and the individual risk-protective score; the local offending prevalence of more well adjusted youths was more influenced (higher) by level of area disadvantage than that of less well adjusted youths (Table 7.7). The overall frequency of offending by less well adjusted youths was more

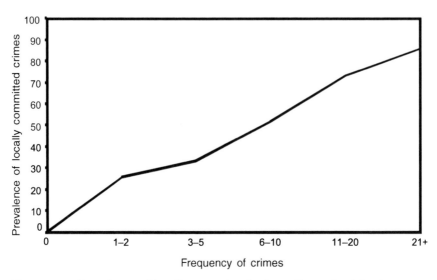

Figure 7.9 Prevalence of locally committed crimes (last crime) by frequency of offending

influenced (higher) by level of area disadvantage than that of more well adjusted youths (Table 7.9).

Youths living in the most advantaged areas have a lower risk of being victimised locally than other youths

So far we have only looked into area of residence risk variations in offending. In this section we will consider the area of residence risk variations in victimisation. The analyses show that there are no significant area of residence structural risk differences in overall prevalence of victimisation. This holds for males and females (Figure 7.10). Nor is there any significant variation by area of residence structural risk in the average number of times victims have been victimised. This holds for boys and girls.

Considering the prevalence of being victimised locally we did not find any significant area of residence structural risk variations, neither totally nor when separately considered for boys and girls (Figure 7.11). However, tested separately, there is a significantly lower risk of local victimisation for females ($p = 0.007$) living in the most advantaged types of area (classes 0 and 1) compared with the rest. The same applied to boys ($p = 0.015$) living in the most advantaged type of area (class 0) compared with the rest. All in all, victimisation does not show any strong variation by area of residence risk, with

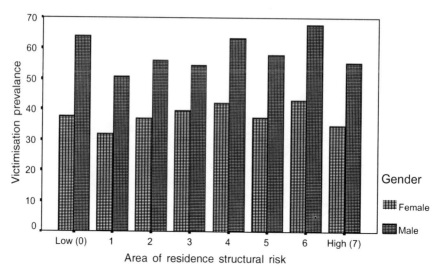

Figure 7.10 Overall prevalence of victimisation by area of residence structural risk group

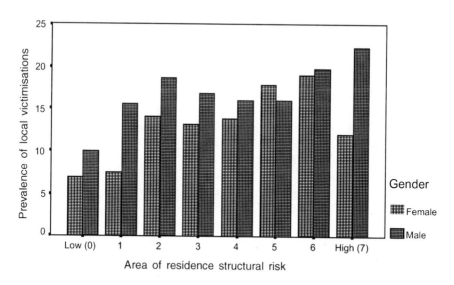

Figure 7.11 Prevalence of victimisation locally by area of residence structural risk group

the exception that those living in the most advantaged areas have a lower risk than others of being victimised locally.

The school context

A significant part of the youths' offending and victimisation takes place in their school context (see Chapter 4). In this section we will explore the link between the schools' structural characteristics and pupils' 1) violent offending in their school; 2) truancy and victimisation by bullying; and 3) victimisation through violence and property crimes in their school.

The school structural risk measure

No independent data of school context were collected for this study. Instead we had to rely on aggregating data about the studied youths' family social class and composition to describe structural variation among the schools.

First, the measure was created by calculating the mean family social class score, and the mean score of the percentage living in a complete family of origin, for the adolescent pupils in each of the 13 included schools and the Link programme (see Chapter 2). Secondly, these two measures were standardised (Z-scores). Thirdly, the two standardised scores were added as a measure of *school structural risk*. Finally, the scale was transformed (by reversing the signs) so that higher values meant more risk and lower values less risk. The resulting measure combines risk aspects of the pupils' family social class position and their family structure. It should be stressed that the school scores are only based on the adolescents included in this study (Year-10 pupils) and therefore do not take into consideration the situation of other pupils at the school. However, it seems to be a fair assumption that variation in school structural risk as represented by one age grade should reflect more generally the structural risk of the school.

Schools with a higher structural risk have more pupils from disadvantaged areas, with weaker school bonds and weaker academic performance

There is a close correspondence between the schools' level of structural risk and the composition of students by their area of residence structural risk. Schools with higher levels of structural risk have more pupils from areas of residence of higher structural risk (Figure 7.12). This illustrates well the segregation in the school system.

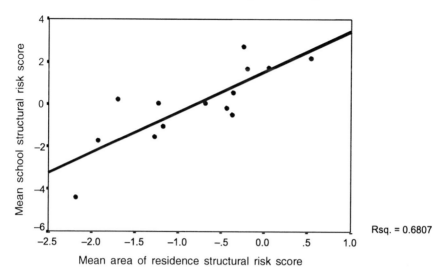

Figure 7.12 Mean school structural risk score by mean area of residence structural risk score

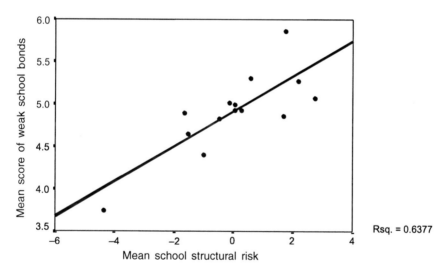

Figure 7.13 Mean score of weak school bonds by mean school structural

An exploration of the level of school structural risk in relation to the pupils' average school bond (for a definition, see Chapter 6) shows that the higher the level of school structural risk, the higher the level of pupils with weak school bonds (Figure 7.13). The measure of school structural risk also has a very strong association to the schools'

155

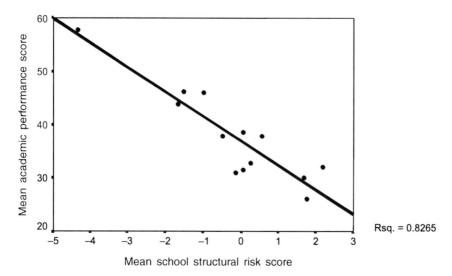

Figure 7.14 Mean academic performance score (pupils aged 15) by mean school structural risk score

average academic performance (based on GCSE/GNVQ results) for 15-year-olds. The higher the school's structural risk, the lower the average academic performance (Figure 7.14). All in all, schools vary in their structural risk. Schools with a higher structural risk tend to have pupils who more often come from disadvantaged areas. Furthermore, schools with a higher structural risk tend to have more pupils who have weaker school bonds and, on average, perform less well academically.

Each youth was assigned his or her school's structural risk score as a measure of his or her school's structural risk. The distribution of the scores is shown in Figure 7.15. The schools were also grouped in four categories based on their average structural risk score (grouped by standard deviations from the mean). The low-risk group contained one school (n = 127), the medium-low-risk group three schools (n = 579), the medium-high-risk group six schools (n = 950) and the high-risk group three schools and the Link programme (n = 301). Each subject was assigned to his or her school's structural risk group for use in graphs and table analyses.

The youths' individual risk-protective score is the strongest predictor of their prevalence of violence in their school environment

In this section we will not be able to provide any information about the subjects' theft offending in their own school. The reason is that

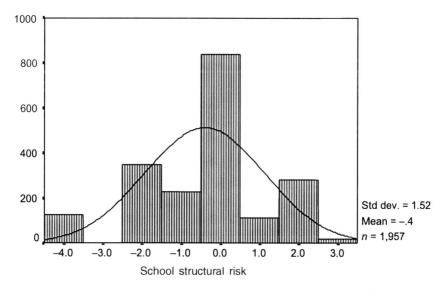

Std dev. = 1.52
Mean = −.4
n = 1,957

School structural risk

Figure 7.15 The distribution of school structural risk scores

the specific types of property crimes included in the study mostly referred to crimes that by definition could not take place in the school environment (shoplifting and residential burglary), or where it was unlikely, or less likely, that they would happen in the school environment (thefts of and from cars and non-residential burglaries), although it is possible that some non-residential burglaries may have been directed towards the subject's own school. Therefore we can only analyse variation in aggressive offending by school structural risk. However, school variations in theft *victimisation* will be analysed in a subsequent section.

Before presenting the findings, two factors which complicate addressing the relationship between school structural context and offending (and victimisation) need to be pointed out. First, the youths were asked whether or not any offence they reported had taken place in their school. However, it is possible that some of the crimes occurring at the school premises may have taken place outside school hours and, if so, have nothing to do with the actual school structural context. For example, some schools may run youth clubs or other activities on their premises in evenings and weekends. To the extent that school variations in aggressive offending partly reflect such activities, a bias was introduced in evaluating the relationship of school structural risk and level of aggressive offending.[6]

Secondly, another complicating factor is that schools have varying rates of truancy (see next section) and, most likely, also varying rates of exclusions of 'problematic' pupils (who in many cases may have been excluded for their violent behaviour). Although we lack data on this, it is a reasonable guess that schools with higher structural risk also have higher rates of school exclusions. The extent to which 'high risk' pupils are excluded, or have a high degree of truancy, may weaken the relationship between school structural risk and violent offending by pupils in that school.

An analysis of the variation in *incidences of aggressive offending* (violence and vandalism) by youths in their own school environment shows that there are no significant differences for boys, but that the difference for girls is significant (see Figure 7.16). A logistic regression of the effect of the subjects' individual scores of school structural risk on their prevalence of aggressive offending in their school showed that this relationship was non-significant for boys but reached significance for girls (odds ratio = 1.21, signf. = 0.042). Aggressive offending is dominated by acts of assault. The pattern for violent crimes only (excluding vandalism) is very similar to that of aggressive offending more generally.

Overall, prevalence of aggressive offending by males in their school was not that different when schools were compared by structural risk group (Table 7.10). However, there are marked variations between

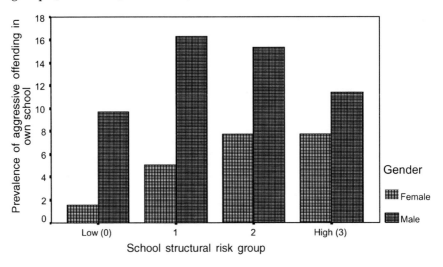

Figure 7.16 Prevalence of aggressive offending (violence and vandalism) committed by pupils in their own school, by school structural risk group and gender

Table 7.10 Prevalence of aggressive offending by school structural risk group and range of variation for individual schools in each group

School structural risk groups/school range	Prevalence of aggressive offending in school		
	Males	Females	Total
Low risk	9.7	1.5	5.5
Range			
Medium low risk	16.3	5.0	10.8
Range	15.1–19.8	3.1–7.0	10.5–11.4
Medium high risk	15.4	7.8	11.6
Range	8.5–30.8	6.0–9.4	8.0–20.0
High risk	11.4	7.7	9.5
Range	4.2–19.4	3.4–10.9	3.8–14.5

individual schools. For example, two schools have markedly lower rates than other schools and one of them belongs to the high school structural risk group. Only one school has a markedly higher rate than the norm.

Whether the violent offending rate variations between individual schools in a given structural risk group depend on factors such as different exclusion and truancy rates; more or less successful school policies against violence and bullying; variation in the 'school climate' (e.g. Rutter *et al.* 1979); and/or the existence (or non-existence) of especially violent gangs that may emerge in an individual school from one year to another, cannot be addressed with the data available in this study. Generally, *one should be careful, without further evidence, not to read too much into an individual school's deviations*, because in some cases they may just reflect 'normal' year-to-year fluctuations and therefore higher prevalence may not always represent more fundamental problems of the school.

A multiple logistic regression of the impact on the prevalence of violent offending by youths in their own school by their school structural risk score, their family structural risk score, their area of residence structural risk score and their individual risk-protective score shows that only their individual risk-protective score has a significant influence on their violent offending in school. Youths with higher risk scores tend more often to have committed violent crimes in their school (Table 7.11). This also holds for boys and girls, with the exception that family social position (structural risk) also

Table 7.11 Multiple logistic regression: prevalence of aggressive offending in own school by school structural risk score, family structural risk score, area of residence structural risk score and individual risk-protective score (total and by gender)

	Total		Male		Female	
	Signif.	Exp. (B)	Signif.	Exp. (B)	Signif.	Exp. (B)
School risk	n.s.	1.04	n.s.	1.02	n.s.	1.01
Family risk	n.s.	0.84	0.026	0.76	n.s.	1.04
Area of residence risk	n.s.	0.96	n.s.	1.01	n.s.	0.86
Risk-protective score	0.000	1.89	0.000	1.70	0.000	1.95

has some influence on boys' violent offending in school. Boys from higher social classes tend to commit acts of violence in school more than other boys in the cohort when controlling for their area of residence, school structural risk and their individual risk-protective score. However, this effect is not very strong. Models allowing for interaction effects were also tried, but none of the interactions was significant.

Every sixth pupil has been truant two times or more

In the study the youths were asked whether during the last year (2000) they had been truant from school, had been bullied and/or had stayed away from school because they were afraid of being beaten up or bullied. The findings show that every sixth pupil had skipped school twice or more without an excuse, every ninth pupil had been bullied at least twice and every eighth pupil had stayed away from school at least once because he or she was afraid of being beaten up or bullied (Table 7.12). There were no significant gender differences in truancy. However, significantly more females reported having been bullied (signf. = 0.000) and that they had stayed away from school because they were afraid of being beaten up or bullied (signf. = 0.000).

Schools with higher structural risks tend to have more truancy and more serious bullying

School levels of truancy and more serious bullying tend to vary by their structural risk (Figure 7.17). There is a highly significant difference in the level of truancy by school structural risk group (signf. = 0.000). This holds for both males (signf. = 0.000) and females

Table 7.12 Prevalence of truancy, bullying and staying away from school because of fear of being beaten up or bullied (total and by gender)

	Total	Male	Female
How often skipped class without an excuse?			
Never	68.1	67.2	68.9
Once	16.2	17.6	14.8
2–4 times	9.2	8.9	9.5
5 or more times	6.5	6.3	6.7
n	1936	970	966
Missing	21		
Have you ever been bullied so you afterwards felt upset or sad?			
Never	71.8	78.4	65.1
Once	16.9	12.9	20.9
2–4 times	8.0	5.9	10.1
5 or more times	3.4	2.9	3.9
n	1940	972	968
Missing	17		
Stayed away from school because of being afraid of being beaten up or bullied?			
Never	87.2	90.2	84.3
Once	8.8	6.8	10.8
2–4 times	2.4	2.2	2.7
5 or more times	1.5	0.8	2.2
n	1928	967	961
Missing	29		

(signf. = 0.000). There are no significant differences in the experience of having been bullied, either totally or for males or females separately. However, the proportion that have stayed home from school because they feared being beaten up or bullied, which may be an indication of the existence of more serious bullying, varies significantly by school structural risk group (signf. = 0.001). It holds for boys (signf. = 0.011), while it just fails to reach significance for girls (signf. = 0.064).

Considering individual schools (Table 7.13), the levels are generally not that different, particularly when considering variation within structural risk groups. There are two schools that stand out (within their structural risk group) as having a markedly higher level of pupils having been truant two times or more, while there is one school that stands out with a very low rate of truancy. The level of pupils reporting that they have been bullied two times or more

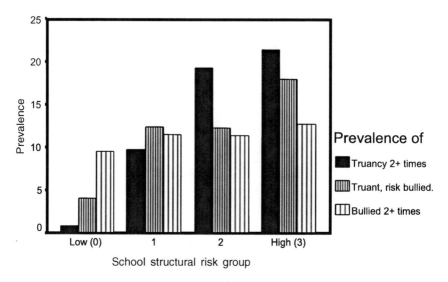

Figure 7.17 Prevalence of truancy (two or more times), truancy because of the risk of being beaten up or bullied and having been bullied (two or more times), by school structural risk

Table 7.13 Prevalence of truancy (two or more times), being bullied (two or more times) and staying away because of being afraid of being beaten up or bullied (at least once), by school structural risk group and range of variation for individual schools in group

School structural risk group/school range	Prevalence of		
	Truancy	Being bullied	Staying away because afraid
Low risk	0.8	9.4	3.9
Range			
Medium low risk	10.1	11.5	12.5
Range	8.2–12.3	10.5–13.4	11.8–13.3
Medium high risk	19.3	11.2	12.3
Range	13.6 – 30.9	7.4 – 16.2	4.6 – 22.6
High risk	21.7	12.5	18.3
Range	14.3–38.2	9.3–14.7	16.0–22.1

does not vary that much between individual schools. Two schools stand out as having markedly lower rates of pupils having stayed away from school because they were afraid of being beaten up or bullied.

The youths' individual risk-protective score is the strongest predictor of their levels of truancy

A multiple logistic regression (Table 7.14) shows that the youths' *prevalence of repeated truancy* (two times or more) is strongly related to their risk-protective score (more high-risk youths are more often

Table 7.14 Multiple logistic regression: prevalence of aggressive offending in own school by school structural risk score, family structural risk score, area of residence structural risk score and individual risk-protective score (total and by gender)

	Truancy*		Bullying**		Bullying risk truancy***	
	Signif.	Exp. (B)	Signif.	Exp. (B)	Signif.	Exp. (B)
Total						
School risk	0.015	1.30	n.s.	1.16	n.s.	1.17
Family risk	0.041	1.19	n.s.	1.17	0.003	1.29
Area of residence risk	n.s.	0.94	n.s.	0.83	n.s.	1.01
Risk-protective score	0.000	3.35	n.s.	0.92	n.s.	1.15
Males						
School risk	n.s.	1.24	n.s.	1.32	n.s.	1.28
Family risk	0.015	1.34	n.s.	1.09	n.s.	1.22
Area of residence risk	n.s.	1.03	n.s.	0.77	n.s.	1.09
Risk-protective score	0.000	2.80	n.s.	0.87	n.s.	0.95
Females						
School risk	0.042	1.39	n.s.	1.07	n.s.	1.12
Family risk	n.s.	1.03	n.s.	1.21	0.013	1.32
Area of residence risk	n.s.	0.85	n.s.	0.87	n.s.	0.95
Risk-protective score	0.000	4.57	n.s.	1.03	0.001	1.41

Note:

All independent variables standardised (Z-scores).

Significant relationships underlined.

  * Truant two or more times.

  ** Bullied two or more times.

  *** Stayed home from school at least once because of fear of being beaten up or bullied.

truant than others), but also to their school structural risk (youths in high structural risk schools are more often truant) and their family social position risk (youths from less advantaged families tend to be truant somewhat more often than others). Considering gender differences, the strongest effect by far for both males and females is their risk-protective score. However, the effect is much stronger for girls than for boys. As regards family social position and school structural risk, it turns out that boys' truancy is only significantly related to their family social position, while girls' truancy is only significantly related to their school structural risk. All in all, high-risk males from less advantaged families, and high-risk females in high structural risk schools, have the highest prevalence of repeated truancy.

None of the included factors significantly predicted whether or not the subject had been *repeatedly bullied* (two or more times). This also holds for boys and girls considered separately (Table 7.14). However, family social position and individual risk-protective score do predict whether or not females had *stayed away from school (at least once) because they were afraid of being beaten up or bullied* (Table 7.14). Females from less advantaged family social positions with higher individual risk scores tended more often than others to have stayed away from school because they were afraid of being beaten up or bullied. For boys none of these factors significantly predicted whether or not they had stayed away from school because they were afraid of being beaten up or bullied. Models allowing for interaction effects were also tried for all three dependent variables, totally and by gender, but in no case were there any significant interaction effects.

The prevalence of victimisations in schools does not vary much by school structural risk

Although there is a weak overall trend that the higher the school's structural risk the less its pupils have been victimised in school (Figure 7.18), these differences are neither significant for boys nor for girls. The same holds true if one considers separately theft, vandalism and violent victimisation in schools (Figure 7.19), although the trend of violence, in contrast to that of theft and vandalism, is a trend of weak increase by school structural risk. This holds for boys and girls.

Considering individual schools (Table 7.15), the overall picture is one of no great variation. Only one school deviates with a markedly higher overall prevalence of victimisation of both boys and girls, and

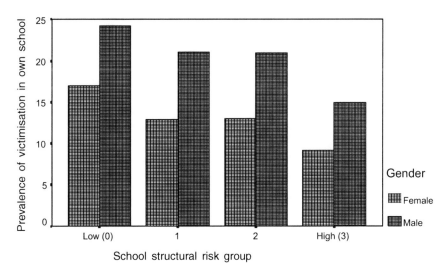

Figure 7.18 Prevalence of overall victimisation in school, by school structural risk group and gender

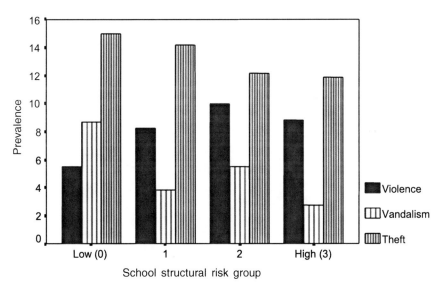

Figure 7.19 Prevalence of theft, vandalism and violence victimisation in school, by school structural risk group

Table 7.15 Overall prevalence of victimisation by school structural risk group and range of variation for individual schools in group

School structural risk groups/school range	Prevalence of overall victimisation in school		
	Males	Females	Total
Low risk	24.2	16.9	20.5
Range			
Medium low risk	21.0	12.9	17.1
Range	18.8–23.5	9.3–16.5	15.9–18.5
Medium high risk	20.9	13.0	17.0
Range	15.9–40.9	6.9–26.0	12.6–33.0
High risk	14.9	9.2	11.9
Range	10.2–25.0	3.6–14.3	7.3–17.1

only one school deviates with a markedly lower prevalence of overall offending for females only.

For violent victimisations the victim was asked whether the offender was a youth from the victim's school or not. Therefore we can explore the prevalence of violent victimisations by fellow pupils (Figure 7.20). As might be expected given that most violent victimisations in school are committed by another pupil at the school (91.4 per cent), the pattern is very similar to that for overall violent victimisations in school.

There are fewer serious violent victimisations in the most advantaged school

It was also possible to explore the level of seriousness of violent victimisations. Comparing the schools' levels of prevalence of violent victimisations with injury (for definitions, see Table 4.9) shows that the main, and statistically significant (signf. = 0.000), dividing line is between the lowest structural school risk (group 0) and the rest, for which the prevalence of violence in school with injuries is two to three times higher (Figure 7.21). No female in the lowest school risk group had been subjected to violence with injury.

The prevalence for individual schools of violent victimisations in school by another pupil is markedly high in one school, and markedly low in two schools. Exactly the same pattern holds for prevalence of violent victimisations in school resulting in an injury (Table 7.16).

A series of multiple logistic regressions were carried out (not shown). They all included as predictors school structural risk, family structural

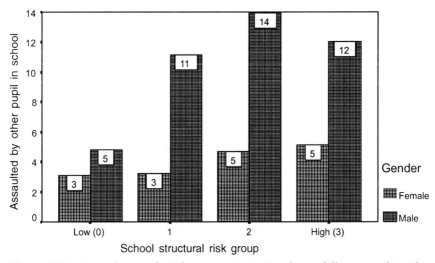

Figure 7.20 Prevalence of violence victimisation by a fellow pupil in the school, by school structural risk group

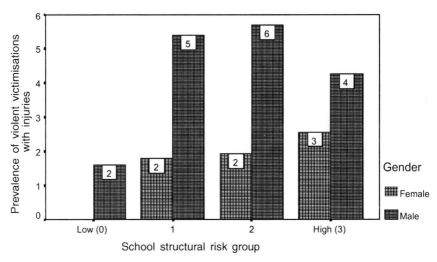

Figure 7.21 Prevalence of violent victimisations with injuries in the school, by school structural risk group

risk, area of residence structural risk, individual risk-protective score and gender. Models with, and without, interactions were tested for 1) overall victimisation in school; 2) violent victimisations in school by a fellow pupil; and 3) violent victimisations that resulted in an injury. When controlling for other predictors, and their interactions, only

Table 7.16 Prevalence of violent victimisations committed by another pupil and of violent victimisations resulting in injury by school structural risk group and range of variation for individual schools in group

School structural risk group/school range	Prevalence of violent victimisation in school	
	By another pupil	With injury
Low risk	3.9	0.8
Range		
Medium low risk	7.3	3.7
Range	5.7–9.2	2.6–4.6
Medium high risk	9.3	3.8
Range	5.8–16.0	2.2–8.5
High risk	8.4	3.4
Range	3.7–13.2	0.9–6.6

gender turned out to be a (highly) significant predictor. Males were much more often victimised in school, much more often subjected to violence by another pupil and, finally, much more often received injuries as a result of a violent victimisation in school.

Pupils who are violent offenders in school are, to a higher degree than others, also victims of violence in school

A study of the relationship between the prevalence of pupils that have been violent in their school and the prevalence of pupils that have been victims of violence in their school shows that there is, as expected, a clear association (Figure 7.22). The more violent pupils in a school, the more pupils who are victims of violence. However, it is far from a one-to-one relationship. For example, one school has a much higher rate of pupils' violent victimisations than could be expected from the number of pupils who have committed violent crimes.

A comparison, on the individual level, shows that there is a strong and significant relationship between being involved in school as an offender and as a victim of violence (signf. = 0.000, gamma = 0.75). Of the violent offenders in school, 29.9 per cent have also been a victim of violence in school (compared with 5.7 per cent of the pupils who have not committed any violence in school). Of those having been a victim of violence in school, as many as 38.4 per cent have also

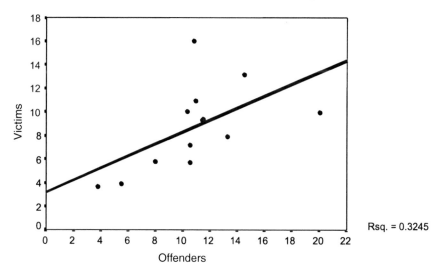

Figure 7.22 Prevalence of pupils being victims of violence in their school by prevalence of pupils who have committed acts of violence in their school

been an offender of violence in school (compared with 8.1 per cent of the pupils who have not been a victim of violence). Another way to illustrate this relationship is to say that of all pupils 3.3 per cent have been both an offender and a victim of violence in their school, 5.1 per cent have only been a victim of violence in their school and 7.4 per cent have only been an offender of violence in their school. This illustrates well the generally strong, although far from perfect, association between being an offender and being a victim of violence (see Table 4.10).

Conclusion

All in all, the exploration into area of residence and school contexts, as represented by their structural characteristics, showed, among other things, that:

- The overall prevalence of offending does not vary by area of residence structural characteristics.

- Youths living in more disadvantaged areas have a higher prevalence of offending locally (i.e. in their neighbourhood) than others.

- Offenders living in more disadvantaged areas have a higher frequency of crime than others.

- There was some evidence that the effect by area of residence structural characteristics on the prevalence of local offending is strongest for youths with more protective factors.

- The youths living in the most advantaged areas are less victimised locally than others.

- The levels of truancy and more serious bullying (youths staying home because they are afraid of being beaten up or bullied) are higher in schools with higher structural risks.

- Aggressive offending in school by girls is higher in schools with higher structural risks.

- The overall prevalence of victimisation in school does not vary much by school structural risk.

- There are fewer serious violent victimisations in school (i.e. with injuries) in the most advantaged school.

Overall, where there are differences between area of residence or school structural contexts, the tendency is that structural advantage may have protective qualities, while structural disadvantage may have risk qualities. As initially discussed in this chapter, with better community context measures (i.e. measures closer to social action) the effects of community contexts on the youths' involvement in crime may prove to be stronger.

Notes

1 This was done by adding the highest negative value (set as positive) to all scores. For example, if the highest negative value was −1.65 this was set to 1.65 and then added to all the values (e.g. 1.65 + −0.41 gives 1.24, while 1.65 + 0.41 gives 2.06). By doing this, the distance between the original scores is kept (in this case 0.82) while the scale is turned into only positive values.
2 Please note that this results in a score including both positive values (high family disruption and low socioeconomic status) and negative values (low family disruption and high socioeconomic status).
3 The reason for this was that, when restricting the data to offenders only, and splitting the data by gender, some categories of area of residence

structural risk had very low frequencies of offenders and therefore the frequency of offending estimates were less reliable.

4 Area of residence structural risk is the third strongest predictor of the four included. The individual risk-protective score is by far the strongest, while the remaining three are much weaker, gender somewhat stronger than family social position risk and area of residence risk (model 1).

5 In this context it should be pointed out that the number of youths in the individual high-risk group in Table 7.9 is substantially lower ($n = 82$) than in the other two groups ($n = 624$ and 637, respectively). This means that much larger differences in frequency are needed for the individual high-risk group to reach statistical significance.

6 However, the fact that most juveniles (91 per cent) assaulted in school were assaulted by another pupil from their school suggests this in not a major source of bias.

Chapter 8

Lifestyles

So far we have dealt with the role of the individuals' family social position, their individual characteristics and the wider community contexts in which their offending and victimisations are embedded. In this chapter we will introduce the concept of lifestyles as an additional and important explanatory factor. We will analyse how lifestyles relate to individual and community characteristics, and to offending and victimisation. We will also look into interaction effects, particularly between lifestyles and other explanatory factors. In the next chapter we will further extend the analysis of the role of lifestyles by bringing in the detailed data on the youths' last-week routines collected in the separate space-time budget study (see Chapter 2).

In criminology, lifestyles have been a strong focus in victimisation research (e.g. Hindelang *et al.* 1979; Garofalo 1986). The basic idea is that an individual's (demographic/structural) characteristics will influence his or her lifestyles which, in turn, will influence his or her degree of exposure to situations entailing higher risks of victimisation. For example, one would expect that females coming from an advantaged social position would have some differences in lifestyle from that of males coming from a disadvantaged social position. It is well documented in criminological research that there is a close link between lifestyles and victimisation risk. However, in this study our main focus will be on the role of lifestyles for offending, a less well researched topic, although we will also report some findings on its relationship to victimisation. As an explanatory factor of offending, just as for victimisation, lifestyles have a natural focus on the role of situations (behaviour settings) for the risk of offending. The main assumed effect of lifestyle is that people with different lifestyles are differently exposed to risk situations (e.g. temptations or provocations) that may, or may not, develop into a crime. A particularly under-researched area is the question of whether lifestyle interacts with community and individual characteristics in producing offending. For example, is the effect on offending by a high-risk lifestyle different for youths with different risk-protective characteristics?

The focus of this chapter will be on lifestyles as represented by the youths' self-reported frequency of time spent in high-risk public environments (shopping-malls, city-centre public space, clubs, bars and discos), the extent of their friends' involvement in crime, and their usage of alcohol and drugs. An overall index of lifestyle risk will be created from these three constructs. The assumption is that youths who spend a lot of time in high-risk public environments, with high-risk friends, and who use alcohol and drugs will have a much higher risk of being involved in crime than those who do the reverse.

Before turning to analysing the impact on offending (and victimisation) of the overall lifestyle risk measure, we will start this chapter by exploring the relationship to offending of the three main components that make up the composite measure: first, peer delinquents; secondly, high-risk public environments; and, thirdly, substance use.

Peer delinquency

That the adolescent offending of boys is, to a large extent, linked to their peers' delinquency is well established in criminological research (e.g. Reiss 1986; Sarnecki 1986; Warr 2002). However, we know less about the role of delinquent peers for adolescent girls' criminality. Although it is well known (at least for boys) that the characteristics of the youths' peers are linked to their offending risk, the causal direction of this influence is somewhat unclear. Whether this relationship is primarily due to the fact that 'delinquent peers' influence (non-delinquent) youths to commit crimes they would not otherwise have committed, or whether already delinquent youths seek out other delinquent youths, or any combination of the two, has not been conclusively answered. For example, it is possible that for some groups of youths they just happen to 'hang around with the wrong crowd' while, for others, it may be a case of 'hanging around with the same crowd' (e.g. other high-frequency delinquents). In the latter case the peer influence may be more on the frequency than on the prevalence of offending.

Seven variables from the questionnaire were chosen to measure the extent to which the youths had friends who were more seriously engaged in criminality. The subject was asked, for each of six different types of crime (ranging from shoplifting to residential burglary), whether he or she had a friend who he or she knew had committed that particular crime. In addition, they were asked whether any of their friends had been caught by the police for a crime. The latter variable was in three categories: 'none', '1–2 friends' and '3 or more friends'. All questions referred to the last year (2000). The measure of peer delinquency was created in the following way. The number of the six specified types of crimes that any friend has committed was summed (note that technically it is possible that the youth has only one friend who has committed all of the six types of crime). The resulting score can vary between 0 and 6. The great majority of the youths (75 per cent) had friends who had committed at least one act of crime. To take into account the seriousness of their friends' offending, but also the frequency of offending by friends, the score for the number of types of crime committed by a friend was then weighted by the number of friends who had been caught by the police (coded 0, 1 and 2 for the three categories specified above). This resulted in a final score varying between 0 and 12 (alpha = 0.82). Youths who did not have a friend whom the police had caught received a score of zero. In this context it should be recalled that the detection rate for the youths' offending was around 10 per cent, and therefore frequent offenders can be expected to be caught by the police sooner or later (see Chapter 4). Those who have been caught by the police more than once are most likely high-frequency offenders.[1] Those who are high-frequency offenders are also likely to have committed more acts of serious crimes (see Figure 4.2). All in all, the peer delinquency measure is a measure that focuses on frequent and serious offending rather than offending in general. The distribution of the scores is shown in Figure 8.1. As may be expected, the distribution is highly skewed. Most youths have low scores on the peer delinquency scale.

The impact of peer delinquency on offending is stronger for females than for males

Peer delinquency is not only related to boys' offending but also to girls' offending. In fact, the relationship between peer delinquency

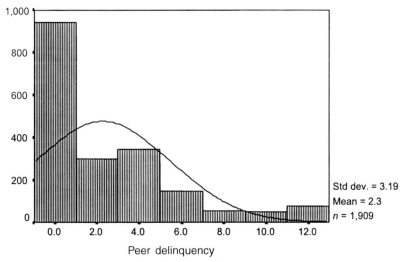

Figure 8.1 Distribution of (high) peer delinquency scores

and prevalence of offending is generally somewhat stronger for girls than for boys.

The effect on overall offending *prevalence* by peer delinquency is highly significant for both males and females (Figure 8.2) but stronger for females (signf. = 0.000, gamma = 0.72) than for males (signf. = 0.000, gamma = 0.52). The same pattern also holds when comparing gender by main groups of crime (serious theft: males gamma = 0.69, females gamma = 0.87; shoplifting: males gamma = 0.58, females gamma = 0.66; aggressive crimes: males gamma = 0.48, females gamma = 0.69).

The impact of peer delinquency on an offender's *frequency* of offending is also somewhat stronger for females' than males' overall offending (males eta^2 = 0.16; females eta^2 = 0.18). However, considering the main categories of crimes, peer delinquency has no significant effect on the frequency of serious thefts and the frequency of shoplifting, only on the frequency of aggressive offending (males eta^2 = 0.12; females eta^2 = 0.09), where the effect is somewhat stronger for boys than girls.

High-risk public environments

Some types of environments are more likely than others to entail risk of creating situations conducive to offending and risk of victimisation.

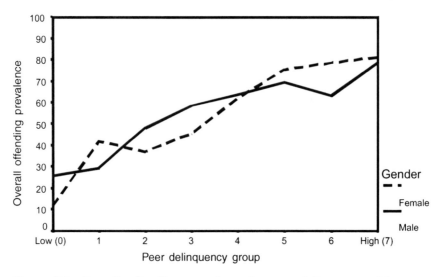

Figure 8.2 Overall offending prevalence by peer delinquency risk group and gender

Generally speaking, it may be assumed that spending more time in public places reflects a lifestyle in which a person is more often confronted with opportunities to offend (and to be victimised by crimes directed towards that person). This is particularly so for what we refer to in this study as common crimes (shoplifting and aggressive crimes). However, it is likely that there is also a more general relationship between a lifestyle involving frequent time spent in high-risk public environments and offending. Youths frequently involved in crime may have a lifestyle that, for example, generally involves a higher participation in public entertainment than other youths. In this latter case there is no direct impact on offending by spending time in a high-risk public environment, merely a correlation. If so, this somewhat complicates the interpretation of the relationship between offending behaviour and time spent in high-risk public environments.

The public environment risk construct was created by adding the scores for four variables referring to the frequency with which the youth normally spent time in 1) shops/shopping-centres; 2) pubs; 3) clubs and discos; and 4) in the city centre of Peterborough. Each variable was coded from 0 to 3 (0 = 'never/almost never', 1 = 'once or twice a week,' 2 = 'most days of a week' and 3 = 'all days of the week'). The final score varies between 0 and 12 (alpha = 0.61). The distribution is shown in Figure 8.3. Since there were very few subjects with scores of 8 and higher, these were added to those with a score of 7 to give a classification for use in table and graph analyses of eight classes.

Time spent in high-risk public environments has a stronger influence on females' than males' offending prevalence, but only affects male offenders' frequency of offending

The analyses of variations in offending *prevalence* revealed that time spent in high-risk public environments had a significant impact on offending, but not as strong an impact as did peer delinquency (Figure 8.4). The influence on overall offending prevalence by time spent in high-risk public environments was somewhat stronger for females (signf. = 0.000, gamma = 0.46) than for males (signf. = 0.000, gamma = 0.32). The same pattern also holds when comparing gender by serious theft (males gamma = 0.43; females gamma = 0.51) and aggressive crimes (males gamma = 0.29; females gamma = 0.45), but not for shoplifting (males gamma = 0.42; females gamma = 0.41), where there was no gender difference in the strength of the relationship.

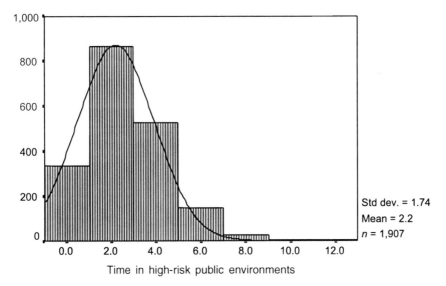

Figure 8.3 Distribution of scores for time spent in high-risk public environments

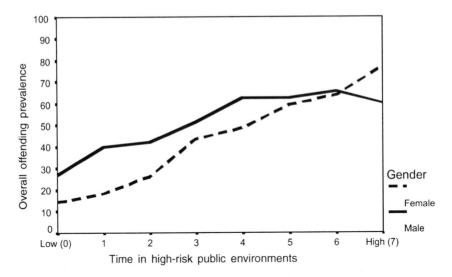

Figure 8.4 Overall offending prevalence by time spent in high-risk public environments and gender

However, the offenders' *frequency* of offending by time spent in high-risk public environments was not significantly different for female offenders, and only for male offenders' overall frequency of offending (males eta^2 = 0.10; females = n.s.), frequency of serious theft (males eta^2 = 0.15; females = n.s.) and aggressive offending (males eta^2 = 0.09; females = n.s.). The effect on frequency of shoplifting by time spent in high-risk public environments was non-significant for both males and females. A separate analysis, restricted to comparing time spent in shops and shopping centres and shoplifters' *frequency* of shoplifting, still showed no significant differences for either boys or girls. However, the *prevalence* of shoplifting was significantly related to time spent in shops and shopping centres for both boys (gamma = 0.44) and girls (gamma = 0.37).

Substance use

The relationship between substance use and offending (and victimisation risk) has already been dealt with in detail in Chapter 4. In this section, the composite measure of alcohol and drug usage employed in the overall lifestyle risk measure will be presented and related to the youths' offending.

There are four alcohol and drug use variables referring to the frequency with which the subject had used alcohol (been drunk), used 'light' drugs like cannabis, used 'hard' drugs like LSD or cocaine and used inhalants (see Chapter 4). The response categories for all four types of substance use were 'no, never', 'yes, once or twice,' 'yes 3–5 times' and 'yes, 6 or more times' (in the last year). These were coded 0–3 and summed resulting in an overall score that varies between 0 and 12 (alpha = 0.66). The overall distribution of substance use is highly skewed; most youths are on the low-frequency end of the distribution (Figure 8.5). Because there were few individuals scoring 8 and higher these were grouped together with those scoring 7 to give a classification of eight groups to be used in tables and graphs.

The effect of substance use is particularly strong on the frequency of serious thefts by male offenders

With the exception of shoplifting, the effect on offending *prevalence* by the alcohol and drug use index score is stronger for females than males (Figure 8.6). The influence on overall offending prevalence by the alcohol and drug use index score was stronger for females (signf. = 0.000, gamma = 0.71) than for males (signf. = 0.000, gamma = 0.52).

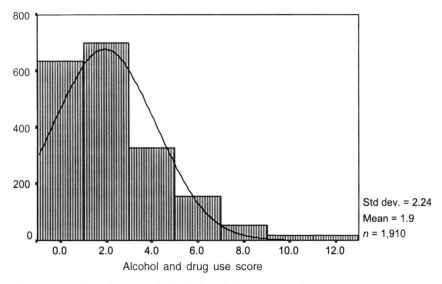

Std dev. = 2.24
Mean = 1.9
n = 1,910

Figure 8.5 Distribution of alcohol and drug use index scores

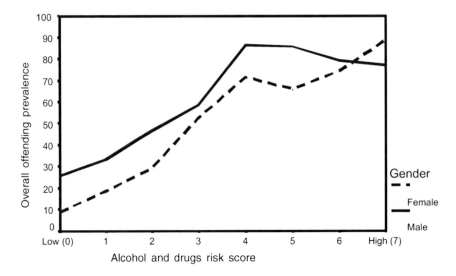

Figure 8.6 Overall offending prevalence by alcohol and drug use index score and gender

The same pattern also holds when comparing by gender for serious theft (males gamma = 0.59; females gamma = 0.87) and aggressive crimes (males gamma = 0.50; females gamma = 0.68). For shoplifting the differences in strength of relationship was small (males gamma = 0.59; females gamma = 0.62).

The alcohol and drug use index score has a strong influence on the offender's *frequency* of offending, particularly so for the boys. For offenders' overall frequency of offending the effect is stronger for males (signf. = 0.000, eta^2 = 0.20) than for females (signf. = 0.000, eta^2 = 0.13). The effect on male offenders' offending is particularly strong for those committing serious thefts (signf. = 0.000, eta^2 = 0.28), while the effect is non-significant for female serious theft offenders. However, it should be recalled that the prevalence of females committing serious thefts is very low (see Table 4.2). In the case of the frequency of aggressive offending, both male and female aggressive crime offenders' frequency of offending is affected by their level of alcohol and drug use (males eta^2 = 0.14; females eta^2 = 0.08), although the effect is stronger for boys. Finally, there are no significant differences in frequency of shoplifting by alcohol and drug-use level for either male shoplifters or for female shoplifters.

The overall lifestyle risk measure

The overall lifestyle risk measure is a composite measure based on the measures developed for the youths' peer delinquency, time spent in high-risk public environments and their levels of substance use. For each of these three measures the lowest third of the scores were re-coded to the value of –1, the middle third scores to the value of 0 and the highest third of the scores to the value of 1. The recoded scores were then added for the three separate measures to give a final measure of *lifestyle risk* that could vary between –3 and 3. Having a score of –3 means that the youth has a score among the lowest third of scores for peer delinquency, for time spent in high-risk environments and for the level of alcohol and drug use. Having a score of 3 means that the youth has a score in the highest third of all three aspects of lifestyle risk. The distribution of the youths by their lifestyle risk scores is shown in Figure 8.7. Most youths have lifestyles at the low-risk end of the distribution. Comparing the distributions for males and females by score of lifestyle risk shows that more males than females tend to have riskier lifestyles, although it is worth while noting that for the highest-risk scores the differences in percentages between boys and girls is small (Figure 8.8).

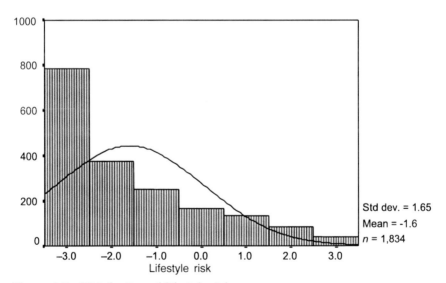

Std dev. = 1.65
Mean = -1.6
n = 1,834

Figure 8.7   Distribution of lifestyle risk scores

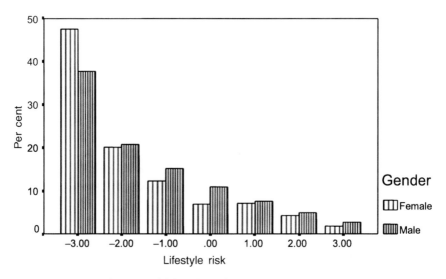

Figure 8.8   Distribution of lifestyle risk scores by gender

Lifestyle risks vary strongly by individual risk-protective scores, but not as much by area of residence structural risk

An analysis of the variation of the mean lifestyle risk scores by area of residence structural risk (see Chapter 7 for definition) shows that the average lifestyle risk varies significantly by area of residence structural risk (Figure 8.9), but that the effect is not very strong (signf. = 0.000, eta^2 = 0.01).

While lifestyle risk does not vary that much by area of residence structural risk, the impact of the youths' risk-protective score on their lifestyle risk is very strong (Figure 8.10). This holds for both males (signf. = 0.000, eta^2 = 0.34) and females (signf. = 0.000, eta^2 = 0.42), although the effect on girls is even stronger than on boys. All in all, the youths' individual risk-protective characteristics are much more important for their lifestyle risk than the area in which they live.

Boys and girls who have a high-risk lifestyle have a much higher prevalence of offending than others

Youths with a low-risk lifestyle, particularly girls with a low-risk lifestyle, do not offend as much as others (Figure 8.11). The effect on offending prevalence is strongest on the protective side while, when a youth reaches lifestyle risk score 2, the initially sharper increase in prevalence peaks and levels off.

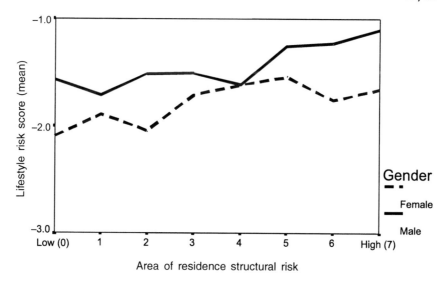

Figure 8.9 Mean lifestyle risk score by area of residence structural risk group and gender

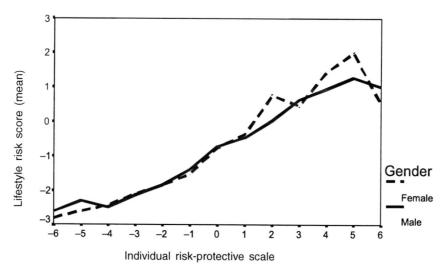

Figure 8.10 Mean lifestyle risk score by individual risk-protective score and gender

183

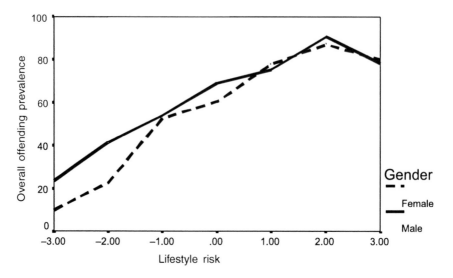

Figure 8.11 Offending prevalence by lifestyle risk group and gender

Offenders with a high-risk lifestyle offend more frequently and are more versatile in their offending than others

Not only the prevalence of offending, but also the offenders' frequency of offending (Figure 8.12), and the offenders' versatility in crime (Figure 8.13), increases significantly by increase in lifestyle risk. The effects of lifestyle risk on the frequency of offending by male (signf. = 0.000, eta^2 = 0.22) and female offenders (signf. = 0.000, eta^2 = 0.17) are quite strong. The same holds for the effects of lifestyle risk on male (signf. = 0.000, eta^2 = 0.24) and female offenders' (signf. = 0.000, eta^2 = 0.27) versatility in offending.

The effect of lifestyle risk on victimisation is not as strong as its effect on offending

Lifestyle has, as expected, a significant effect on risk of victimisation. However, and perhaps somewhat surprisingly (Figure 8.14), the effect of lifestyle risk is less strong on the prevalence of victimisation (Figure 8.14; males signf. = 0.000, gamma = 0.29; females signf. = 0.000, gamma = 0.40) than on the prevalence of offending (see Figure 8.12; males signf. = 0.000, gamma = 0.58; females signf. = 0.000, gamma = 0.75). The same even holds if one only considers victimisations of violent crimes (Figure 8.15; males signf. = 0.000; gamma = 0.26;

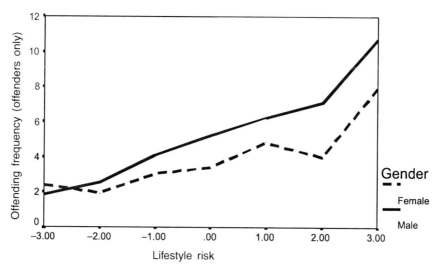

Figure 8.12 Offenders' frequency of offending by lifestyle risk group and gender

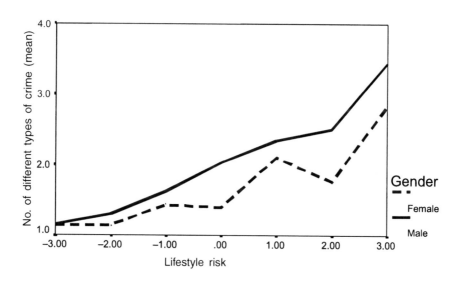

Figure 8.13 Offenders' versatility in offending by lifestyle risk group and gender

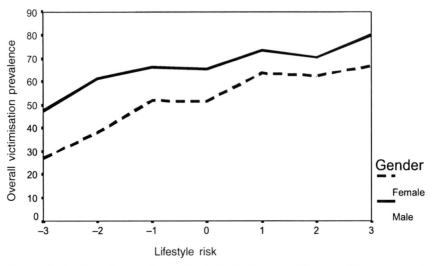

Figure 8.14 Prevalence of overall victimisations by lifestyle risk group and gender

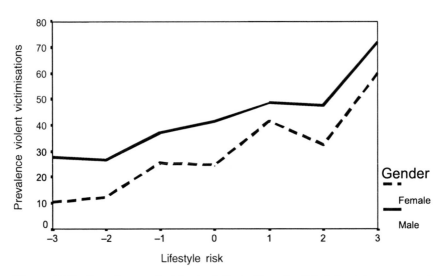

Figure 8.15 Prevalence of violent victimisations by lifestyle risk group and gender

females signf. = 0.000; gamma = 0.45). It is worth while highlighting that the lifestyle effect on prevalence of victimisations is stronger for girls than for boys.

There are no significant effects by lifestyle risk on female victims' frequency of being victimised

Looking into how often the victims have been victimised (Figure 8.16), there are no significant differences by lifestyle risk for girls. However, for boys a higher lifestyle risk, particularly if they belong to the highest-risk group, means a higher risk of being repeatedly victimised (signf. = 0.000, eta^2 = 0.05).

Lifestyle risk and other explanatory factors: a multiple regression analysis

In this section of the chapter we will bring together all the various explanatory factors with which we have previously dealt, and include lifestyles in one concluding analysis of their potential independent and interactive effects on youth offending. The included explanatory factors are *area of residence structural risk* (see Chapter 7), *school structural risk* (see Chapter 7), *family structural risk* (see Chapter 5), *individual risk-protective factors* (see Chapter 6) and *lifestyle risk*. We will also include *gender* among the predictors. On the basis of the findings presented in Chapter 4, we will focus our analysis on four dependent variables: overall offending, serious theft (as a measure of more serious youth offending), shoplifting (a crime where females dominate) and aggressive offending – that is, violence and vandalism combined (a crime where males dominate).

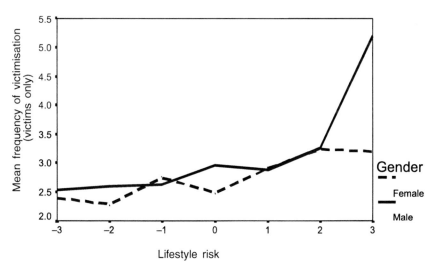

Figure 8.16 Victims' mean frequency of victimisations by lifestyle risk group and gender

A series of multiple regression analyses (OLS) were performed including all the above-mentioned explanatory factors, and all possible interactions between them, except with gender (Table 8.1). The findings show that:

- The model explained 39 per cent of the variance for overall offending, 22 per cent for serious theft, 16 per cent for shoplifting and, finally, 33 per cent for aggressive offending.

- The individuals' risk-protective scores were a strong predictor for all categories of crime, but somewhat less for serious theft.

- Lifestyle risk was also a strong predictor of offending for all categories of crime, but somewhat lower for serious theft.

- Lifestyle risk also had a strong interaction effect with the individual risk-protective score (a fact that we will explore more in the subsequent section), particularly for serious theft and overall offending, and less strongly for shoplifting and aggressive crimes.

- School structural risk had a significant impact on overall offending and shoplifting. This may reflect the rather strong correlation, particularly for girls, between frequency of truancy and frequency of shoplifting (for females $r. = 0.38$; for males $r. = 0.23$), since schools with higher structural risks tend to have higher rates of truancy (see Chapter 7).

- Gender had a significant impact on all categories of crime, and on overall offending. Being female decreased the risk of overall offending, serious thefts and aggressive crimes, while increasing the risk of committing a crime of shoplifting.

All in all, the youths' lifestyle risks, their individual risk-protective characteristics, and the interaction between the two, appear to be the most important explanatory factors of their overall involvement in offending. The interaction between an individual's characteristics and their lifestyle appears to be a particularly interesting aspect. Therefore, we will explore this interaction in greater depth in the next section.

Lifestyle risk, individual risk-protective scores and offending: exploring the interaction effects

Findings of interaction effects in a multiple regression analysis do not necessarily tell us much about the nature of these interactions.

Table 8.1 OLS multiple regression: frequencies of overall offending, serious theft, shoplifting and aggressive crimes by gender and key explanatory factors

	Overall offending		Serious theft		Shoplifting		Aggressive crimes	
	Beta	Prob.	Beta	Prob.	Beta	Prob.	Beta	Prob.
Female	-0.09	0.001	-0.09	0.000	0.08	0.002	-0.14	0.000
Area risk	0.00	n.s.	-0.01	n.s.	-0.03	n.s.	0.02	n.s.
School risk	0.05	0.030	0.02	n.s.	0.07	0.017	0.03	n.s.
Family risk	-0.03	n.s.	-0.03	n.s.	-0.03	n.s.	-0.02	n.s.
Individual risk	0.26	0.000	0.12	0.000	0.20	0.000	0.24	0.000
Lifestyle risk	0.23	0.000	0.07	0.029	0.16	0.000	0.24	0.000
Area*school risk	0.01	n.s.	-0.01	n.s.	0.04	n.s.	0.00	n.s.
Area*family risk	0.01	n.s.	-0.06	0.039	0.04	n.s.	0.03	n.s.
Area*individual risk	0.02	n.s.	-0.03	n.s.	0.02	n.s.	0.03	n.s.
Area*lifestyle risk	0.00	n.s.	0.03	n.s.	-0.02	n.s.	0.00	n.s.
School*family risk	0.01	n.s.	0.05	n.s.	-0.03	n.s.	0.01	n.s.
School*individual risk	0.07	0.033	0.06	n.s.	0.05	n.s.	0.05	n.s.
School*lifestyle risk	-0.04	n.s.	-0.04	n.s.	0.01	n.s.	-0.05	n.s.
Family*individual risk	-0.05	n.s.	-0.04	n.s.	0.01	n.s.	-0.06	n.s.
Family*lifestyle risk	0.01	n.s.	-0.04	n.s.	-0.03	n.s.	0.06	n.s.
Individual*lifestyle risk	0.24	0.000	0.36	0.000	0.10	0.001	0.15	0.000
Multiple R^2 × 100 =	39		22		16		33	

Note:
Significant coefficients underlined. Interaction terms were calculated by first centring each of the two variables and then multiplying them.

189

The strong interaction between lifestyle risk and the individual risk-protective score means that the relationship between lifestyle risk and offending is somehow dependent on the youths' individual risk-protective score. To explore the nature of this interaction, offending frequency by main categories of the youths' lifestyle risk (high, medium and low risk) and their individual risk-protective characteristics (protective, balanced and risk) were analysed.[2] The statistical significance and measures of strength of association of the relationship between offending and lifestyle risk were computed for each of the three main groups of individual risk-protective scores.

Lifestyle risk has the strongest impact on the offending by youths with balanced individual risk-protective scores

For overall offending frequency[3] the difference by lifestyle group is significant for youths in the protective and the balanced group (Figure 8.17). However, the effect on offending frequency is much stronger for the balanced group (signf. = 0.000, eta^2 = 0.17) than for the protective group (signf. = 0.000, eta^2 = 0.05). There are very few individuals who have the combination high individual risk and low lifestyle

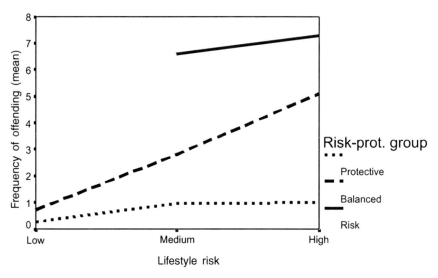

Figure 8.17 Mean offending frequency by combinations of groups of lifestyle risk and individual risk-protective scores
Note:
There are few subjects (n = 6) in the low-risk lifestyle and high individual risk group. This data point has therefore been excluded

risk (n = 6). We decided not to include this data point in the graph because of the low reliability associated with such a small number of subjects. For illustrative purposes, the relationship is also shown when using the full range of lifestyle risk scores (Figure 8.18).

Considering frequency of *serious thefts* (Figure 8.19), the pattern is that there is no lifestyle effect for those youths belonging to the protective group (very few in this group have committed a serious theft), while there is a significant effect for those in the group of balanced risk-protective scores (signf. = 0.000, eta^2 = 0.08) and those in the group of high risk-protective scores (signf. = 0.016, eta^2 = 0.04).

The strongest influence by lifestyle risk on frequency of *shoplifting* is for the balanced group (signf. = 0.000, eta^2 = 0.06), followed by the protective group (signf. = 0.000, eta^2 = 0.04), while the differences are non-significant for the risk group of youths (Figure 8.20). The frequency of *aggressive crimes* is strongly affected by lifestyle for the youths in the balanced risk-protective group (signf. = 0.000, eta^2 = 0.14), and somewhat for those in the protective group (signf. = 0.000,

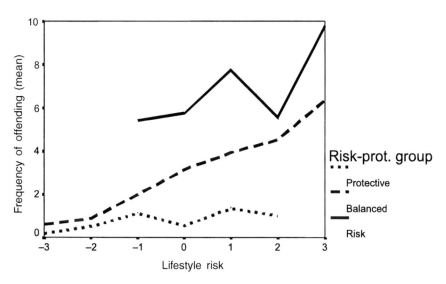

Figure 8.18 Mean offending frequency by combinations of groups of lifestyle risk and individual risk-protective scores
Note:
Figure 8.18 includes the full range of lifestyle risk scores. Since there are very few subjects (single figures) who have a low-risk lifestyle (i.e. scores of −3 or −2) among those in the individual risk group they have been excluded from the graph. No subject in the protective group had a lifestyle risk score of 3.

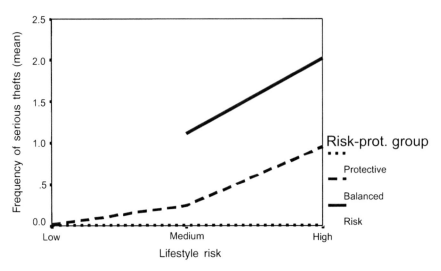

Figure 8.19 Mean frequency of serious thefts by combinations of groups of lifestyle risk and individual risk-protective scores
Note:
There are very few subjects (n = 6) in the low-risk lifestyle and high individual risk group. This data point has therefore been excluded

eta^2 = 0.03). The differences between classes of lifestyle risk are non-significant for the youths in the risk group (Figure 8.21).

Considering *gender differences* by comparing the zero-order correlations between offending and lifestyle risk for the main groups of individual risk-protective scores shows no great difference between boys and girls (Table 8.2). The strongest influence on offending by lifestyle risk is among the youths who have balanced individual risk-protective scores (particularly as regards the frequency of overall offending and the frequency of aggressive crimes). This holds for both boys and girls.

All in all, the analyses of the interaction effects between lifestyle risk and individual risk-protective scores indicate that:

- Lifestyle risk has only a small effect on offending by youths who have high individual protective scores.

- Lifestyle risk has a strong effect on offending for youths who have balanced individual scores (i.e. neither particularly high-risk nor high protective scores), particularly for their involvement in aggressive crimes.

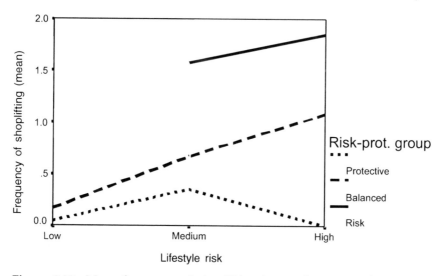

Figure 8.20 Mean frequency of shoplifting by combinations of groups of lifestyle risk and individual risk-protective scores
Note:
There are very few subjects (*n* = 6) in the low-risk lifestyle and high individual risk group. This data point has therefore been excluded

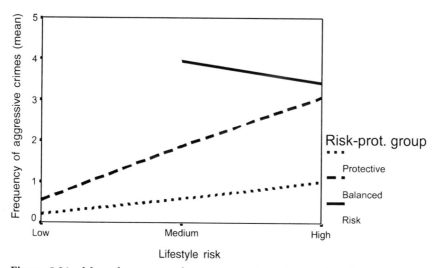

Figure 8.21 Mean frequency of aggressive crimes by combinations of groups of lifestyle risk and individual risk-protective scores
Note:
There are very few subjects (*n* = 6) in the low-risk lifestyle and high individual risk group. This data point has therefore been excluded

Table 8.2 Zero-order correlations between offending frequency (overall and for main types of crimes) and lifestyle risk score by main group of individual risk-protective score, total and by gender

Type of crime	Individual risk-protective group		
	Protective	Balanced	Risk
Total			
Overall offending	0.23	0.44	0.20
Serious thefts	(−0.01)	0.29	0.24
Shoplifting	0.13	0.25	0.13
Aggressive crimes	0.20	0.40	(0.08)
n =	725	760	94
Males			
Overall offending	0.17	0.45	(0.26)
Serious thefts	(0.00)	0.33	0.28
Shoplifting	(0.04)	0.27	(0.22)
Aggressive crimes	0.17	0.40	(0.05)
n =	286	430	53
Females			
Overall offending	0.28	0.44	(0.15)
Serious thefts	(−0.03)	0.26	(0.23)
Shoplifting	0.19	0.23	(0.00)
Aggressive crimes	0.24	0.43	(0.13)
n =	439	329	41

Note:
Figures in brackets indicate a non-significant relationship. The much lower *n* for the individual risk group means a much stronger correlation is needed to obtain statistical significance.

- Lifestyle risk does not have much effect on offending by youths with high individual risk scores, the exception being that of serious theft offending.

Poor parental monitoring and high lifestyle risk go together

In the analyses carried out in Chapter 6 (see Table 6.19) it was pointed out that parental monitoring may, foremost, be a factor influencing the situational risk of the youths. An analysis of the relationship between the youths' mean lifestyle risk score and their level of parental monitoring shows that there is a strong association between the two. Boys (signf. = 0.000, eta^2 = 0.25) and, particularly, girls (signf. = 0.000, eta^2 = 0.35) who have poorer parental monitoring tend more often to live a riskier lifestyle (Figure 8.22).

The effect on frequency of offending by levels of (poor) parental monitoring is stronger for youths with balanced risk-protective scores than for youths with scores on the protective end of the distribution (Figure 8.23). For youths in the individual risk group (not shown in the graph since there are too few individuals in the group to get meaningful rates for each level of parental monitoring) the relationship is non-significant and negative – i.e. the higher the amount of parental monitoring, the higher the frequency of crime (Table 8.3).

Three groups of adolescent offenders?

The idea that there are different types of offenders is central within developmental criminology. Longitudinal research has suggested that there is a small group of offenders with a long duration and high frequency of crime who are responsible for a large proportion of a cohort's crime, and another, much larger, group of offenders who have a short duration and a low frequency of crime (e.g. Wolfgang *et al.* 1972; Wikström 1987; Farrington 1998). Therefore it has become

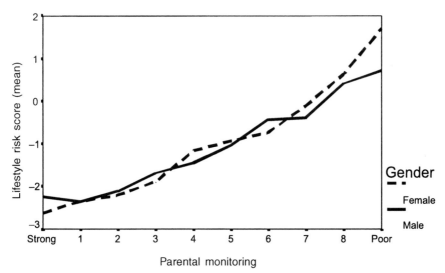

Figure 8.22 Mean lifestyle risk score by level of (poor) parental monitoring

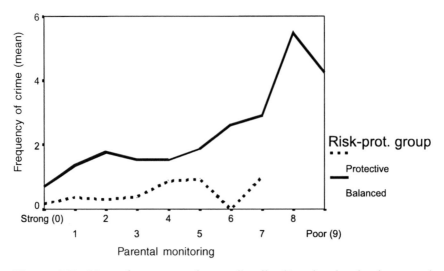

Figure 8.23 Mean frequency of overall offending by level of parental monitoring, separately for youths with a protective and youths with a balanced individual risk-protective score

Table 8.3 Overall offending frequency by level of (poor) parental monitoring: bivariate regressions for main groups of individual risk-protective scores

Risk-protective group	b	Beta	Signif.	$R^2 \times 100$	n
Protective	0.11	0.15	0.000	2	739
Balanced	0.36	0.20	0.000	4	785
Risk	−0.41	−0.11	n.s.	1	101

'conventional' to talk about two major groups of offenders based on their offending patterns.

The most recent and most elaborate attempt to define these two groups is by Moffitt (1993). She talks about *life-course persistent* and *adolescence-limited* offenders. The first group emerges early in life as having 'problematic' behaviour and continues through adolescence and adulthood with a high prevalence and frequency of many different types of offending behaviour. This group's development and emerging consistency of 'problematic' and offending behaviours over the life-course is seen, in a stepping-stone fashion, as a result of the interplay between the child's neuropsychological deficiencies and the environmental response (parents, teachers, etc.) to the manifestations of these neuropsychological characteristics (e.g.

'difficult temperament' and 'conduct problems'). The second group's offending starts in adolescence, their 'criminal career' is short lived and not related to any deeper individual psychological or social problems. Moffitt hypothesises that adolescence-limited offending has to do with the fact that adolescence is a period of transition to adulthood when (more well adjusted) youths, as part of developing independence (e.g. seeking mature status), may want to imitate the anti-social behaviour of life-course persistent teens.

Moffitt's classification has been much debated as regards the empirical support for the existence of two main groups of offenders, and the explanation of their crime involvement. There is an increasing body of empirical research within criminology that searches for the presence of distinct trajectories in offending. Nagin and Land (1993) introduced the use of 'non-parametric, mixed poisson' analysis to reveal heterogeneity in longitudinal sequences of offending existing among groups of offenders and non-offenders. Conviction data from the age of 10 to 32 years from the Cambridge Study of Delinquent Development was used. In their initial analysis, one non-offending group and three 'trajectories' of offending were proposed: *high-rate chronics*, *adolescence-limited* and *low-rate chronics*. Despite the similar nomenclature to Moffitt's (1993) scheme, there were some important differences between the classification as proposed by Moffitt and by Nagin and Land's empirically derived groups. The first potential inconsistency between the two lies in the persistence of the *life-course persistence/high-rate chronic* grouping. Nagin and Land (1993: 348) note that, while their *high-rate chronic* group offend consistently throughout their teenage years, after the age of 22, their offending frequency begins to drop – an occurrence not predicted by Moffitt. This, however, could be explained by a heterotypic continuity (that is, acts that are *'conceptually* consistent' with offending; Moffitt 1993: 100 emphasis as original) in so far as anti-social behaviour may expand beyond the range of acts included in Nagin and Land's dependent measure. For instance, Moffitt (1993: 101) argues that, as offenders age, so the manifestations of the perpetuating trait may vary from the offences typically associated with adolescent offending to conceptually homogeneous acts (e.g. family neglect). Given that these might be less likely to result in convictions for the offender, it may appear that previously high-rate offenders are desisting, whereas in fact it is only the nature of the anti-social behaviour that is altering. As Moffitt (1993: 101) succinctly puts it, 'there is no reason to expect that life-course-persistents miraculously assume prosocial tendencies after an antisocial tenure of several decades'.

The *adolescence-limited* group revealed through Nagin and Land's analysis much more closely matches the group of the same name hypothesised by Moffitt. For this group, Nagin and Land's analysis revealed that the frequency of offending peaks at the age of 14 and then drops rapidly so that, by the age of 22, their offending has essentially ceased.

The third offending group identified by Nagin and Land, but not predicted by Moffitt, is the *low-rate chronics*. The low-rate chronics have the lowest rate of offending during their teenage years, but by the age of 20 their offending trajectory crosses that of the *adolescence-limited*, reaching a peak at the ages of 22–24, before starting to decline once again.

Nagin and Land also attempted to identify distinctive risk factors that were associated with each trajectory group. At the ages of 8–11, in comparison with the non-offending group, members of all the offending groups were significantly (at the 5 per cent level) more likely to have low IQs, a daring disposition, a parent with a criminal record, to be troublesome, live in poor-quality housing and to be physically neglected by their parents. Between the ages of 12 and 15, the members of the three offending groups were more likely to be truant from school, whereas between the ages of 16 and 19 offenders were more likely to be hostile to the police, have unstable employment records, to drink and to gamble. With regard to between-offending-group differences, the *high-rate chronics* were significantly (at the 10 per cent level) more troublesome than the *adolescence-limited* and the *low-rate chronics* and seemed to be particularly prone to heavier alcohol use and employment instability. In terms of behaviours and characteristics particularly associated with the *high-rate chronic* group, this group was the only one where members were significantly more likely to lack concentration, lie chronically, have delinquent siblings and smoke marijuana. Poorer performance at junior school and greater popularity among peers between the ages of 8 and 11 specifically characterised the *adolescence-limited* group. Finally, the *low-rate chronics* were distinguished by having very low IQ scores.

As Nagin and Land (1993: 356–8) note, one question that poses itself is to what extent the trajectories identified make up discrete entities and configurations, or whether they reflect points on a continuous dimension. Another issue is the extent to which the behaviours and characteristics found to be associated with the trajectory groupings may be considered to be causes, risk factors or simply correlates.

Nagin *et al.* (1995) extended both the ages of the offenders examined and the analysis of the characteristics associated with the offending groups from that of Nagin and Land (1993). Of considerable interest here was that:

> The seeming reformation of the adolescence-limiteds, however, was less than complete. They continued to drink heavily, use drugs, and get into fights. While their official criminal records ceased many years before, they were still committing criminal acts, such as stealing from their employers, according to self reports (Nagin *et al.* 1995: 112).

Indeed, at the age of 32, while the adolescence-limiteds had no convictions (in keeping with the never-convicted group), on a self-report measure of general delinquency (burglary, vehicle theft, theft from a vehicle, shoplifting, vandalism, violence and drug use) and a self-report theft measure, the offending behaviour of the so-called adolescence-limiteds was broadly the same as for the high and low-level chronic offenders.

In terms of what may be described as the lifestyle characteristics of the *adolescence-limited* group, Nagin *et al.* (1995: 128–32) found that they did display some signs of adaptation to a more conventional lifestyle. In comparison with the other two offending groups, the adolescence-limited group had, by the age of 32, managed to engender greater employment stability after having had unstable employment histories similar to the other offending groups at the age of 18. While all the offending groups were more likely than the non-offending groups to have evidenced instability in their personal relationships during their lifetime (divorced or separated and have a child living elsewhere), the *adolescence-limited* group reported better relationships with their partners and lower levels of violence towards their partner than did the *high-level chronic* and *low-level chronic* groups.

Nagin *et al.* (1995: 132) interpret the *adolescence-limited* group's (AL's) findings thus:

> The ALs appear to be engaged in what might be characterized as circumscribed deviance. At age 32 they seem to be careful to avoid committing crimes with a high-risk of conviction, which might jeopardize their stable work careers, or to engage in behaviors, like spousal assault, that might harm their familial relationships. Instead, they seem to restrict their deviance to behaviors less likely to result in official sanction or disrupt intimate attachments.

While this would support Moffitt's (1993) contention that the cessation of offending may be more apparent than real as a result of the comprehensiveness of the dependent variable used, in this instance it is not for the life-course persistent (or *high-level chronics* in Nagin and Land's terminology), but rather for the perhaps somewhat-inappropriately labelled *adolescence-limited* group (see also Hirchi and Gottfredson 2000).

Recently, the utility of the analyses of offending trajectories has been questioned. Laub and Sampson (2003) have reanalysed the Gluecks' dataset that has been updated to include official offending up to the age of 70 years for cohort members. Using the data to test empirically the relationship between age and crime, they found evidence of the existence of a number of different offending trajectory groups. All these tended to share a similar basic shape to the aggregate age–crime pattern, but with a great deal of variation in their actual forms. Laub and Sampson also found no evidence of the existence of a group of stable, high-rate offenders across the life-course as per Moffitt's *life-course persistents*, but, rather, that the norm is for all offenders to age out of crime. They also used a range of childhood and adolescent individual risk factors to assess whether these could differentiate between different group membership and it was found that they could not.

What do trajectory analyses actually tell us? First, empirically, the evidence would appear to suggest that there are indeed different trajectories of offending which, broadly speaking, conform to the basic shape of the aggregate age–crime curve. However, they conform to such varying degrees that to call the relationship between age and crime 'invariant' for all individuals stretches that term beyond any reasonable definition (see e.g. Cohen and Vila 1996; D'Unger *et al.* 1998; Laub and Sampson 2003).

Predicatively, Laub and Sampson's (2003) long-term follow-up of the Gluecks' men has indicated that although different offending trajectories are identifiable, group membership is not predictable from a range of childhood 'risk factors'. Hence, their analyses suggest that the different trajectory groups are not 'types of offenders' in the classic sense of the phrase, in so far as they do not appear to relate to qualitatively different groups of individuals with their own aetiologies. Laub and Sampson (2003: 110) note: 'although latent classes of offenders appear to yield distinct trajectories of offending, supporting Nagin and Land (1993), group membership is not easily, if at all, predictable from individual, childhood, and adolescent risk factors'. It is more difficult to identify where such trajectories leave us theoretically. Does trajectory analysis do any more than simply divide a continuous distribution into groups, or does it reveal something more substantive? We believe a particularly understudied influence of crime is the role that social contexts play, in interaction with individual characteristics, in determining different trajectories in offending (see also McCord 2000; Wikström and Loeber 2000). Social contexts appear so far to have been largely ignored as a potential influence in trajectory analyses, where the primary focus has been on establishing the existence of such trajectories and then looking at the impact of various configurations of individual characteristics upon group membership. This seems to repeat the omission identified previously in much criminal career research, where there has been a lack of an integrated approach in the study of individuals and their social contexts (see Farrington *et al.* 1993).

One possible mechanism through which social contexts may act to influence offending trajectories is their impact on individuals' lifestyles (Wikström and Sampson 2003), which then, in interaction with individual characteristics (especially as hypothesised here, those relating to individuals' self-control and morality), act to perpetuate or help diminish involvement in offending. It seems reasonable to believe that a more holistic examination of individuals operating within their social contexts will provide a more complete picture of individual differences in offending trajectories than is presently available.

The present study is not longitudinal and therefore it is not possible to study the development of offending over longer periods of time. However, the knowledge accumulated in longitudinal and other research may help to give some background to the interpretation of the cross-sectional findings of this study into adolescent offending. A particularly important contribution of this study may be the analysis of the interaction between individual risk-protective characteristics and lifestyle risk, which may help to further the state of knowledge, especially as regards the aetiology of different groups of offenders.

Classifying offending groups by individual risk and behavioural contexts rather than by offending patterns.

While Moffitt's strategy of classification is to create groups defined by their offending patterns over the life-course and then to look for explanations of the offending of these groups, we will approach the problem from the opposite angle. We will suggest that there are different groups of adolescents (defined by their individual social situation and disposition) operating in different behavioural contexts (defined in this study by their lifestyles) and that individual-behavioural context combinations determine their crime involvement. We will argue that this approach to 'groups of offenders' better represents reality and also has the great advantage that it allows for a less deterministic approach to explaining individual trajectories in offending. For example, changes over the life-course in individuals' social situation and their behavioural contexts may cause changes in their crime involvement (see Wikström 2005 for an elaboration of this argument in terms of explaining individual development and change and its relation to crime involvement).

Main groups of adolescent offenders

A possible *interpretation* of the findings presented in this chapter is that, broadly speaking, there are three main categories of adolescent offenders defined by the aetiology of their offending:

1 *Propensity-induced offenders*: Youths at the risk end of the risk-protective score distribution.
2 *Lifestyle dependent offenders*: Youths having balanced risk-protective scores.
3 *Situationally limited offenders*: Youths at the protective end of the risk-protective score distribution.

The first group (i.e. *propensity-induced offenders*), which is small in number, consists of youths who are poorly individually adjusted and who are likely to have a high overall offending prevalence, regardless of their lifestyle risk. This is mainly due to the high level of aggressive offending at each level of lifestyle risk (for shoplifting and serious theft, their prevalence of offending is somewhat higher in the high-risk compared with the medium-risk lifestyle group). Very few subjects in this group have a low lifestyle risk (Table 8.4).

This group's (high) offending frequency does not vary much by lifestyle risk. Overall, the offending by this group of offenders may be interpreted as being more about their individual dispositions (propensity to offend) than about situational risk. This group consists of only 6 per cent of the youths (Table 8.5), but this 6 per cent have committed 28 per cent of the overall crimes (during 2000) and almost half of the cohorts' crimes of serious thefts (46 per cent).[4]

The second group (i.e. *lifestyle-dependent offenders*) are youths who are neither individually very well adjusted nor individually poorly

Table 8.4 Per cent in main lifestyle risk group by main individual risk-protective score group

Risk-protective group	Lifestyle risk group				
	Low	Medium	High	Total	n
Protective	85.4	13.8	0.8	100	725
Balanced	49.9	41.8	8.3	100	760
Risk	6.4	57.4	36.2	100	94

Table 8.5 Per cent subjects, and per cent of the crimes (overall offending and main types of crime), committed by main risk-protective group

Risk-protective group	Per cent subjects	Per cent of the crimes committed by group			
		Overall offending	Serious thefts	Shoplifting	Aggressive
Protective	45.4	10.3	2.4	9.9	11.9
Balanced	48.3	62.1	51.6	60.5	64.4
Risk	6.2	27.6	46.0	29.6	23.7
$n =$	1,957	2,489	289	618	1,602

Note:
n in the first column refers to number of subjects in the study, while in the other columns n refers to the number of crimes committed. The skewness of the distribution of offending by risk-protective group is most likely underestimated since only a maximum of six crimes has been counted for each type of crime (see Chapter 4).

adjusted. This is the group of youths who appear to run the highest risk of getting into frequent offending by having a high-risk lifestyle. This is a group for which the enactment of their (medium) level of propensity to offend may be highly dependent on whether or not they have a lifestyle that frequently brings them into situations of risk. All the three different constructs that make up the overall lifestyle risk measure significantly predict variation in this group's overall offending frequency, and in particular having peers who are delinquent and high levels of alcohol and drug use (Table 8.6). This is a group of youths for whom a major reason for offending may be peer influence.

Table 8.6 Overall offending frequency by main lifestyle risk constructs: multiple regressions for main groups of individual risk-protective scores*

| Lifestyle risk construct | Risk-protective group* | | | |
| | Protective | | Balanced | |
	Beta	Signif.	Beta	Signif.
Peer delinquency	0.08	0.034	0.25	0.000
Risk public environment	0.05	n.s.	0.18	0.008
Alcohol and drug use	0.22	0.000	0.26	0.000
Multiple $R^2 \times 100$	9		22	

Note:
* Model non-significant for individual risk group (not shown).

The final group (i.e. *situationally limited offenders*) – individually well adjusted youths (that is, youths who have strong social bonds, self-control and morality as regards offending) who live a more risky lifestyle (medium risk) – may occasionally offend, in particular committing an occasional aggressive crime. Few youths in this group have a high-risk lifestyle (Table 8.4). Considering the different constructs that make up the overall lifestyle risk measure, it also looks like it is primarily alcohol and drug use that gets this group into occasional trouble (Table 8.6). However, they are not likely to be frequent offenders (Table 8.5). Crime by offenders in this group appears more to be about occasionally strong situational risks (related to drinking or using drugs) than about their propensity to offend.

Looking into gender and key family structural characteristics of the youths in the three main groups of individual risk-protective scores (Table 8.7), the proportion of females is somewhat higher in the protective group than in the balanced and risk groups, the proportion of youths from the middle classes is much lower in the high-risk group compared with others, and there are fewer youths living in complete families of origin in the high-risk group. There are no significant differences in the proportion of youths with a non-UK background.

Somewhat simplified, the findings suggest that there may be three different groups of adolescent youth offenders, which may warrant different strategies of prevention. For the high individual risk adolescent offenders it may be a question of addressing more fundamental problems arising from their developmental history and

Table 8.7 Gender and selected family structural characteristics by main individual risk-protective group

Per cent	Individual risk-protective group			
	Protective	Balanced	Risk	Signif.
Females	60.1	42.7	42.7	0.000
Middle class*	47.0	40.7	19.4	0.000
Complete family of origin	68.6	60.8	50.5	0.000
Non-UK**	23.0	19.8	17.0	n.s.

Notes:
* Lower middle and upper middle class.
** First or second-generation immigrants.

their current (family and school) social situation, rather than primarily addressing a risky lifestyle, which could simply be a consequence of these factors. For the offenders in the group with a balanced individual risk-protective score, prevention strategies may focus more on influencing their lifestyles (and possibly also their parents because of the strong link between poor parental monitoring and lifestyle risk) to promote a less risky way of life. Finally, the offenders in the group already having strong protective factors do not appear to be strongly influenced by lifestyle risk. If they live a high-risk lifestyle some of them will occasionally commit a crime, predominantly an aggressive crime. However, their offending appears perhaps best described as 'uncharacteristic' and not a sign of any high risk of potential development into more frequent and serious offending.

Notes

1 This claim may be supported by the fact that the zero-order correlation between the youths' self-reported offending frequency and whether or not they have been caught by the police is $r. = 0.36$.
2 Risk-protective scores were grouped as follows: protective (scores −6 to −3), balanced (scores −2 to 2) and risk (scores 3 to 6). Lifestyle risk scores were grouped as follows: low (scores −3 to −2), medium (scores −1 to 1) and high (scores 2 to 3).
3 It should be noted that in this section the ANOVA analyses (and graphs) of frequency data include non-offenders (i.e. scores of 0), while in previous sections the ANOVA analyses (and graphs) only included offenders who

have committed a crime, or the particular crime in question. However, the OLS regression analyses have always included non-offenders.

4 When comparing the distribution of offending from this study with the distribution of offending in longitudinal studies, please recall that this study only covers offending during one year. Thus the proportion of crimes committed by the high-risk group is most likely less than it would have been had a longer period been studied.

Chapter 9

Youth routines and involvement in crime: some preliminary findings from the space-time budget study

In addition to the questionnaire study of all Year 10 pupils in Peterborough, a special space-time budget study was carried out for a randomly selected subsample (see Chapter 2). In this chapter we will present some preliminary findings from this study. The method's full potential as a tool for studying the influence of adolescents' behavioural contexts on crime involvement is currently taken forward in the research carried out in the ongoing Peterborough Adolescent Development Study (PADS).

Time-budgets show, in our case hour by hour over one week, what the youths were doing and with whom (see Pentland *et al.* 1999 for an overview of time-budget studies). As far as we are aware, time-budget techniques (at least at this level of detail) have never before been employed in the study of adolescent offending. The main advantage with a time-budget technique over questionnaire-based descriptions is that one gets a much more detailed picture of the youths' day-to-day social life. As Robinson states, time-budgets (or, as they are alternatively called, 'time-diaries') 'represent complete accounts of daily activity' and they 'allow one to generate estimates of how much societal time is spent on the complete range of human behaviour' (1999: 48).

Time-budgets can be analysed in many different ways. We have analysed the time-budget data 1) with the individual as the unit, and 2) with time (hour) as the unit. The latter makes it possible to describe hour by hour where the youths were and what they were doing. Thus one can explore patterns in the time and space flow of the youths' social life and to study how this varies, for example, by their individual characteristics. This aspect of the space-time budget study, which is probably the most interesting one, will not be presented in this book but be the topic of a forthcoming study (Wikström *et al.* 2006). Here we will concentrate on some preliminary exploration of how much time the youths spend engaged in different types of activities, and how this relates to their individual characteristics and community contexts and, moreover, how all this relates to their offending and victimisation patterns.

The space-time budget interviews were carried out over a six-month period – i.e. the first half of year 2001 (the second and third term of Year 10). The data refers to events during one week. The youths were talked through their last seven days retrospectively. This is a longer recall period than is 'normally' recommended: 'The *general view* of *experienced* time-diary researchers is ... that recall should not be attempted for more than 2 days in arrears' (Harvey 1999: 23 emphasis added). The possibility of recall is obviously dependent on the temporal detail that is sought. Some time-budget studies code activities in minutes, and if that is the case obviously one cannot get reliable data over longer recall periods. In our case we opted for coding by the hour. It may still be argued that this is too detailed when covering a whole week. For what it is worth, the interviewers in this study judge that the youths generally had a good recall of what happened to them over the last week, although it cannot be excluded that the recall of more distant days was less precise. Minimally, we would argue that the space-time budget data give a much more detailed picture of the adolescents' social life than is possible to achieve through the use of a battery of questions administered through a questionnaire.

One can say that we traded the risk of some potential errors in recall to cover a longer period in time. It was felt that we needed to capture a whole week of the youths' activities to get a complete picture of their social life. The alternative, for example to ask about the two last days (which then would vary for each individual depending on what day the interview was conducted), was for our purposes viewed less satisfactory for at least two major reasons. First, as youth routines vary so much by day of the week, particularly between weekends and other days, it would be difficult, for example, to analyse the relationship between the youths' day-to-day routines and their individual characteristics if the pair of days studied varied between the youths (e.g. for some it may be Monday and Tuesday and for others Saturday and Sunday). Secondly, even if one can construct an 'average' week from the accounts of the last two days it would have meant, compared with asking about the full week, that we would have had substantially fewer observations relating to each weekday.

Since several different activities can occur during an hour one has to make a choice which one to code. It was decided simply to code the most prevalent activity. However, this leads to an underestimation of certain types of activities that normally have a short duration, for example, making a telephone call or sending an e-mail. Coding by main hourly activity applies to the questions regarding geographical location (i.e. enumeration district), place (e.g. school yard), activity (e.g. sleeping) and with whom the youths spent their time (e.g. peers only). For the specific questions referring to offending, victimisation, substance use, fear, risk situations, carrying of weapons and truancy, the coding was made so that every hour in which this activity occurred was coded as one hour regardless of the duration of the activity.

Although one hour is the smallest unit of measurement, in the presentation of mean frequencies the results will show hours and minutes. So, for example, a mean of 1.5 hours has been recalculated to show 1.30 (i.e. 1 hour and 30 minutes). This should not be taken to indicate a higher level of precision than there actually is. The subjects' accounts of their location, place, activity, etc., were coded according to preset categories. During the actual interview process some (not foreseen) extra categories were added to the original classification to ensure that all main activities reported by the youths were covered. The coding was very detailed (see Appendix B). However, in this report the analyses will focus on broader categories only.

All in all, although there may be some imprecision in our accounts of the youths' routines it can be argued that it is much more precise and detailed than is normally the case in studies of adolescent offending.

It should be stressed that we only have time-budget data for a subsample (n = 339) of the studied population. Therefore the power of the analyses will generally be less than the analyses presented in the preceding chapters. The main implication of less power is that greater differences are needed to get statistically significant results (using the same criteria for a statistically significant difference as in previous chapters). Another implication of the lower number of subjects is that we cannot break down the analyses by as many variable combinations and categories as was possible when using the larger data-set from the questionnaire study (because the n's of the cells in some cases become too small to give reliable estimates).

The first step of the analyses presented in this chapter is to describe the general patterns in adolescent routines. The second step is to explore whether there are any differences in activity patterns by gender, family social position, individual risk-protective characteristics and community and school contexts. The third step is to create main dimensions of adolescent youth routines and then study their link to offending and victimisation. The final step is to return to the three major groups of adolescent offenders suggested in the lifestyle chapter and specifically explore variations in individual routines between those youths who belong to the protective and the balanced group of individual risk-protective scores. The purpose of this analysis is to see whether we can validate the findings (presented in Chapter 8) showing the greater importance of lifestyle for offending by youths in the balanced compared with youths in the protective group of individual risk-protective scores. But before doing all this, we will start by exploring offending and victimisation as reported in the space-time budget study.

Offending and victimisation

In contrast to the questionnaire study, there was no restriction in what types of crime were included in the space-time budget study. About 5 out of 100 youths offended at least once during the studied week (5.6 per cent counting all types of crime and 4.7 per cent counting only crimes of theft, vandalism and violence – see Table 9.1). Of the 31 crimes reported for the studied week, there were 5 bike thefts, 2 cases of shoplifting, 1 car theft, 1 non-residential burglary, 9 acts of vandalism, 2 motoring offences, 9 acts of violence and 2 acts of molestation (i.e. aggressively harassing someone). The prevalence of victimisations was somewhat less – about 2 out 100 youths (2.4 per cent) were victimised during the studied week (Table 9.1).

Given the findings of longitudinal research showing that, among all offenders, there is a small group of highly persistent offenders (i.e. having a high frequency and a high duration in crime), one would expect a correlation between the frequency of offending during year 2000 (as reported by the youths in the questionnaire study) and the frequency of offending during a single week in 2001 (as reported by the youths in the space-time budget study). This is also the case. The zero-order correlation is 0.35 (signf. = 0.000), regardless of whether the correlation includes all crimes committed last week or only crimes of violence, vandalism and theft. Another way to illustrate

Table 9.1 Prevalence of offending and victimisation during one week in 2001

	Per cent
Offending	
Theft	1.5
Vandalism	2.2
Violence	2.7
Driving offences	1.5
Other	0.6
Overall offending	5.6
Overall offending (excl. driving offences and other crimes)	4.7
Victimisation	
Theft	1.2
Vandalism	0.0
Violence	1.2
Overall victimisation	2.4

this relationship is to look at the youths' prevalence of offending during the studied week in 2001 in relation to their offending frequency in 2000. This analysis shows, by and large, that the higher the frequency of crimes committed in 2000, the more likely it is that the youths have also committed a crime during the studied week in 2001 (Figure 9.1).

A similar calculation was also made for frequency of *victimisation* (between the full year of 2000 and one week in 2001). This showed that, although there was a significant association (i.e. more of the youths, than would be expected by chance, of those victimised during the year 2000 were also victimised during one week in 2001), the strength of the association was much less than for offending ($r. = 0.13$, signf. = 0.017).

Almost all the youths' crimes were committed in the presence of peers and the great majority of the crimes occurred in public spaces

Of all crimes committed by the youths (during one week), 92 per cent were committed with other peers present (active or passive in the crime), while the remaining 8 per cent were committed by the youth alone or with both peers and adults present. Moreover, most of the crimes were committed in public spaces (64 per cent), predominantly in streets (40 per cent of all crimes) and parks/

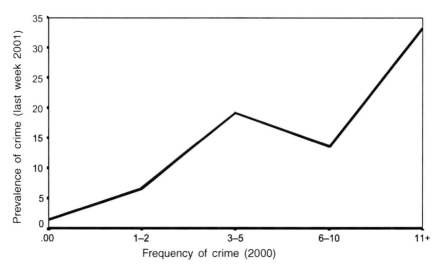

Figure 9.1 Prevalence of offending (last week 2001) by frequency of offending in 2000

recreational grounds or fields (20 per cent of all crimes). The rest of the crimes were committed at various other locations, such as shopping centres, others' homes and school grounds[1] In most cases the crime took place when the offender was not involved in any particular organised activity. Face-to-face socialising (i.e. chatting to others) was the most common activity (56 per cent). This shows that youth offending is predominantly conducted when socialising with peers in public spaces and therefore routine activities involving peers in public spaces may be regarded as particularly high risk. However, as we know from the previous lifestyle analyses (in Chapter 8) different groups of youths, depending on their individual risk-protective scores, may be differently affected by situational factors (a topic we will return to below).

Offenders offend, on average, less than two hours a week

Calculating the mean time that offenders spent offending during the studied week showed that offenders spent between one and two hours a week offending (the mean being 1 hour and 38 minutes). Put differently, offenders spend, on average, less than 3 per cent of their waking time offending. The most time any offender spent offending in the studied week was 3 hours (which is 5 per cent of their waking time). Note that the actual duration of the offending is probably much less because an hour is the smallest unit of measurement. In most cases it could be a question of minutes rather than hours. All in all, this is a finding of considerable interest since it shows that offending, in terms of time, is a very marginal activity of all activities carried out during a week by young offenders.

Main patterns of the youths' routine activities

In this section we will briefly consider the main pattern of the youths' routine activities as represented by time spent according to three main dimensions: 1) *place* (including some geographical location information); 2) *type of activity*; and 3) *with whom they spent time*. This information will give us some basic data about the pattern of the adolescents' social lives.

Youths spend most of their time at home and in school

Looking into time spent by main category of place (Table 9.2) shows that youths spend most of their time at home or in school (78.6 per cent if including sleeping time, 65.7 per cent if excluding sleeping time). The remaining third (34.3 per cent) of their waking time they predominantly spend 'in others' homes', 'in transit' (e.g. public transport, private transport or walking with a fixed destination) or 'in streets or squares' (Table 9.3).

Table 9.2 Average time spent by main location (hours per week)

Location	Total hours	Per cent	Discounting sleeping time*	Per cent
Place of residence	103	61.3	40	38.1
Other place in neighbourhood	21	12.5	21	20.0
School	29	17.3	29	27.6
Other place	15	8.9	15	14.3
Total	*168*	*100.0*	*105*	*100.0*

Note:
* The average time sleeping is 63 hours. In these calculations it has been assumed that the youths sleep at home, which is overwhelmingly the case, although a marginal error is introduced by the fact that some youths at some times have slept in other locations (most commonly friends' homes).

Table 9.3 Average time spent by location outside the home and the school, in order of rank of time spent (hours per week)

Location	Hours*	Per cent time of the week	
		Total	Discounting sleeping time**
Others' home	12.00	7.1	11.4
Transport (bus, etc.)	7.48	4.6	7.4
Street, squares	6.18	3.7	6.0
Shops/shopping centres	2.24	1.4	2.3
Locales of entertainment	2.12	1.3	1.9
Sports grounds	1.48	1.1	1.7
Other	3.30	2.1	3.3
Total	*36.00*	*21.3*	*34.0*

Notes:

* Figures refer to hours and minutes. For example, 1.24 means 1 hour and 24 minutes.
** The average time sleeping is 63 hours. In these calculations it has been assumed that the youths sleep at home, which is overwhelmingly the case, although a marginal error is introduced by the fact that some youths at some times have slept in other locations (most commonly friends' homes).

Youths spend most of their time in the presence of family members or school staff

Discounting time spent sleeping, the youths' four main activities by time spent doing that activity are, in rank order: attending classes and lectures, media consumption, eating and personal care, and face-to-face socialising (i.e. chatting to others). These four main activities account for 68 per cent of the youths' waking time activities (Table 9.4).

Looking into whom the youths spend time with (Table 9.5), and discounting sleeping time, most time is spent 1) with family members only, followed by 2) situations where both peers and non-family adults are present (this almost exclusively reflects time in school, other adults in this case refers, with few exceptions, to teachers and other school staff) and, finally, 3) time spent with peers only.

At least two general observations, perhaps not unexpected but nevertheless of great importance for thinking about the aetiology and prevention of crime can be made from these findings. First,

Table 9.4 Average time spent by main activity, in order of rank of the 10 most frequent activities (hours per week)

Activity	Hours*	Per cent time of the week	
		Total	Discounting sleeping time
Sleeping	63.18	37.7	
Classes and lectures	24.42	14.7	23.6
Media consumption	18.30	11.0	17.7
Eating/personal care	16.30	9.8	15.8
Face-to-face socialising	11.24	6.8	10.9
In transit**	7.00	4.2	6.7
Hobbies and games	6.30	3.9	6.2
Domestic activities***	4.18	2.6	4.1
Homework (school)	4.12	2.5	4.0
Sports	4.00	2.4	3.8
Other****	7.36	4.5	7.2
Total	168.00	100.1	100.0

Notes:
* Figures refer to hours and minutes. For example, 1.24 means 1 hour and 24 minutes.
** On public transport, private transport or walking with a fixed destination.
*** For example, cleaning, washing up, cooking, gardening.
**** Includes, for example, paid and voluntary work, meetings of clubs and societies, cultural activities, indirect socialisation (i.e. phone, e-mail, etc.) and being ill in bed.

it is clear that adolescents do spend most of their time with their key agents of socialisation (parents and teachers) and therefore that these agents (at least potentially) have a great role to play in the social fostering (parents) and social education (teachers) of the youths. However, time spent with parents and teachers does not tell us much about the content and quality of these interactions, only about the potential, although one would expect a general relationship between time spent with parents and the quality of the interaction. Secondly, since we know that most of the youths' crimes are committed when they are with peers only (see above), this puts the focus on the situational risks that may be involved when adolescents socialise in a peer-only environment.

Table 9.5 Average time spent, by whom time spent with (hours per week)

Activity	Hours*	Per cent time of the week	
		Total	Discounting sleeping time*****
Myself (solitude)	4.12	2.5	4.0
Family only (including adults)	100.00	59.5	35.2
Family only (no adults)	2.36	1.6	2.5
Peers only**	17.48	10.6	16.9
Others only (including 1 adult)	1.36	1.0	1.5
Others only (no adults)	0.18	0.2	0.3
Family and peers (including adults)	3.12	1.9	3.0
Family and peers (no adults)	0.24	0.2	0.4
Family and others (including adults)	2.54	1.7	2.8
Family and others (no adults)	0.12	0.1	0.2
Peers and others (including adults)***	32.36	19.4	31.0
Peers and others (no adults)	0.24	0.2	0.4
Mixed****	1.48	1.1	1.7
Total	*168.00*	*100.0*	*99.9*

Notes:

    * Figures refer to hours and minutes. For example, 1.24 means 1 hour and 24 minutes.

    ** Youths of roughly the same age group.

    *** Predominantly in the school setting, teachers and schoolmates.

    **** Family, peers and others.

    ***** In these calculations it has been assumed that the youths sleep at home in the presence of their family, which is overwhelmingly the case, although a marginal error is introduced by the fact that some youths at some times have slept in other locations (most commonly friends' homes). The hours slept have been deducted from the category of time spent with family only (i.e. no. of hours spent with family only is set to 37 hours).

The general impact on offending risk by time spent with peers has been shown in previous research. Osgood *et al.* (1996) report from the findings of a longitudinal study of a national US sample of 18–26-year-olds strong empirical support for their hypothesis that 'situations conducive to deviance are especially prevalent in unstructured socializing activities with peers that occurs in the absence of authority figures'. However, as already pointed out above, situational factors may affect youths differently according to their individual risk-protective characteristics. This question has not been adequately addressed in previous research.

Differences in the youths' routine activities by gender, family social position and ethnicity

One reason why there is a significant (but modest) relationship between the youths' structural position (as determined by their genders, their families' social positions and ethnicities Table 9.6) and their offending is that structural characteristics may have some impact on the youths' patterns of routine activities, and therefore on their exposure to situations conducive to offending. For example, the youths' routine activities may vary due to the influence of gender roles, and social class and ethnic differences in social and economic resources and culture.

Gender differences in routine activities appear predominantly to reflect 'traditional' gender roles

A good illustration of this is the *gender* differences in routine activities (recall that all figures refer to time spent during one week). Boys spend, on average, more time *on streets and in squares* (8 hours v. 4 hours and 12 minutes for girls), while girls spend slightly more time in *shops and shopping centres* (2 hours and 54 minutes v. 2 hours for boys) (Table 9.7).

Boys spend much more of their time on *hobbies and games* (10 hours and 6 minutes v. 2 hours and 18 minutes for girls) and doing *sports* (6 hours and 30 minutes v. 1 hours and 12 minutes for girls),

Table 9.6 Average time spent by main location (hours per week) by gender, family structural risk and ethnic background

Location	Gender		Family structural risk		Ethnic group	
	Signif.	Eta²	Signif.	Eta²	Signif.	Eta²
Place of residence	n.s.	–	n.s.	–	0.010	0.03
Other place in neighbourhood	n.s.	–	n.s.	–	n.s.	–
School	n.s.	–	0.051	0.03	n.s.	–
Other place	n.s.	–	n.s.	–	n.s.	–

Table 9.7 Average time spent by location outside the home and the school by gender, family structural risk and ethnic background (hours per week)

Location	Gender		Family structural risk		Ethnic group	
	Signif.	Eta²	Signif.	Eta²	Signif.	Eta²
Others' home	n.s.	–	n.s.	–	n.s.	–
Transport (bus, etc.)	n.s.	–	n.s.	–	0.041	0.02
Street, squares	0.000	0.05	0.006	0.04	0.054	0.02
Shops/shopping centres	0.002	0.03	n.s.	–	n.s.	–
Locales of entertainment	n.s.	–	n.s.	–	n.s.	–
Sports grounds	0.000	0.06	n.s.	–	n.s.	–

Note:
Other places not included due to the great heterogeneity of places covered by this class.

while girls spend more of their time in *face-to-face socialising* (13 hours and 36 minutes vs. 9 hours and 30 minutes for boys), doing *domestic work* (5 hours and 18 minutes v. 3 hours and 30 minutes for boys) and *homework from school* (5 hours and 6 minutes v. 3 hours and 24 minutes) (Table 9.8).

Boys spend somewhat more *time by themselves* (5 hours v. 3 hours and 6 minutes for girls) and with *peers only* (19 hours and 6 minutes v. 16 hours and 12 minutes) (Table 9.9). All in all, one might say that the emerging picture of gender differences in the adolescents' routine activities is that boys spend more time in risky settings than girls.

Differences in the youths' routine activities by family structural risk are surprisingly small

The differences in routine activities by the youths' *family structural risk* are much less than were the gender differences. Youths from the lowest structural risk group (middle class and complete family of origin) tend to spend a couple of hours more in school than others (Table 9.6). Youths from the lowest structural risk group also tend to spend somewhat less time *in streets and squares* than others (3 hours and 36 minutes compared with a range between 5 hours and 36 minutes to 8 hours and 6 minutes for the other three categories) (Table 9.7).

The only significant differences in *activities* are that youths from families in the two categories of lowest structural risk spend less time on *domestic activities* than others (3 hours and 42 minutes compared with 4 hours and 30 minutes and 6 hours and 18 minutes for the youths in the two highest categories of family structural risk) but more time on *homework from school*, where the rate of time spent decreases by increasing family structural risk (from 6 hours, to 5 hours, to 3 hours and, finally, to 2 hours and 54 minutes) (Table 9.8).

There are no significant differences regarding with whom time is spent by family structural risk (Table 9.9). All in all, the differences between adolescents by family structural risk are surprisingly small. However, were there are differences they are (with the exception of time spent on domestic work) all in the direction of higher risk – i.e. less time spent in school, more time spent in streets and squares and less time spent on school homework.

Asians are more family oriented in their routine activities than others

In general the *ethnic* differences in routine activities (between UK natives, Asians and non-Asian foreigners) are basically a question of the greater home orientation in the activities by Asians. Asians spend more of their *time in the home* (113 hours compared with 100 for the other two groups) (Table 9.6), and less of their time in *streets and squares* (3 hours and 36 minutes compared with 6 hours and 48 minutes for UK natives and 5 hours and 42 minutes for non-Asian foreigners). They also spend less time *in transit* (4 hours and 36 minutes compared with 8 hours for UK natives and 8 hours and 12 minutes for non-Asian foreigners) (Table 9.7). A not easily explained difference is that Asian youths tend to *sleep* somewhat more than others (66 hours and 42 minutes compared with 63 hours for UK natives and 62 hours and 48 minutes for non-Asian foreigners), although this fact may be related to their greater home centredness (Table 9.8).

Asians spend less time than others *by themselves* (1 hour and 36 minutes compared with 4 hours and 12 minutes for UK natives and 5 hours and 30 minutes for non-Asian foreigners) and with *peers only* (10 hours and 54 minutes compared with 18 hours and 42 minutes for UK natives and 16 hours and 6 minutes for non-Asian foreigners), but more time with *family and other adults* (8 hours and 36 minutes compared with 2 hours and 42 minutes for UK natives and 1 hour for non-Asian foreigners), the latter possibly reflecting cultural differences in patterns of family socialisation with friends. All in all, the major ethnic difference in routine activities appears to be the greater family orientation of the Asian youths.

Table 9.8 Average time spent by main activity by gender, family structural risk and ethnic background (hours per week)

Location	Gender		Family structural risk		Ethnic group	
	Signif.	Eta^2	Signif.	Eta^2	Signif.	Eta^2
Sleeping	n.s.	–	n.s.	–	0.019	0.02
Classes and lectures	n.s.	–	n.s.	–	n.s.	–
Media consumption	n.s.	–	n.s.	–	n.s.	–
Eating/personal care	n.s.	–	n.s.	–	n.s.	–
Face-to-face socialising	0.000	0.05	n.s.	–	n.s.	–
In transit	n.s.	–	n.s.	–	n.s.	–
Hobbies and games	0.000	0.27	n.s.	–	n.s.	–
Domestic activities	0.000	0.04	0.051	0.03	n.s.	–
Homework (school)	0.001	0.03	0.000	0.06	n.s	–
Sports	0.000	0.20	n.s.	–	n.s.	–

Table 9.9 Average time spent, with whom, by gender, family structural risk and ethnic background (hours per week)

Location	Gender		Family structural risk		Ethnic group	
	Signif.	Eta^2	Signif.	Eta^2	Signif.	Eta^2
Myself (solitude)	0.001	0.03	n.s.	–	0.013	0.03
Family only (including adults)	n.s.	–	n.s.	–	n.s.	–
Family only (no adults)	n.s.	–	n.s.	–	n.s.	–
Peers only	0.042	0.01	n.s.	–	0.009	0.03
Others only (including adults)	n.s.	–	n.s.	–	n.s.	–
Others only (no adults)	n.s.	–	n.s.	–	0.010	0.03
Family and peers (including adults)	n.s.	–	n.s.	–	n.s.	–
Family and peers (no adults)	n.s.	–	n.s.	–	n.s.	–
Family and others (including adults)	n.s.	–	n.s.	–	0.019	0.02
Family and others (no adults)	n.s.	–	n.s.	–	n.s.	–
Peers and others (including adults)	n.s.	–	n.s.	–	n.s.	–
Peers and others (no adults)	n.s.	–	n.s.	–	n.s.	–

Note:
Mixed category not included.

It may be interesting to note that, by and large, the variations in risk routine activities by gender, family structural risk and ethnicity show some correspondence to their (mostly modest) differences in offending levels (see Chapters 4 and Chapter 5). Males tend to engage somewhat more in risk activities than females, and Asians tend to engage less in risk activities than others[2] (i.e. spending time in streets and in squares and together with peers only). As regards family structural risk there is a difference in time spent in streets and squares but not as regards time spent with peers only.

Differences in the youths' routine activities by their individual risk-protective characteristics

Earlier in this chapter it was shown that most of the youths' offending occurred when they spent time with other peers only in public spaces (i.e. streets, squares, parks and recreational grounds). The analyses in the previous section showed, among other things, that females, youths from families of lower structural risk and youths of Asian origin tend to spend less time in streets and squares, and that females and youths of Asian origin tend to spend somewhat less time with peers only. In this section we will address the differences in the youths' routine activities by their individual risk-protective scores.

The youths' routine activities analysed by main groups of risk-protective scores (i.e. protective, balanced and risk groups) show that the youths' routine activities vary, sometimes strongly, by their risk-protective characteristics, and particularly so for time spent in activities linked to levels of offending (e.g. time spent in streets and squares and with peers only).

Youths belonging to the protective group, compared with youths in the balanced and the risk groups, spend more *time at home* (106 hours and 36 minutes compared with 100 hours and 6 minutes for the balanced group and 99 hours and 54 minutes for the risk group), and less time in their *neighbourhood outside the home* (18 hours and 54 minutes compared with 25 hours and 30 minutes for the balanced group and 24 hours and 24 minutes for the risk group). The more protective characteristics a youth has the more time he or she spends *in school* (31 hours and 12 minutes for the protective group, 27 hours and 36 minutes for the balanced group and 25 hours and 48 minutes for the risk group) (Table 9.10).

Table 9.10 Average time spent by main location (hours per week) by main groups of individual risk-protective score, area of residence structural risk and school structural risk

Location	Individual risk-protective score		Area of residence structural risk		School structural risk	
	Signif.	Eta²	Signif.	Eta²	Signif.	Eta²
Place of residence	0.011	0.03	n.s.	–	n.s.	–
Other place in neighbourhood	0.054	0.02	n.s.	–	0.001	0.05
School	0.002	0.04	0.007	0.03	0.000	0.09
Other place	n.s.	–	n.s.	–	n.s.	–

Youths belonging to the protective group tend to spend somewhat less time in *others' homes* (10 hours and 6 minutes compared with 13 hours and 36 minutes for the balanced group and 16 hours and 42 minutes for the risk group), and much less time out *in streets and in squares* (3 hours and 36 minutes compared with 8 hours and 36 minutes for the balanced group and 13 hours and 42 minutes for the risk group) than youths in other groups (Table 9.11).

The higher the youths' individual risk the more of their time they spend in *face-to-face socialising* (9 hours and 6 minutes for the protective group, 13 hours and 18 minutes for the balanced group and 15 hours and 42 minutes for the risk group) and less in *classes and lectures* (26 hours and 18 minutes for the protective group, 23 hours and 36 minutes for the balanced group and 22 hours and 30 minutes for the risk group) (Table 9.12).

Finally, youths in the protective group spend much less time with *peers only* (13 hours and 24 minutes compared with 22 hours for the balanced group and 24 hours and 12 minutes for the risk group). A not easily explained finding is that the youths in the balanced group spend somewhat less time than others with *family only* (95 hours and 36 minutes compared with 105 hours and 30 minutes for the protective group and 104 hours for the risk group) (Table 9.13).

All in all, the findings show that youths in the individual risk group spend much more time in risk activities (i.e. time spent in streets and squares and with peers only) than those in the balanced group, and that those in the balanced group engage far more in risk

Table 9.11 Average time spent by main location outside the home and the school (hours per week) by main groups of individual risk-protective score, area of residence structural risk and school structural risk

Location	Individual risk-protective score		Area of residence structural risk		School structural risk	
	Signif.	Eta²	Signif.	Eta²	Signif.	Eta²
Others' home	0.045	0.02	n.s.	–	0.035	0.02
Transport (bus, etc.)	n.s.	–	0.014	0.03	0.000	0.13
Street, squares	0.000	0.13	0.001	0.05	0.012	0.03
Shops/shopping centres	n.s.	–	n.s.	–	n.s.	–
Locales of entertainment	n.s.	–	n.s.	–	n.s.	–
Sports ground	n.s.	–	n.s.	–	n.s.	–

Table 9.12 Average time spent by main activity (hours per week) by main groups of individual risk-protective score, area of residence structural risk and school structural risk

Location	Individual risk-protective score		Area of residence structural risk		School structural risk	
	Signif.	Eta²	Signif.	Eta²	Signif.	Eta²
Sleeping	n.s.	–	n.s.	–	n.s.	–
Classes and lectures	0.007	0.03	0.011	0.03	0.000	0.11
Media consumption	n.s.	–	n.s.	–	0.006	0.04
Eating/personal care	n.s.	–	n.s.	–	0.031	0.04
Face-to-face socialising	0.002	0.06	0.024	0.03	0.008	0.03
In transit	n.s.	–	0.010	0.03	0.000	0.13
Hobbies and games	n.s.	–	n.s.	–	n.s.	–
Domestic activities	n.s.	–	n.s.	–	n.s.	–
Homework (school)	0.000	0.12	0.013	0.03	0.000	0.12
Sports	n.s.	–	n.s.	–	n.s.	–

Note:
Other activities not included due to the great heterogeneity of activities covered by this class.

activities than those in the protective group. The effects (as judged by Eta²) are much stronger than was the case for gender, family structural risk or ethnicity.

Table 9.13 Average time spent, with whom, by main groups of individual risk-protective score, area of residence structural risk and school structural risk

Location	Individual risk-protective score		Area of residence structural risk		School structural risk	
	Signif.	Eta^2	Signif.	Eta^2	Signif.	Eta^2
Myself (solitude)	n.s.	–	n.s.	–	n.s.	–
Family only (including adults)	0.001	0.05	n.s.	–	0.028	0.03
Family only (no adults)	n.s.	–	n.s.	–	n.s.	–
Peers only	0.000	0.12	0.006	0.04	0.002	0.04
Others only (including adults)	n.s.	–	n.s.	–	n.s.	–
Others only (no adults)	n.s.	–	n.s.	–	n.s.	–
Family and peers (including adults)	n.s.	–	n.s.	–	n.s.	–
Family and peers (no adults)	n.s.	–	0.017	0.03	n.s.	–
Family and others (including adults)	n.s.	–	n.s.	–	n.s.	–
Family and others (no adults)	n.s.	–	n.s.	–	n.s.	–
Peers and others (including adults)	n.s.	–	0.031	0.02	0.003	0.04
Peer and others (no adults)	n.s.	–	n.s.	–	n.s.	–

Note:
Mixed category not included.

Differences in the youths' routine activities by their community context

The main differences in the youths' routine activities by their community context (neighbourhoods and schools) relate to time spent on school and peer-related activities, but not on time spent on family-oriented activities.

Youths living in areas of higher structural risk spend somewhat more time than others on activities related to situational risks of offending

Youth routines differ somewhat by *area of residence structural risk* (areas of structural risk have been grouped in three categories for this analysis – scores 0–2, 3–4 and 5–7 have been combined – for a general definition of the construct, see Chapter 7). The effect sizes of area of residence structural risk on routine activities is quite small (see Tables 9.10–9.13). However, the strongest differences relatively speaking (as judged by eta^2) regard activities that may entail higher situational risks of offending – that is, time spent in streets and squares and time spent with peers only. Youths living in areas of higher structural risks also tend to spend somewhat less time on school-related activities (e.g. classes and lectures and doing homework for school) than others.

Youths living in areas of residence of higher structural risk spend more time *in streets and in squares* (8 hours compared with 5 hours and 12 minutes for the middle group and 4 hours and 30 minutes for the area of residence low structural risk group). The same holds for time spent with *peers only* (20 hours and 36 minutes compared with 15 hours and 24 minutes for the middle group and 15 hours and 54 minutes for the low area of residence structural risk group) and for time spent on *face-to-face socialising* (13 hours and 36 minutes compared with 10 hours and 6 minutes for the middle group and 10 hours and 36 minutes for the low area of residence structural risk group). Youths from areas of residence of higher structural risk tend to spend somewhat less time *in transit* (5 hours and 6 minutes compared with 7 hours and 42 minutes for the middle group and 7 hours and 6 minutes for the low areas of residence structural risk group). A possible reason for this is that youths from more disadvantaged areas, to a higher degree, attend local schools since a large part of the time youths spend in transit is going to and from school.

Youths residing in areas with a low structural risk spend marginally more time *in school* than others (31 hours and 36 minutes compared with 28 hours for the middle group and 28 hours and 24 minutes for the youths from the area of residence high structural risk group). This difference is also, as expected, reflected in time spent in *classes and lectures* (26 hours and 30 minutes compared with 23 hours and 36 minutes for the middle group and 23 hours and 42 minutes for the youths from the area of residence high structural risk group). The time spent on *homework from school* decreases with increasing structural risk of the area of residence (from 5 hours for those in the area of residence low structural risk group, over 4 hours and 18 minutes for those in the middle group, and 3 hours and 12 minutes for those in the area of residence high structural risk group). Also reflecting the lesser time spent on school activities is the fact that youths from areas of residence of higher structural risk spend less time in situations with *peers and non-family adults* (the latter being predominantly school staff). Finally, there is also a significant difference in time spent with non-adult family members and peers. Youths from area of residence low structural risk tend to spend more time together with non-adult family members (mostly siblings) and peers (48 minutes compared with 6 minutes for the two other groups), although, in terms of time, this is a very marginal activity for all youths.

Youth routines differ by school structural risks, particularly as regards time spent on school-related activities, and also, but less strongly so, as regards time spent on activities related to situational risks of offending

The youths' routine activities differ significantly by the *school structural risk* (for a definition of the four groups compared by school structural risk, see Chapter 7). This is particularly so for school-related activities such as time spent in classes and lectures and time spent on doing homework from school (the former is at least partly related to higher truancy levels in schools with higher structural risks). The variations in non-school-related activities are not as strong as for the school-related activities. However, it is of interest to note that youths, particularly in the low structural risk school, spend much less time in activities that may entail situational risks for offending (e.g. time spent in streets and squares and with peers only).

The strongest variation between the youths' routine activities according to their school's structural risk relates to their school activities. In schools with lower structural risk the youths spend more time *in school*. Youths in the school with the lowest structural risk spend, on average, 37 hours and 30 minutes in school, that is 12 hours more compared with those in the two groups of schools with the highest structural risk (both 25 hours and 30 minutes), and 7 hours more than those in the remaining group of school structural risk (30 hours and 42 minutes) (Table 9.10). This is, as expected, also reflected in the amount of time spent in *classes and lectures* (31 hours and 54 minutes in the school with the lowest structural risk compared with 22 hours and 12 minutes in the groups of school with the highest structural risk) (Table 9.12). Youths in low structural risk schools also spend more time doing *homework for school* (9 hours and 42 minutes for the low structural risk school compared with only 2 hours and 42 minutes for the groups of schools with the highest structural risk) (Table 9.12), but also more time *in transit* (probably just indicating that schools with lower structural risks tend to be more attractive and therefore draw students from a larger geographical area). One reason why the amount of time spent in school varies by school structural risk is that the levels of truancy are higher in schools with higher structural risk (the zero-order correlation between time spent in school and time spent being truant is $r. = -0.28$, signf. = 0.000). This finding is also consistent with the findings in the questionnaire study regarding the relationship between school structural risk and repeated truancy (see Figure 7.17).

The youths' routine activities by school structural risk also vary for many non-school-related activities (see Tables 9.10–9.13), but not as strongly as for the school-related activities (as judged by eta^2). Youths in the low structural risk school spend much less time in their *neighbourhood outside the home* (6 hours and 48 minutes increasing up to 28 hours and 24 minutes for the youths in the group of schools with the highest structural risk), *in others' homes* (7 hours and 48 minutes increasing up to 16 hours and 42 minutes for the youths in the group of schools with the highest structural risk), *in streets and in squares* (1 hour and 36 minutes increasing up to 7 hours and 54 minutes for youths in the group of schools with the highest structural risk), *in face-to-face socialising* (5 hours and 54 minutes increasing up to 13 hours and 30 minutes for youths in the group of schools with the highest structural risk), and with *peers only* (8 hours and 6 minutes increasing up to 19 hours and 18 minutes for the youths in the group of schools with the highest structural risk). In many of these cases, there is a particularly big jump in time spent between the school with the lowest structural risk and the next group of schools by level of structural risk.

In addition to the already-mentioned significant differences in routine activities by school structural risk, there are also significant differences as regards time spent on media consumption, on eating/

personal care, and with peers and non-family adults. The latter just reflects the already-noted difference that youths from lower structural risk schools tend to spend more time in school (time spent with peers and non-family adults is predominantly time spent with peers and school staff). Differences in media consumption show no clear pattern of increase or decrease by school structural risk. Rather, youths at the two extremes tend to have a slightly higher media consumption than those in the two middle groups (note that, in this report we have not explored any differences in type of media consumed, just overall time spent on any media). As regards eating/personal care there is a weak tendency of increase by school structural risk – youths in the low structural risk school spend about one hour less on eating/personal care than those in the group of schools with the highest structural risk.

Family, school and peer centred activities: a factor analysis

The analyses conducted so far indicate that three broad dimensions of the youths' activities can be described as family, school and peer-oriented activities. An oblique factor analysis of selected variables, referring to key aspects of time spent by place, activity and with whom, from the space-time-budget study (Table 9.14), resulted in three dimensions (three factors with an eigenvalue above 1, explaining 63 per cent of the variance) that could be interpreted as representing peer centredness (factor 1), family centredness (factor 2) and school centredness (factor 3). Peer centredness and family centredness were negatively correlated – that is, youths who were peer centred tended not to be family centred, while school centredness was not significantly related to family centredness, and only very weakly (negatively) to peer centeredness (Table 9.15).

Peer centredness, time spent in high-risk situations and offending

Only peer centredness independently predicts offending rates, and poor parental monitoring goes together with a high degree of peer centredness

The correlations between the three main dimensions of youths' routine activities and offending, as represented by the overall 2000 annual frequency of offending and the overall 2001 one-week frequency of offending, showed that school centredness was not significantly related to offending levels, family centredness only

Table 9.14 Factor analysis: oblique rotation, selected youth routine variables

Time spent	Factor 1 (peer centred)	Factor 2 (family centred)	Factor 3 (school centred)	h^2
Home*	−0.45	0.89	−0.11	0.85
Family only***	−0.44	0.81	−0.04	0.71
Other home*	0.21	−0.84	−0.21	0.76
School*	−0.31	−0.18	0.71	0.63
Cultural activities**	0.04	0.11	0.70	0.53
Homework (school)**	−0.49	0.25	0.40	0.36
Streets/squares*	0.84	−0.18	−0.06	0.72
Face-to-face socialising**	0.69	−0.40	−0.15	0.52
Peers only***	0.82	−0.46	0.09	0.76
Substance use	0.67	−0.23	−0.18	0.46
Explained variance	37.3	14.8	11.0	

Note:

Loadings 0.40 and higher underlined.
  * Place.
 ** Activity.
*** With whom.

Table 9.15 Zero-order correlations of main youth activity orientation factors and frequency of crime year 2000 and (last week) year 2001

	Peer centredness	Family centredness	School centredness	Crime 2000	Crime 2001
Peer centredness	1.00				
Family centredness	−0.31	1.00			
School centredness	−0.13	(0.02)	1.00		
Crime frequency 2000	0.35	−0.13	(−0.04)	1.00	
Crime frequency 2001	0.30	−0.13	(−0.00)	0.35	1.00

Note:

Correlations in brackets are non-significant.

weakly (negatively) related to offending levels, while peer centredness showed a much stronger relationship to offending levels (Table 9.15). A multiple regression analysis showed that the three variables together explained 13 per cent of the variance in the overall 2000 annual offending frequency and 9 per cent in the overall 2001 one-week frequency of offending (Table 9.16). However, in both cases, only peer centredness was a significant predictor.

In the lifestyle chapter we showed that lifestyle risk was related to poor parental monitoring (see Figure 8.22). The same holds for the relationship between (poor) parental monitoring and the degree to which the youths' activities are peer centred ($r. = 0.38$, signf. = 0.000).

One in seven of the youths spends time in a high-risk situation during a week

Having established that peer-centred activities are the activities most closely linked to offending risk, the next question to be addressed is whether there is a relationship between peer centredness and actual time spent in high-risk situations.

A *high-risk situation* is defined as any of the following: having an argument with another person, being harassed/provoked by another person, witnessing someone having an argument, witnessing someone being harassed/provoked or witnessing an incidence of violence. Having an argument with others (40.3 per cent), being harassed/provoked by someone else (26.9 per cent) or witnessing a violent incident (17.9 per cent) were the three most common of the five types of risk situations included in the index. It should be stressed that the high-risk situation index predominantly is relevant

Table 9.16 Multiple regression: frequency of crime (year 2000 and 'last week' year 2001) by main dimensions of activity orientation

	Beta	Signif.
Dependent: frequency of crime 2000 (annual)		
Peer centredness	0.34	0.000
Family centredness	−0.03	n.s.
School centredness	−0.01	n.s.
Multiple $R^2 \times 100 = 13$		
$n = 330$		
Dependent: frequency of crime 2001 (last week)		
Peer centredness	0.30	0.000
Family centredness	−0.04	n.s.
School centredness	0.04	n.s.
Multiple $R^2 \times 100 = 9$		
$n = 338$		

to risk of getting involved in crimes directed towards the person (e.g. aggressive crimes, personal theft).

Of all youths, 15 per cent have spent at least some time during a week in a high-risk situation and, on average, these youths have spent 1 hour and 17 minutes in such situations (the mean calculated for all youths is 12 minutes). There is no gender difference in time spent in high-risk situations (14.8 per cent of the females and 15.2 per cent of the males spent time during a week in a high-risk situation).

Peer-centred youths spend more time in high-risk situations

Youths who display higher levels of peer centredness more often find themselves in high-risk situations[3] (Figure 9.2). The zero-order correlation between (the full scales) of peer centredness and time spent in high-risk situations is $r. = 0.27$ (signf. = 0.000).

Youths who spend more time in high-risk situations offend more than others

To explore the relationship between time spent in high-risk situations and offending, the mean frequency of crimes committed by the number of hours spent in high-risk situations during the studied week was calculated (Table 9.17). Although the number of crimes

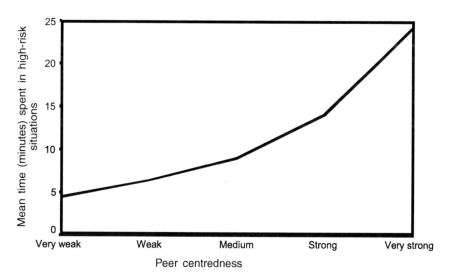

Figure 9.2 Time spent in high-risk situations by degree of peer centredness

Table 9.17 Mean frequency of crimes by frequency of time spent in high-risk situations

Time spent in high-risk situations	Total	Theft	Vandalism	Violence	n
None	0.08	0.01	0.02	0.02	288
1 hour	0.09	0.00	0.02	0.02	43
2+ hours	0.62	0.25	0.12	0.25	8
Signif.	0.001	0.000	n.s.	0.000	339
$Eta^2 =$	0.04	0.09	–	0.05	

committed during a week is rather few (31 crimes during 'the week' we studied) and the number of youths who have repeatedly been in a high-risk situations was very few (8 in our studied week), the results show that there are significant differences by time spent in high-risk situations for total crimes, and for the subcategories of crimes of theft and violence, but not for vandalism (although the trend for the latter is the same as for the others). In this context it should be pointed out that most of the thefts reported in the space-time budget study concern personal thefts, which is important to remember when comparing with the questionnaire study data on theft that refer to shoplifting and serious thefts only.

The same analysis as is reported in Table 9.17 was also conducted using data on the annual mean frequency of offending in 2000. For this analysis to make sense, one has to assume that there is some correspondence between the time the youths spent in high-risk situations during one week in 2001 and the time they spent in such situations during the whole of year 2000. The findings show that the annual mean frequency of aggressive offending in year 2000 was significantly related to the time youths spent in high-risk situations (one week in 2001). The mean frequency of aggressive offending for those who had not spent any time in a high-risk situation was 1.3, compared with 2.9 for those who had spent 1 hour in a high-risk situation and 3.5 for those who had spent 2 hours or more in a high risk situation. As regards mean frequency of shoplifting, and of serious thefts, there were no significant relationships to time spent in high-risk situations.[4]

The relationship between key dimensions of youth routine activities and offending: a comparative analysis of youths with protective and balanced individual risk-protective scores

In the final analysis of this chapter we will return to the question of whether the way youths live their lives has a greater impact on offending levels for those who have balanced compared with the those who have protective individual risk-protective scores. The risk group of youths is not included in the space-time budget study because the number of such youths who took part is very low (n = 12) and therefore estimates of relationships will be highly unreliable for this group. Partly the analyses in this section are made to see whether we can validate the findings reported in the lifestyle chapter (Chapter 8), which shows that the youths with balanced risk-protective scores are more affected by the way they live their lives than those with protective individual risk-protective scores.

Peer centredness has a greater impact on offending levels for youths with balanced rather than protective risk-protective scores

Comparing frequency of crime by peer centredness for the balanced and the protective group shows that while the frequency of crime does not vary much by level of peer centredness (and is non-significant) for the protective group, it increases steadily by level of peer centredness for the balanced groups. This holds both when the 2000 annual mean frequency of crime is analysed (Figure 9.3; for the balanced group: signf. = 0.009, eta^2 = 0.06) and when the 2001 last week mean frequency of crime is analysed (Figure 9.4; for the balanced group: signf. = 0.013, eta^2 = 0.09).

It should be noted that the peer centredness measure is a more general measure of peer-related activities than the lifestyle risk measure, which specifically targeted risk aspects of youth lifestyles (having peer delinquents, being drunk and using drugs, and spending time in risky public environments). The zero-order correlation between peer centredness and lifestyle risk is quite strong (r. = 0.46, signf. = 0.000) but it is far from being a one-to-one relationship (see also Figure 9.5).

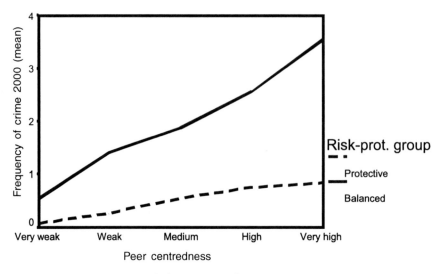

Figure 9.3 Mean annual frequency of crime 2000 by peer centredness compared for the protective and balanced groups of individual risk-protective scores

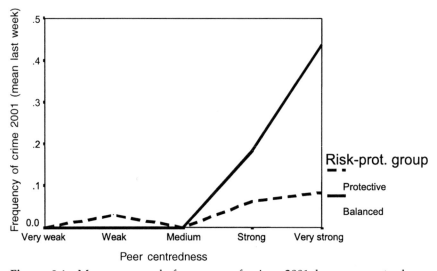

Figure 9.4 Mean one-week frequency of crime 2001 by peer centredness compared for the protective and balanced groups of individual risk-protective scores

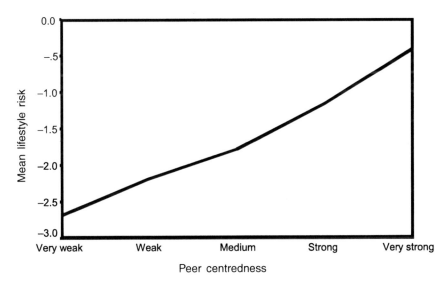

Figure 9.5 Mean lifestyle risk score by peer centeredness

Youths with balanced risk-protective scores and a strong family centredness tend to offend less than others, while level of school centredness does not affect offending levels for either the balanced or the protective groups of youths

The pattern of variation in offending by level of family centredness was the same both when using the 2000 annual frequency of crime (Figure 9.6) and the 2001 one-week frequency of crime (Figure 9.7). There was no great variation for the protective group but a significant drop in mean frequency for those at the stronger end of family centredness. Overall these differences did not reach significance, but when those who have strong and very strong family centredness were compared with the rest, the differences were significant for the 2000 annual mean frequency of crime (signf. = 0.019, eta^2 = 0.04). As regards school centredness there were no distinct patterns, and no significant differences, as regards offending frequencies by level of school centredness.

All in all, the analyses of offending frequencies by main dimensions of the youths' routine activities (peer, family and school centredness) support the findings presented in the lifestyle chapter (Chapter 8); the offending of youths with balanced individual risk-protective factors is more influenced by the way they live their life than is the case for youths with protective individual risk-protective scores.

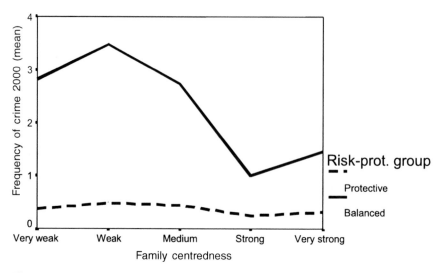

Figure 9.6 Mean annual frequency of crime 2000 by family centredness compared for the protective and balanced groups of individual risk-protective scores

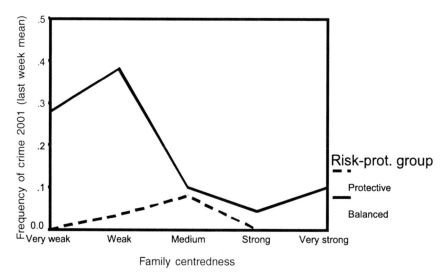

Figure 9.7 Mean one-week frequency of crime 2001 by family centredness compared for the protective and balanced groups of individual risk-protective scores

Notes

1 The more general findings from the questionnaire study (see Chapter 4), pointed to the youths' school and neighbourhood as two main places of offending. In the space-time budget study the schools do not rank high as a place of (last week) offending. This may be a consequence of a lower annual frequency of offending in schools compared with other locations, despite a high annual prevalence (recall that we only had access to prevalence data for offending by place of occurrence of the youths' last crime committed).

2 In this case the large difference in offending between Asian males and females should be recalled. To what degree the overall Asian patterns in routine activities are also highly influenced by a markedly different pattern for the Asian females or not we do not know. The time-budget data do not allow for a reliable breakdown by gender for Asians due to the much lower number of subjects in the time-budget study than in the questionnaire study.

3 The scores for peer centredness have been divided into five groups with equal numbers of subjects. In most previous analyses when scales have been made into classes for use in graphs and tables we have made the classes by making groups of equal ranges of scores. The reason why we opted for groups with equal numbers of subjects rather than equal ranges of scores was the much lower number of subjects in the space-time budget study compared with the questionnaire study. If we had chosen equal ranges of scores some of the extreme classes would have had very few subjects.

4 In this context it may be reported that the zero-order correlation between time spent in shops and shopping centres (as reported in the space-time budget study) and frequency of shoplifting (as reported in the questionnaire study) was very low and non-significant. Also recall the earlier reported finding that the prevalence of shoplifting, but not the frequency of shoplifting, was related to time spent in shops and shopping centres (based on the youths' reports in the questionnaire study).

Chapter 10

Key findings and their explanation

The context of the study

This is a study of adolescent involvement in crime in a medium-sized city

The study gives a snapshot in time of 14–15-year-old adolescents' individual characteristics, their lives and involvement in crime in a medium-sized UK city (Peterborough). Adolescence is the time in life when involvement in crime peaks. This study focuses on current offending and victimisation as they relate to the youths' individual characteristics and their behavioural context. Since this is a cross-sectional study we do not know from where the youths are coming (their past childhood developmental history), or to where they are going (their future development into adulthood). Therefore we cannot provide any data about how their individual differences (related to involvement in crime) have emerged or any data on how their current behavioural context impacts on their future life chances and involvement in crime. However, it is entirely reasonable to argue that we can use the findings from existing longitudinal studies (developmental and criminal career studies) to help in the interpretation of the findings of patterns and correlates of adolescent involvement in crime as reported in this study. We will use the knowledge on developmental patterns from longitudinal studies particularly when discussing the existence of different types of groups of adolescent offenders.

A particular strength of this study is its focus on the youths' behavioural contexts (as represented by lifestyles/routines) *and* their individual characteristics, especially the interaction between the two. This is an aspect that has been largely ignored in most longitudinal (and other) studies, which predominantly focus solely on the role of individual characteristics (and their development) for offending risk. In addition to our lifestyle and youth routine activities measures, we also have measures of community contexts (neighbourhood and school characteristics), another aspect largely neglected in developmental research. However, our community context constructs are, at best, rudimentary. They only give a rough picture of the structural characteristics of the community but no in-depth knowledge about aspects of neighbourhood and school social life and control, which may be assumed more directly to influence the youths' behaviour.

Involvement in crime

Offending of a less serious nature is a widespread but not normal experience in adolescence

Having committed a common crime like an act of aggression or shoplifting is a rather common experience in adolescence. More serious offending is rare. Also victimisation experiences are common. This is in accordance with what has been found in previous studies of self-reported offending and victimisation in adolescent populations. While adolescent offending may not be regarded as a statistically highly deviant phenomenon, this is not the same as to say that there are no differentiating factors between those who have and those who have not offended, or between those who offend occasionally and those who offend more frequently. On the contrary, there are significant individual and lifestyle differences, as this study clearly shows. This is an important insight since it is sometimes claimed that committing crime is a natural, almost inevitable, part of being an adolescent. Although adolescence may generally be a more risky period of life for crime involvement, whether adolescents will be involved in crime or not (and the extent to which they will be involved) is rather a question of the interplay between who they are and in what behavioural contexts they operate than the fact that they are adolescents. Of particular importance to note here is the finding that adolescents with protective individual characteristics were unlikely to commit acts of crime regardless of their behavioural contexts (lifestyles).

High-frequency adolescent offenders are versatile in their offending and this versatility normally also includes having committed more serious crimes

It seems reasonable to assume that high-frequency offenders have a higher propensity than others to infringe upon the rules of the law (and possibly also to break rules more generally). For example, this study shows that those who have weak pro-social values as regards offending, and who report anticipating low levels of shame if they were caught offending, offend much more than others. The fact that high-frequency offenders in most cases are versatile in their offending (i.e. commit many different types of crime), a finding also demonstrated in several previous studies, suggests that their propensity to offend is generalised rather than specific. This, in turn, suggests that it may be a more fruitful starting point for the explanation and understanding of adolescent offending to analyse variation in (generalised) offending propensity rather than to focus on propensities to commit certain types of crime (that is, focus on explaining 'offending' rather than on 'burglary', 'shoplifting', 'car theft', etc.). It seems plausible that individual variations in the mix of crime types committed by high-frequency offenders (cross-sectionally and over time), or the variation in types of crime committed by occasional offenders, may primarily be explained by situational factors rather than any particularly strong inclination to commit specific types of crimes.

The fact that most of the serious crimes have been committed by high-frequency offenders is in line with findings from longitudinal research on developmental pathways showing that persistent offenders generally proceed from minor acts of crime to offending behaviour that also includes more serious crimes. It is therefore plausible that many of the high-frequency offenders in this study, in contrast to most of the occasional offenders, have had an extensive previous general history of 'anti-social behaviour' and crime.

Adolescent offenders only spend a marginal amount of time on offending

Although offending is a widespread experience in adolescence, the amount of time the adolescent offenders spend on offending is marginal.[1] Even the most persistent offender will only offend in a limited number of circumstances and the weekly time spent on offending can be counted in hours or perhaps even in minutes. This suggests the great importance of taking into account the role played by behavioural contexts (situational factors) and, particularly, their interaction with individual characteristics related to offending risk, when developing explanations of adolescent offending. The fact that even the most prolific offenders spend so little time offending, and that they are likely to encounter a much larger number of 'good opportunities' to offend than actually materialise into acts of crime, makes it unlikely that highly deterministic (individual or situational) explanatory models will fully capture the complexities of offending behaviour. This, in turn, suggests the need for an improved understanding of how individual perception of action alternatives and processes of choice, as affected by individual characteristics and behavioural contexts, influences the occurrence of acts of crime (Wikström 2006).

Adolescent offenders are more often victimised than others

Being an offender, particularly a frequent offender, increases the risk of also being a victim of crime. The relationship is especially strong between frequent violent offending and violent victimisations. This is likely to reflect a more generalised link between offending and victimisation through the youths' individual characteristics and their lifestyles. For example, it may be a reasonable hypothesis that youths with high individual risk characteristics and strong lifestyle risks more often get into 'trouble', which sometimes results in them committing a crime, but at other times results in their being victimised (particularly being a victim of a violent crime). The implication of this is that, when we talk about high-frequency adolescent offenders, we are likely to talk about adolescents who are also repeatedly victimised and, therefore, the offender and victim roles for this group may be somewhat blurred.

Explanatory factors

Adolescent offending is best interpreted as the consequence of perception of action alternatives and processes of choice made against the background of the interplay between the youths' individual characteristics and their behavioural contexts

It is beyond the scope of this book to deal with all the complexities involved in explaining adolescent offending. However, a brief sketch of the main theoretical arguments, as laid out in the 'situational action theory of crime causation', and on which the interpretations of the findings of this study are based, may be warranted (see further Wikström and Sampson 2003; Wikström 2004, 2005, 2006):

1 Crimes are acts of moral rule breakings defined in law and explanations of crime have to explain why individuals come to break moral rules as defined in law. It is the rule breaking (e.g. driving drunk when it is illegal) rather than the act itself (driving when drunk) that should be explained by a theory of crime causation.

2 Individual action (including acts of crime) is ultimately a result of how individuals see their action alternatives and make choices. This is the key *situational mechanism* that links individual characteristics and experiences and the behavioural contexts in which they operate to their actions.

3 What alternatives for action an individual sees and what choices an individual makes depend on who they are (their individual characteristics and experiences) and the features of the behavioural contexts in which they operate (Figure 10.1). The most important *individual differences* are those relating to an individual's morality and executive functions (the latter is important as regards their capability to exercise self-control). The most important features of a *behavioural setting* are those relating to its moral context (moral rules and their enforcement and sanctioning) and the temptations and provocations they provide. It is the interplay between an individual's morality and capability to exercise self-control on the one hand, and the moral contexts in which the individual faces temptations and provocations on the other hand, which determine what alternatives for action he or she will see, what choices he or she will make and, consequently, what action will follow (including any acts of crime).

4 Individuals are different and they operate in different behavioural contexts. Systemic factors (e.g. inequality and segregation) and individuals' developmental history do not explain why individuals commit acts of crime, but why they become different and why they come to operate in different behavioural contexts. In other words, their role in crime causation is important but indirect (they are the causes of causes – that is, they influence the individual and environmental factors that, in turn, make individuals see certain action alternatives and make certain choices that may cause them to commit acts of crime). The process through which systemic factors and developmental factors influence individual development of characteristics and experiences and exposure to behavioural contexts may be referred to as *social mechanisms* – that

is, the processes that link macro-features to individual development and exposure to behavioural contexts.

Although not specifically designed to test the situational action theory of crime causation, the main finding in the study of the importance of the interaction between individual characteristics (morality and self-control) and lifestyle (exposure to risky settings) is broadly in accord with some of the key assumptions made in the situational action theory of crime causation. Before moving on to discuss particular findings of the study, two implications of the theoretical framework of particular relevance to these discussions should be mentioned.

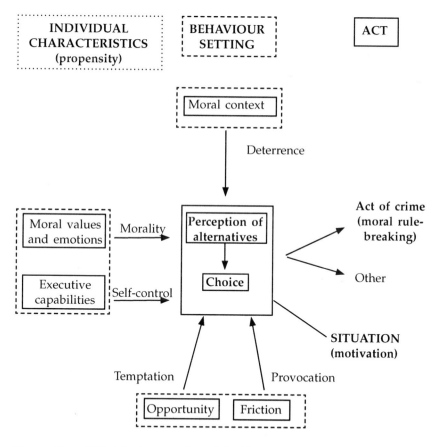

Figure 10.1 Wikström's general model of key situational factors influencing individuals' acts of crime

The first implication is that, while all social acts like crimes will necessarily involve some influence both by the individual's characteristics and the features of the setting in which the behaviour occurs, it is plausible to argue that in some cases individual factors, and in others environmental factors, may be the more important antecedents of the particular act (e.g. an act of crime). Moreover, focusing on individual differences, it is also plausible to argue more generally that for some individuals offending may be more propensity driven while for others offending may be more a result of particularly strong environmental inducements.

A second implication is that any effects of more distant structural factors (like family social position) are primarily mediated through the proximate factors as represented in the situational model (see, for example, Figures 6.31 and 7.1). This, in turn, means that to develop a better understanding of the role of structural disadvantage we should focus our efforts on improving our understanding of the social mechanisms through which structural disadvantage (developmentally and situationally) impacts on the aspects of individual characteristics and experiences and day-to-day living which more directly influence offending behaviour (see Wikström and Sampson 2003). For example, family and neighbourhood structural characteristics set the context in which child rearing and parenting operate, and school structural characteristics set the context in which teaching and social education have to operate. It is reasonable to assume that successful parenting and schooling are generally more difficult to achieve in disadvantaged as opposed to advantaged structural contexts, and therefore that the expected 'success rate' of socialisation, for example, as measured by the adult outcomes of health, educational achievement, wealth, psychological well-being and pro-social behaviour, would be somewhat lower in more disadvantaged circumstances.

The impact of gender on adolescent offending behaviour is quite modest

Although adolescent males offend more overall than adolescent females, knowing whether an adolescent is a male or a female does not help much in predicting whether they have offended or not. The latter also holds as regards violent and serious offending, where males offend about twice as much as females, and also for shoplifting, where females offend significantly more than males. Most, but not all, of the modest variance in offending frequency explained by gender can be accounted for by the fact that, compared with males, there are more females with strong protective factors (the gender differences being strongest for self-control and shaming) and fewer females with high-risk lifestyles. The same factors that explain adolescent male variation in offending, explain equally well, or sometimes slightly better, adolescent female involvement in crime. This fact would suggest that there is no great need to develop gender-specific models for the proximate adolescent factors influencing offending. Instead it suggests that the focus on explaining the modest gender differences in adolescent offending should be directed towards the more distant and indirect factors, explaining, for example, why females tend to have more protective factors than males.

Family structural characteristics have a modest impact on adolescent offending

Neither social class nor family type or ethnic background, separately or taken together, has any strong direct influence on adolescent offending (and victimisation). However, they do have an important effect on the youths' individual risk-protective scores. Adolescents in more disadvantaged circumstances tend more often to have high-risk factors, while youths from advantaged circumstances tend more often to have strong protective factors. This is congruent with the assumption that structural factors have a distant and indirect influence on offending, which is further supported by the fact that structural characteristics do not have any significant effect on adolescent offending when controlling for the youths' risk-protective factors.

Adolescent crime is not particularly a lower-class phenomenon. Adolescent involvement in crime does not vary much by (family) social class. The small social class differences in offending prevalence apply to crimes of theft only (particularly serious theft) and, in this case, are basically a difference between the middle classes, particularly the upper and upper middle class, and the rest. Offenders from lower social classes tend to be somewhat more active in aggressive crimes than others, but the effect is modest. Youths from upper and middle-class families tend to have somewhat stronger school bonds, self-control and levels of shaming than others.

Youths living with foster parents or in care have higher rates of offending than others. This may, at least partly, be explained by the fact that, particularly being in care, but possibly also living with foster parents, is often a consequence of a placement by social authorities initiated by the youth's social problems or those of his or her family, that may have involved criminality and substance abuse. There is no great difference in offending, and there is only a difference for girls, between youths living in a complete family of origin and those in a split family (i.e. with a single parent, with a biological and step-parent or moving between families). One has to bear in mind that nowadays it is not a very unusual experience for youths to live in a split family and therefore the social significance of being a child in a split family may be much less than in the past. Youths living in split families tend to have somewhat less strong social bonds (family and school bonds) and self-control than those living in a complete family of origin. This applies primarily to those living with a single parent or with a step-parent, but not to those moving between families. However, youths living with foster parents or in care tend to have less strong social bonds, self-control, pro-social values and shaming than all other youths, although the differences are not that large.

The adolescents' family ethnic background does not have much impact on the adolescents' offending, with one main exception, and that is the substantially lower rate of offending (and victimisation) for girls (but not boys) from Asian families. A probable explanation for this difference is that Asian girls tend to have much stronger individual protective factors than others. However, one has to bear in mind that the analysis in this study of family ethnic background has focused on comparing native and Asian youths, while the remaining youths with other ethnic backgrounds have been grouped together in one very heterogeneous category. The implication of this is that there may be ethnic subgroups within the group of youths with a non-Asian foreign background who have significantly higher or lower offending rates compared with natives.

There is no evidence for a social class or neighbourhood-disadvantaged-based adolescent 'subculture' of anti-social values (i.e. of pro-crime values)

The overwhelming majority of youths have strong pro-social values (i.e. do not think it is acceptable for youths their age to engage in crime). There are no differences in the adolescents' pro-social values by family social class or by area of residence structural risk. This finding therefore indicates that there are no social class or neighbourhood-disadvantage-based 'subcultures' of crime and delinquency. This is not the same as saying that the degree of pro-social values the youth has is irrelevant for his or her offending. On the contrary, youths with strong pro-social values are much less likely to offend than others. Interpreting the fact that youths who frequently offend are more likely to have peers who also offend frequently, and that they are all likely to have more positive attitudes towards offending, as evidence for the existence of a subculture of crime and delinquency is another matter. However, one has to bear in mind, as the findings of this study clearly show, that youths who frequently offend are likely to have a wide range of different individual and lifestyle risk factors. They are not simply a group with weak pro-social values. Perhaps positive attitudes towards offending in adolescence may rather be a question of individual morality linked to lifestyle risk than a question of belonging to a subculture of crime and delinquency.

The youths' social situations and dispositions are strong predictors of their risk of offending

It is evident from the analyses conducted in this study that the adolescents vary strongly in their dispositions (self-control and morality, the latter as represented by pro-social values and shaming) and social situations (family and school bonds and level of parental monitoring). In turn the individual variation in all the studied aspects of dispositions and social situation is strongly related to their prevalence and frequency of offending. However, the two social bonds constructs lose their significance as predictors when controlling for the disposition constructs. This may be interpreted as supporting the view that aspects of the individual closer to action (perception of alternatives and decision-making as regards choices whether to engage in a criminal act or not) tend to have a greater direct importance than those that are more distant.

However, the findings show that the different disposition and social situation constructs are quite strongly correlated and may be represented as one risk-protective dimension. The more risk characteristics the youths have the more likely they are to offend, to offend frequently, to commit more serious crimes and to be versatile in their offending, while the reverse holds true for those youths who have more protective characteristics. All this can be interpreted as showing that the youths' propensity to offend is highly dependent on their risk-protective characteristics as defined by their social situation and dispositions.

The youths' individual routines and the related lifestyle risks are strong predictors of offending

Adolescents vary strongly in the way they live their lives, as the findings of this study clearly show. The analyses showed that the adolescents vary by the degree to which they were family, school and peer centred in their time use and activities. The analyses further showed that variations in the youths' routine activities were strongly influenced by their individual risk-protective characteristics, but also, to a lesser degree, by their family structural characteristics and their community (neighbourhood and school) structural characteristics. Particularly youths with a high degree of peer-centred time use and activities, but also (and most likely as a consequence of the high degree of peer centredness) youths with a low degree of family-centred time use and activities, tended to be more involved in offending than others. The more the youths activities were peer centred the more likely it was that they also had a strong lifestyle risk, as measured by time spent with delinquent peers, time spent in public high-risk environments and frequency of alcohol and narcotic drugs use. The offending level was particularly high for those whose peer-centred time use and activities also included a strong lifestyle risk.

It seems to be a reasonable assumption that variations in the way youths live their lives mean that they are differently exposed to behaviour settings that have characteristics which may entail a higher than average situational risk for offending (e.g. through high levels of temptation or provocation). The findings of the study provide some empirical evidence for such a link. It was shown that youths with more peer-centred time use and activities did spend more time in high-risk situations than others, and, in turn, that those who spent more time in high-risk situations did offend more often than others. However, this analysis was restricted to time spent in a particular type of high-risk situation (situations where the subject was involved in or witnessed arguments or harassment or witnessed violence between others) and further analyses may reveal links between a broader range of different types of high-risk situations and offending levels.

Lifestyle has a stronger impact on offending for some groups of youths than for others

Although the adolescents' individual risk-protective characteristics, and their individual routine activities/lifestyles, are both strong independent predictors of their offending levels, perhaps the most interesting finding of this study is the strong interaction effect between individual risk-protective characteristics and lifestyle risk. Youths with high individual risk factors tend to offend regardless of their level of lifestyle risk (although very few of them have a low lifestyle risk), while youths with high individual protective factors only occasionally offend if they have a higher lifestyle risk. The group in-between, those with balanced risk-protective factors, seems to be the group of adolescents most influenced by their type of lifestyle. For this group of youths the level of offending increases with increased lifestyle risk. The findings of this study suggest – when taking into account the knowledge we have from developmental and other studies – the existence of three main groups of adolescent offenders, as defined by the hypothesised causal background to their crime involvement.

Propensity-induced offenders
This group is very small in number and consists of youths who are poorly individually adjusted and who are likely to have a high level of overall offending, regardless of their lifestyle risk (although very few have a low-risk lifestyle). The offending by this group of offenders may be interpreted as being more about their individual dispositions (propensity to offend) than about situational risk.

Lifestyle-dependent offenders
This group of youths are neither individually very well adjusted, nor individually poorly adjusted. They appear to be the group of youths who run the highest risk of getting into frequent offending by having a high-risk lifestyle. This is a group for which whether their (medium) level of propensity will materialise in offending may be highly dependent on whether or not they have a lifestyle that frequently brings them into situations of risk. Peer influence may be a major reason for this group's offending.

Situationally limited offenders
This is a group of individually well adjusted youths who, if they live a more risky lifestyle, may occasionally offend (in particular committing an occasional aggressive crime) without any greater risk of developing a 'criminal career'. Crime by offenders in this group appears more to be about occasionally strong situational risks (primarily related to drinking or using drugs) than about their underlying propensity to offend.

Youths living in disadvantaged areas tend to offend more locally and the offenders living in disadvantaged areas tend to be more active than others

There are no large differences in the number of youths who have had an offending experience by their level of area of residence structural disadvantage. However, the criminality by offenders living in more disadvantaged areas tends to be more frequent and they do appear to offend more locally (in their neighbourhood) than others. This finding may be interpreted as indicating that youths living in more disadvantaged areas are more often introduced locally (in their neighbourhood) to criminogenic behaviour settings than those youths living in advantaged areas.

A particularly interesting finding is that the influence on local offending prevalence by area of residence structural risk appears to be strongest for the adolescents who have high individual protective characteristics, somewhat less for those with balanced individual risk-protective characteristics, and none at all for those with high individual risk characteristics. This finding is congruent with the assumption that situational inducements are more important for adolescents with lower than for those with higher individual risk characteristics. In addition it is also interesting to highlight that area of residence structural risk only has an impact on the overall frequency of offending for youths with balanced risk-protective characteristics. This may reflect the fact mentioned earlier that this is the group of youths for whom lifestyle risk (and particularly peer influence) has a special importance for their offending levels and area of residence structural risk may have some implications for their exposure to delinquent peers.

Schools with higher structural risk have more truancy and the truancy levels are highest among the youths who have the highest individual risk scores

Adolescents who are truant from school are more often involved in offending behaviour. The levels of truancy tend to be higher in schools with higher structural risk (particularly as regards female truancy), and youths with high individual risk scores are the most truant. Being truant may be regarded as a situational risk for offending (e.g. being in an unsupervised context). On the basis of the previous discussion of the differential impact on offending by situational factors for different groups of adolescents, one would assume that truancy will have the strongest impact on offending for youths with lower rather than higher individual risk characteristics (the latter would offend regardless of any stronger situational inducements).

To test this, analyses, not previously reported, of, respectively, the prevalence of offending, and the frequency of offending, by levels of truancy for different groups of youths by their individual risk-protective characteristics were conducted. The findings showed that the effect on prevalence of offending by truancy level was strongest for the youths with protective individual characteristics (signf. = 0.000, gamma = 0.61), followed by the youths with balanced individual risk-protective scores (signf. = 0.000, gamma = 0.48), while for youths with high individual risk scores the differences were non-significant. The pattern of offending frequency by truancy showed this to be non-significant for the youths with high individual risk characteristics, while the effect was strongest for youths with balanced individual risk-protective characteristics (signf. = 0.000, eta^2 = 0.08) and less for youths with protective individual characteristics (signf. = 0.000, eta^2 = 0.03). This finding suggests again that lifestyle risks are most important for the offending levels of youths with balanced risk-protective characteristics. The fact that the impact on prevalence (but not frequency) is strongest for the youths with protective individual characteristics (as it was also with regards to the influence of area of residence structural risks) may be interpreted as suggesting that situational risk has an important influence on their occasional offending, while it doesn't influence their risk for more frequent offending. If this is correct, it means that lifestyle risk may have a more lasting impact on offending by those with balanced individual risk-protective scores than for those with protective characteristics. The former group (the balanced group) will more regularly (since they have a higher propensity) be influenced by the situational inducement to which a high lifestyle risk exposes them, while in the latter case (the protective group), presumably only very strong situational inducements will occasionally make them offend.[2]

Implications for crime prevention

The prevention of adolescent offending should focus on developing strategies targeting the background to and circumstances of the criminality of different groups of adolescent offenders

This is not a crime prevention study. It is a study of the basic patterns of adolescent offending and some of their possible causes. As such it may constitute a foundation on which to build and develop adolescent crime prevention strategies. It may help to focus crime prevention efforts towards areas and measures that are likely to have a significant effect on adolescent offending. One lesson that may be drawn from this study is that there are different types of adolescent offenders. This may warrant different strategies of prevention. More generally, the implications of the findings of this study suggest that lifestyle and situationally oriented prevention approaches may work best for the group of youths labelled 'lifestyle dependent' offenders. By the same token, it is less likely that lifestyle and situationally oriented strategies in isolation would have any great prospect of being very effective for the group of youths we have labelled 'propensity-induced offenders'.

The findings of this study stress the great potential role that parents and teachers can play in crime prevention. The adolescents spend most of their time with their family or in school. It is likely that what parents and teachers do, and what they do not do, can therefore make a real difference. For example, poor parental monitoring and adolescent truancy from school are two strong correlates of offending risk. This raises questions about how effectively to motivate and engage parents and teachers in the fostering, monitoring and the social education of youths, and also raises questions about what kind of social and economic support, and given to whom, may be needed to achieve this. It is likely that social and economic support needs to be specifically targeted at those parents (families) and teachers (schools) operating in the more disadvantaged contexts. All in all, the main argument being made is that strategies to influence the day-to-day activities of the family and the school should be the cornerstone of a local crime prevention strategy.

However, it is less likely that strategies which build on involving parents and teachers, for example, strengthening parental monitoring and combating truancy, will be successful in having any major impact on the criminality of the adolescents with the highest individual risk characteristics.[3] For this group, whose socially problematic backgrounds are quite well documented in longitudinal studies, it may predominantly be a question of addressing more fundamental problems arising from their developmental history (their social heritage) and in their current (family and school) social situation. This may involve anything from neuropsychological problems needing treatment to current situations of substance abuse. It appears less likely that situationally oriented crime prevention strategies (e.g. CCTV, street lighting, target hardening) would have much of an impact on this group's criminality (which is not the same as to say that situational crime prevention is not effective in protecting specific targets). In addition, one may also question whether deterrence is an effective strategy to deal with this group's criminality. This is the group of adolescents who generally report experiencing the least degree of shame if caught offending, and perceive the detection risk if committing a crime to be low, and the consequences for them if caught to be not very serious. They also tend to have personality characteristics, like low self-control, that may make them less likely to consider the consequences of their behaviour. In addition to all this, they may have substance abuse problems, which may further diminish their ability to consider whether their acts would have any future negative consequences for them. However, this is not to say that criminal justice measures should not be part of dealing with this group's offending. Some kind of repressive measures may be necessary to manage and control the more serious aspects of this group's offending.

However, to tackle this group's criminality fundamentally (in the longer term) there is much to be said in favour of developing early prevention strategies (with a strong focus on family conditions and parenting styles and the early educational system) to attempt to reduce the number of youths ending up with high individual risk characteristics and a high-risk lifestyle in adolescence (for a discussion of potential concrete measures to include in an early prevention strategy, see Wikström and Torstensson 1999).

For the lifestyle-dependent adolescent offenders (those with balanced risk-protective characteristics who may offend more frequently if living a more risky lifestyle) it may be another story. In this case, measures to involve parents, for example, by promoting more effective parental monitoring of the youths' leisure activities outside the home, and teachers, for example, encouragement to supervise better what goes on in school during break-times and free lessons (given that a lot of crime takes place in the school environment) and to develop measures against truancy and bullying, may stand a better chance to be effective in reducing this group's involvement in crime. This is also a group of youths whose offending may be more influenced by levels of formal and informal social control in their neighbourhoods and in non-residential public spaces (like city centres). It is more likely that situational crime prevention measures may influence this group's offending.

Particular consideration may also be given to prevention strategies which address the potential role that high-frequency offenders might play in the criminality of youths with balanced risk-protective characteristics, because their offending behaviour appears particularly related to peer delinquency. For example, the level of offending by youths with balanced risk-protective characteristics may be strongly influenced by a high-risk lifestyle bringing them into contact with more 'experienced' adolescent or older offenders (see, for example, Reiss 1988; Reiss and Farrington 1991).

The fact that the adolescents' involvement in crime is closely linked to their individual characteristics, their lifestyles, and the interaction between the two, suggests that any successful adolescent crime prevention strategy has to build on an integrated approach, including social/developmental, situational and criminal justice elements that target the particular problem of prevention related to the different groups of adolescent offenders. It is further plausible that a strategy aiming permanently to affect the social conditions and day-to-day living of the adolescents (rather than a set of short-term projects), and which, as part of the broader strategy, targets or involves the key players in crime prevention (i.e. parents and teachers), will be the one which holds the most promise for making a real difference.

Notes

1 Note that this finding is from the space-time budget interview study, where there were no restrictions on what types of crimes were included.
2 In this context it is important to bear in mind that, although the effect by community context structural characteristics may be strongest for the adolescents with high individual protective factors, they still, at every level of structural risk, have a lower prevalence of offending than others.
3 In many cases their parents may even be a main cause or part of these youths' adjustment problems. When parents have social and other problems of their own they may be more difficult to engage in helping solve their child's problems.

Appendices

Appendix A: Wording of offending, victimisation and substance use questions

Offending

1 During the *last year* (year 2000) have you ever stolen anything from a shop (for example, CD records, cosmetics, computer games)?
2 During the *last year* (year 2000) have you ever purposely damaged or destroyed property not belonging to you (for example, smashed windows, scratched car paintwork, sprayed graffiti on a wall)?
3 During the *last year* (year 2000) have you ever used a weapon or force to take money or things from other people?
4 Not counting events you told us about in the previous question, during the *last year* (year 2000) have you ever beaten up or hit someone, for example, punched, kicked or head-butted someone (do not count fights with your brothers or sisters)?
5 During the *last year* (year 2000) have you ever broken into a house to steal something?
6 During the *last year* (year 2000) have you ever broken into a non-residential building to steal something (for example, broke into a shop, warehouse, school, company)?
7. During the *last year* (year 2000) have you ever stolen a car or broken into a car to steal something?

Victimisation

1 During the *last year* (year 2000), have you had anything that belongs to you stolen (do not count thefts by your brothers or sisters)?
2 During the *last year* (year 2000) has anyone, against your will, vandalised (destroyed) something that belongs to you?
3 During the *last year* (year 2000) have you ever been beaten up or hit, for example, punched, kicked, head-butted or bitten by an adult or another youth (do not count fights with your brothers or sisters)?

Substance use

1 During the *last year* (year 2000) have you ever been drunk?
2 During the *last year* (year 2000) have you ever tried marijuana or hashish (grass, pot)?
3 During the *last year* (year 2000) have you ever tried other drugs like amphetamine (speed), acid, LSD, ecstasy, heroin, cocaine, coke or crack?
4 During the *last year* (year 2000) have you ever tried inhalants such as glue, gas or aerosol spray?

Appendix B: Space-time budget codes

Geographical location

Code enumeration district
If OUTSIDE PETERBOROUGH

Code

1111	=	Yaxley
2222	=	Eye
3333	=	Glinton
4444	=	Farcet
5555	=	Ailsworth/Castor
6666	=	Other village/rural area close to Peterborough
7777	=	Other place in Cambridgeshire
8888	=	Outside Cambridgeshire

With whom

10 By yourself

20 Family only (other family guardians, e.g. grandparents = parents)

    21 Parents only
    22 Siblings only
    23 Parents + siblings
    24 Others, including adult/s
    25 Others, not incl. adult/s

30 Peers only (incl. boy and girlfriends)

    31 1 male peer
    32 1 female peer
    33 2 or more male peers
    34 2 or more female peers
    35 Mixed male and female peers

40 Others only

    41 Adult guardian
    42 No adult guardian

50 Family + peers

    51 Parents + peers
    52 No parents + peers

60 Family + others

    61 Parents + others
    62 No parents + others, incl. adult guardian
    63 No parents + others, no adult guardian

70 Peers + others

    71 Adult guardian
    72 No adult guardian

80 Family + peers + others

    81 Incl. parents
    82 Incl. other adult guardian
    83 No parents, no other adult guardians

Place

10 Home

20 Others' home

30 School

    31 Classroom
    32 Other place in school buildings
    33 Outdoors school grounds

40 Shops/shopping malls

    41 Queensgate shopping centre
    42 Rivergate shopping centre
    43 Other shopping local
    44 Serpentine shopping centre
    45 Orton garden centre

50 Entertainment

    51 Game arcades
    52 Theatre
    53 Cinema
    54 Pub
    55 Disco/club
    56 Restaurant
    57 Café
    58 Youth club/community centre
    59 Library

60 Sport

    61 Peterborough United football ground
    62 Rugby ground
    63 Cricket ground
    64 Athletics ground
    65 Ice rink
    66 Snooker club
    67 Golf course
    68 BMX track
    69 Sports centre
    70 Lido swimming pool
    71 Other swimming pool

72 Bowling alley
73 Other
74 Skate park (indoors)
75 Shooting range
76 Hockey pitch
77 Tennis courts

80 Streets, squares, etc.

81 Street/street corner
82 Parks/recreation grounds/meadows/fields
83 Car park
84 Petrol station/garage
85 Industrial estate
86 Bus station/stop
87 Railway station
88 Airport
89 Other

90 Official building

91 Police station
92 Social services locale
93 Youth justice locale
94 Court
95 Other

100 Other

101 Hospital
102 GP's office
103 Dentist
104 Hairdresser
105 Beauty salon
106 Church/religious centre
107 Hotel
108 Holiday accommodation
109 Other

110 Moving around
111 By foot
112 By bike
113 By moped/motorcycle
114 By car

115 By bus
116 By train
117 By aeroplane
118 Other

Activity

10 **Domestic**

11 Housework (cleaning, etc.)
12 Gardening
13 Shopping
14 Childcare
15 Adult care
16 Pet care
17 Walking the dog

20 **Personal**

21 Eating
22 Sleeping
23 Personal care (e.g. washing, dressing, etc.)
24 Medical care (treatment, etc.)
25 Ill in bed/at home
26 Dental care
27 Physical exercise (running/weightlifting, etc.)
28 Prayer

30 **Educational**

21 Classes and lectures
22 Homework
23 Other

40 **Work**

41 Work (paid)
42 Voluntary work
43 Work experience

50 **Leisure**

51 *Sport*

510 *Individual*
    511   Boxing
    512   Marshal arts
    513   Tennis
    514   Golf
515 Motor sports
516 Badminton
517 Table-tennis
518 Athletics
519 Other

520 *Team sport*
521 Rugby
522 Football
523 Cricket
524 Ice-hockey
525 Land-hockey
526 Other
527 Rounders

53 *Meetings of clubs/societies*

531 Drama
532 Dance/music
533 Art/photography/multimedia
534 Computer
535 Guides/Scouts
536 Cadets
537 Church/religious
538 Political
539 Other specified club/society/organisation

54 *Hobbies/games*

541 Hobbies (e.g. collecting, writing poetry, needlework, painting)
542 Rollerblading/roller-skating
543 Cycling/BMX
544 Bowling
545 Darts
546 Snooker
547 Traditional game playing (e.g. arcade, board or solo games)

548 Computer/console games
549 Computers (e.g. programming)
550 Internet (browsing)
551 Fishing
552 Fairground/theme rides
553 Playing a musical instrument

56 *Media consumption*

561 Television watching
562 Watching film/video/DVD
563 Reading cartoons
564 Reading magazines
565 Reading newspapers
566 Reading books
567 Listening to radio/music

57 *Socialising (no organised activity)*

571 Talking (face to face)
572 Talking by phone
573 Communication by e-mail (chat rooms, etc.)
574 Communication by mobile phone/texting

58 *Hanging around (no socialising)*
59 *Walking/transportation*
60 *Cultural activities (e.g., museums, art galleries)*
61 *Official meeting/appointment with social authority*
62 *Watching sports event*

Truancy

80 *Truancy*

Risk situations

Directly involved

10 Argument

11 Incl. threats
12 Not incl. threats

20 Being harassed/provoked

21 Sexual

22　Non-sexual

30　Harassing/provoking
   31　Sexual
   32　Non-sexual

Witnessing

40　Argument

   41　Incl. threats
   42　Not incl. threats

50　Being harassed/provoked

   51　Sexual
   52　Non-sexual

60　Harassing/provoking

   61　Sexual
   62　Non-sexual

Weapons

Carrying a weapon (any object intended to be used as a weapon):

10　Gun
20　Air-gun/rifle
30　Knife
40　Other sharp instrument (e.g. razor)
50　Other blunt instrument (e.g. baseball bat)
60　Other

Consumption of alcohol and drugs

10　Drinking alcohol
   11　Cider
   12　Beer
   13　Wine
   14　Spirits
   15　Combinations of above

20　Using drugs

   21　Cannabis, marijuana, hashish, grass, pot

22 Amphetamine, speed, acid, LSD, ecstasy, heroin, cocaine, coke, crack, etc.
23 Combinations of above

30 Using inhalants (e.g. glue, gas, aerosol spray)

Victimisation

10 Theft

11 Worth less than £5
12 Worth between £6 and £24
13 Worth between £25 and £99
14 Worth £100 or more

20 Vandalism

21 Worth less than £5
22 Worth between £6 and £24
23 Worth between £25 and £99
24 Worth £100 or more

30 Violence

31 No injuries (just pain or less)
32 Minor injuries (e.g. bruises and marks, nose bleeding that did not need treatment by a doctor)
33 More serious injuries (e.g., wounds or broken limbs that needed treatment by a doctor)

Offending

10 Theft

11 From a shop (shoplifting)
12 Directly from a person (personal belongings) using threats or violence
13 Directly from a person (personal belongings) *not* using threats or violence
14 Broke into a house
15 Broke into a shed/stole something from a house ground
15 Broke into a non-residential building
16 Broke into a car
17 Stole a car

18 Stole a moped or MC
19 Stole a bike

20 Other crimes

    20 Driving offences
    21 Other

30 Vandalism

    31 Vehicle (car, lorry, etc.)
    32 Moped/MC
    33 Bike
    34 Private house
    35 Non-residential building
    36 Street lights
    37 Other

40 Violence

    41 Male/s – acquaintance
    42 Female/s – acquaintance
    43 Mixed sex – acquaintance
    44 Male/s – known by appearance
    45 Female/s – known by appearance
    46 Mixed – known by appearance
    47 Male/s – total stranger
    48 Female/s – total stranger
    49 Mixed sex – total strangers

Note:
If at least one of the victims is an acquaintance code, 'acquaintance'. Else, if at least one is known by appearance code, 'known by appearance'. Else, if all are total strangers, code, 'total strangers'.

Fear

10 Scary or frightening location
    11 Scary or frightening people present
    12 Scary or frightening environment (e.g. dark and empty)

Appendix C: Parental monitoring questions

Table C1 Variables used to create the parental monitoring construct

Variable	Code	n	%
Parents know where you are?			
Always	0	682	35.2
Most of the times	1	762	39.3
Sometimes	2	413	21.3
Never	3	80	4.1
Total		1,937	99.9
Missing 20			
Parents know what you do?			
Always	0	489	25.3
Most of the times	1	679	35.1
Sometimes	2	576	29.8
Never	3	191	9.9
Total		1,935	100.1
Missing 22			
Parents know what friends you are with?			
Always	0	645	33.4
Most of the times	1	732	37.9
Sometimes	2	469	24.3
Never	3	86	4.5
Total		1,932	100.1
Missing 25			

Note:
All questions refer to when subject is out by him or herself or with friends in the evening.

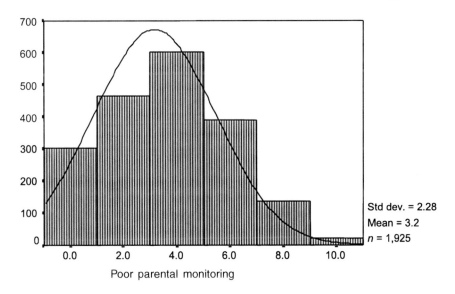

Std dev. = 2.28
Mean = 3.2
n = 1,925

Poor parental monitoring

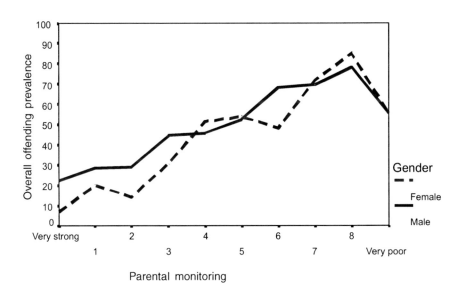

Parental monitoring

Appendix D: Self-control scale questions

Do you agree or disagree with the following statements about yourself?

A   When I am really angry, other people better stay away from me.
B   I often act on the spur of the moment without stopping to think.
C   I always feel guilty when I misbehave.
D   I sometimes find it exciting to do things for which I might get in trouble.
E   I don't devote much thought and effort preparing for the future.
F   Sometimes I will take a risk just for the fun of it.
G   If things I do upset people, it's their problem not mine.
H   I often try to avoid things that I know will be difficult.
I   I never think about what will happen to me in the future.
J   I always try to avoid upsetting or hurting other people's feelings.
K   I easily get bored with things.
L   I often feel bad when I do something wrong.
M   I lose my temper pretty easily.

Appendix E: Pro-social values scale questions

How wrong do you think it is for someone of your age to do the following?

A   Skip school without an excuse.
B   Lie, disobey or talk back to adults such as parents and teachers.
C   Purposely damage or destroy property that does not belong to you.
D   Steal something worth less than £5.
E   Steal something worth £25.
F   Steal something worth £100.
G   Go into or try to go into a building to steal something.
H   Go joyriding, that is, take a motor vehicle such as a car or motorcycle for a ride without the owner's permission.
I   Hit someone with the idea of hurting that person.
J   Attack someone with a weapon with the idea of seriously hurting that person.
K   Use a weapon or force to get money or things from other people.
L   Sell drugs such as cannabis, heroin, cocaine.
M   Use cannabis, hashish or pot.
N   Use hard drugs such as heroin.

Appendix F: Deterrence construct

Table F1 Variables used to create the deterrence construct

Variable	Code	n	%
Do you think that there is a great risk of being detected if you were to steal something from a shop, for example a CD record or cosmetics?			
No risk at all	0	76	3.9
A small risk	1	534	27.6
A great risk	2	909	46.9
A very great risk	3	418	21.6
Total		1,937	100.0
Missing 20			
Do you think that there is a great risk of ever being caught by the police if you broke into a car, for example, to steal a car stereo?			
No risk at all	0	61	3.1
A small risk	1	404	20.8
A great risk	2	801	41.2
A very great risk	3	676	34.8
Total		1,942	99.9
Missing 15			
If you were caught stealing something in a shop, do you think you would be in a lot of trouble?			
No, nothing would happen	0	23	1.2
No, not very much trouble	1	120	6.2
Yes, some trouble	2	694	35.7
Yes, a lot of trouble	3	1,107	56.9
Total		1,944	100.0
Missing 13			
If you were caught for breaking into a car, do you think you would be in a lot of trouble?			
No, nothing would happen	0	24	1.2
No, not very much trouble	1	45	2.3
Yes, some trouble	2	387	19.9
Yes, a lot of trouble	3	1487	76.5
Total		1,943	99.9
Missing 14			

References

Anderson, S., Kinsey, R., Loader, R. and Smith, C. (1994) *Cautionary Tales – Young People, Crime and Policing in Edinburgh.* Aldershot: Avebury.

Armstrong, D., Hine, J., Hacking, S., Armaos, R., Jones, R., Klessinger, N. and France, A. (2005) *Children, Risk and Crime: The On-track Youth Lifestyles Surveys.* Home Office Research Study 278. London: Home Office Research, Development and Statistics Directorate.

Bailey, K.D. (1994) *Typologies and Taxonomies: An Introduction to Classification Techniques. Sage University Paper Series on Quantitative Applications in the Social Sciences* 07–102. Thousand Oaks, CA: Sage.

Batta, I.D., McCulloch, J.W. and Smith, N.J. (1975) 'A study of juvenile delinquency amongst Asians and half-Asians: a comparative study in a northern town based on official statistics', *British Journal of Criminology,* 15: 32–42.

Beinart, S., Anderson, B., Lee, S. and Utting, D. (2002) *Youth at Risk? A National Survey of Risk Factors, Protective Factors and Problem Behaviour among Young People in England, Scotland and Wales.* London: Communities that Care.

Belson, W.A. (1975) *Juvenile Theft: The Causal Factors.* London: Harper & Row.

Bhopal, K. (1997) *Gender, 'Race' and Patriarchy: A Study of South Asian Women.* Aldershot: Ashgate.

Blumstein, A., Cohen, J. and Farrington, D.P. (1988a) 'Criminal career research: its value for criminology', *Criminology,* 26: 1–35.

Blumstein, A., Cohen, J. and Farrington, D.P. (1988b) 'Longitudinal and criminal career research: further clarifications', *Criminology,* 26: 57–74.

Blumstein, A., Cohen, J., Roth, J.A. and Visher, C.A. (1986) *Criminal Careers and Career Criminals. Volume 1.* Washington, DC: National Academy Press.

Bottoms, A.E. and Wiles, P. (1997) 'Environmental criminology' in M. Maguire *et al.* (eds) *The Oxford Handbook of Criminology* (2nd edn). Oxford: Clarendon Press.

Bowling, B. (1990) 'Conceptual and methodological problems in measuring "race" differences in delinquency', *British Journal of Criminology*, 30: 483–492.

Bowling, B. and Phillips, C. (2001) *Racism, Crime and Justice.* Harlow: Longman.

Boxford, S.H. (2003) 'The Cardiff School Study: an investigation of pupil offending in secondary schools'. Unpublished PhD thesis, University of Cambridge, Institute of Criminology.

Braithwaite, J. (1981) 'The myth of social class and criminality reconsidered', *American Sociological Review*, 46: 36–57.

Briar, S. and Piliavin, I. (1965) 'Delinquency, situational inducements, and commitment to conformity', *Social Problems*, 13: 413–23.

Bronfenbrenner, U. (1979) *The Ecology of Human Development: Experiments by Nature and Design.* Cambridge, MA: Harvard University Press.

Brooks-Gunn, J., Duncan, G.J., Klebanov, P.K. and Sealand, N. (1993) 'Do neighborhoods influence child and adolescent development?', *American Journal of Sociology*, 99: 353–95.

Brown, S. (1995) 'Crime and safety in whose "community?" Age, everyday life, and problems for youth policy', *Youth and Policy*, 48: 27–48.

Bursik, R.J. and Grasmick, H.G. (1993) *Neighborhoods and Crime.* New York, NY: Lexington Books.

Cambridgeshire County Council Research Group (2000) *The DETR Index of Multiple Deprivation 2000 and its Component Domain Indices of Deprivation 2000 – Cambridgeshire and the East of England.* Cambridge: Cambridgeshire County Council Research Group.

Cambridgeshire County Council Research Group (2001) *Supplement to the DETR IMD 2000 Report. IMD Scores in Cambridgeshire and Peterborough.* Cambridge: Cambridgeshire County Council Research Group.

Chung, I.-J., Hill, K.G., Hawkins, J.D., Gilchrist, L.D. and Nagin, D.S. (2002) 'Childhood predictors of offense trajectories.' *Journal of Research in Crime and Delinquency*, 39: 60–90.

Cohen, L.E. and Felson, M. (1979) 'Social change and crime rate trends: a routine activity approach', *American Sociological Review*, 44: 588–608.

Cohen, L.E. and Vila, B.J. (1996) 'Self-control and social control: an exposition of the Gottfredson–Hirschi/Sampson–Laub debate', *Studies on Crime and Crime Prevention*, 5: 125–50.

Coleman, J.S. (1988) 'Social capital in the creation of human capital', *American Journal of Sociology*, 94 (Supplement): 95–120.

Communities that Care (2002) *Youth at Risk? A National Survey of Risk Factors, Protective Factors and Problem Behaviour among Young People in England, Scotland and Wales.* London: Communities that Care.

Dion, K.K. and Dion, K.L. (2001) 'Gender and cultural adaptation in immigrant families', *Journal of Social Issues*, 57: 511–21.

D'Unger A.V., Land, K.C., McCall, P.L. and Nagin, D.S. (1998) 'How many latent classes of delinquent/criminal careers? Results from mixed poisson regression analyses', *The American Journal of Sociology*, 103: 1593–630.

Eggleston, E.P., Laub, J.H. and Sampson, R.J. (2004) 'Methodological sensitivities to latent class analysis of long-term criminal trajectories', *Journal of Quantitative Criminology*, 20: 1–26.

Elliott, D.S. and Ageton, S.S. (1980) 'Reconciling race and class differences in self-reported and official estimates of delinquency', *American Sociological Review*, 45: 95–110.

Elliott, D.S., Wilson, W.J., Huizinga, D., Sampson, R.J., Elliott, A. and Rankin, B. (1996) 'The effects of neighborhood disadvantage on adolescent development', *Journal of Research in Crime and Delinquency*, 33: 389–426.

Farrington, D.P. (1973) 'Self reports of deviant behavior: predictive and stable?', *Journal of Criminal Law and Criminology*, 64: 99–110.

Farrington, D.P. (1989) 'Self-reported and official offending from adolescence to adulthood', in M.W. Klein (ed.) *Cross-national Research in Self-reported Crime and Delinquency*. Dordrecht: Kluwer.

Farrington, D.P. (1992) 'Criminal career research: lessons for crime prevention', *Studies on Crime and Crime Prevention*, 1: 7–29.

Farrington, D.P. (1993) 'Have any individual, family or neighbourhood influences on offending been demonstrated conclusively?', in D.P. Farrington *et al.* (eds) *Integrating Individual and Ecological Aspects of Crime*. Stockholm: National Council for Crime Prevention.

Farrington, D.P. (1998) 'Individual differences and offending', in M. Tonry (ed.) *The Handbook of Crime and Punishment*. Oxford: Oxford University Press.

Farrington, D.P. (2000) 'Explaining and preventing crime: the globalization of knowledge – the American Society of Criminology 1999 Presidential Address', *Criminology*, 38: 1–25.

Farrington, D.P. (2002) 'Developmental criminology and risk-focused prevention', in M. Maguire *et al.* (eds) *The Oxford Handbook of Criminology* (3rd edn). Oxford: Oxford University Press.

Farrington, D.P. (2002) 'What has been learned from self-reports about criminal careers and the causes of offending.' Unpublished report for the Home Office (downloaded from http://www.homeoffice.gov.uk/rds/pdfs/farrington.pdf).

Farrington, D.P. (2003) 'Developmental and life-course criminology: key theoretical issues – the 2002 Sutherland Award Address', *Criminology*, 41: 221–55.

Farrington, D.P., Loeber, R., Stouthamer-Loeber, M., Van Kammen, W. B. and Schmidt, L. (1996) 'Self-reported delinquency and a combined delinquency seriousness scale based on boys, mothers, and teachers: concurrent and predictive validity for African-Americans and Caucasians', *Criminology*, 34: 493–517.

Farrington, D.P., Sampson, R.J. and Wikström, P.-O.H. (1993) *Integrating Individual and Ecological Aspects of Crime*. Report 1993: 10. Stockholm: Allmänna Förlaget.

Fergusson, D.M., Horwood, L.J. and Nagin, D.S. (2000) 'Offending trajectories in a New Zealand birth cohort', *Criminology*, 38: 525–51.

Flood-Page, C., Campbell, S., Harrington, V. and Miller, J. (2000) *Youth Crime: Findings from the 1998/99 Youth Lifestyles Survey. Research Study* 209. London: Home Office.

Furnstenberg Jr, F.F., Cook, T.D., Eccles, J., Elder Jr, G.H. and Sameroff, A. (1999) *Managing to Make It*. Chicago, IL: University of Chicago Press.

Garofalo, J. (1986) 'Lifestyles and victimisation: an update', in E.A. Fattah (ed.) *From Crime Policy to Victim Policy – Reorienting the Justice System*. London: Macmillan.

Gibbons, D.C. (1971) 'Observations on the study of crime causation', *American Journal of Sociology*, 77: 262–78.

Gibbons, D.C. (1975) 'Offender typologies – two decades later', *British Journal of Criminology*, 15: 140–56.

Gibbons, D.C. (1985) 'The assumption of the efficacy of middle-range explanation: typologies', in R.F. Meier (ed.) *Theoretical Methods in Criminology*. Beverly Hills, CA: Sage.

Gibbons, D.C. (1994) *Talking about Crime and Criminals: Problems and Issues in Theory Development in Criminology*. Englewood Cliffs, NJ: Prentice Hall.

Gold, M. (1966) 'Undetected delinquent behavior', *Journal of Research in Crime and Delinquency*, 3: 27–46.

Gottfredson, M. and Hirschi, T. (1986) 'The true value of lambda would appear to be zero: an essay on criminal careers, career criminals, selective incapacitation, cohort studies, and related topics', *Criminology*, 24: 213–34.

Gottfredson, M. and Hirschi, T. (1988) 'Science, public policy, and the career paradigm', *Criminology*, 26: 37–55.

Gottfredson, M.R. and Hirschi, T. (1990) *A General Theory of Crime*. Stanford, CA: Stanford University Press.

Gottfredson, D.C., McNeill III, R.J. and Gottfredson, G.D. (1991) 'Social area influences on delinquency: a multilevel analysis', *Journal of Research in Crime and Delinquency*, 28: 197–226.

Graham, J. and Bowling, B. (1995) *Young People and Crime*. London: Home Office.

Grasmick, H.G., Tittle, C.R., Bursik Jr, R.J. and Arneklev, B.J. (1993) 'Testing the core implications of Gottfredson and Hirschi's general theory of crime', *Journal of Research in Crime and Delinquency*, 30: 47–54.

Hagan, J. (1992) 'The poverty of a classless criminology – the American Society of Criminology 1991 Presidential Address', *Criminology*, 30: 1–19.

Harvey, A.S. (1999) 'Guidelines for time use data collection and analysis', in W.E. Pentland *et al.* (eds) *Time Use Research in the Social Sciences.* New York, NY: Kluwer Academic/Plenum Publishers.

Hawkins, D.F., Laub, J.H. and Lauritson, J.L. (1998) 'Race, ethnicity, and serious juvenile offending', in R. Loeber and D.P. Farrington (eds) *Serious and Violent Juvenile Offenders: Risk Factors and Successful Interventions.* Thousand Oaks, CA: Sage.

Hedström, P. and Swedberg, R. (1998) *Social Mechanisms: An Analytical Approach to Social Theory.* Cambridge: Cambridge University Press.

Herrenkohl, T.I., Hawkins, D.J., Chung, I-J., Hill, K.G. and Battin-Pearson, S. (2001) 'School and community risk factors and interventions', in R. Loeber and D.P. Farrington (eds) *Child Delinquents: Development, Intervention and Service Needs.* Thousand Oaks, CA: Sage.

Hindelang, M.J., Gottfredson, M.R. and Garofalo, J. (1978) *Victims of Personal Crime: An Empirical Foundation for a Theory of Personal Victimization.* Cambridge, MA: Ballinger.

Hindelang, M.J., Hirschi, T. and Weis, J.G. (1979) 'Correlates of delinquency: the illusion of discrepancy between self-report and official measures', *American Sociological Review*, 44: 995–1014.

Hindelang, M.J., Hirschi, T. and Weis, J.G. (1981) *Measuring Delinquency. Sage Library of Social Research.* Volume 123. Beverly Hills, CA: Sage.

Hirschi, T. (1969) *Causes of Delinquency.* Berkley, CA: University of California Press.

Hirschi, T. and Gottfredson, M. (1983) 'Age and the explanation of crime', *American Journal of Sociology*, 89: 552–84.

Hirschi, T. and Gottfredson, M. (1986) 'The distinction between crime and criminality', in T.F. Hartnagel and R.A. Silverman (eds) *Critique and Explanation: Essays in Honor of Gwynne Nettler.* New Brunswick, NJ: Transaction.

Hirschi, T. and Gottfredson, M.R. (1995) 'Control theory and the life-course perspective', in A. Piquero and P. Mazerolle (eds) (2001) *Life-course Criminology: Contemporary and Classic Readings.* Belmont, CA: Wadsworth.

Hirschi, T. and Gottfredson, M.R. (2000) 'In defense of self-control', *Theoretical Criminology*, 4: 55–69.

Horney, J., Osgood, D.W. and Marshall, I.H. (1995) 'Criminal careers in the short-term: intra individual variability in crime and its relation to local life circumstances', *American Sociological Review*, 60: 655–73.

Janson, C.-G. (1982) *Delinquency amongst Metropolitan Boys. Project Metropolitan 17.* Stockholm: Department of Sociology, University of Stockholm.

Janson, C.-G. and Wikström, P.-O.H. (1995) 'Growing up in a welfare state: the social class–offending relationship', in Z. Smith Blau and J. Hagan (eds) *Current Perspectives on Ageing and the Life Cycle: Delinquency and Disrepute in the Life Course.* Greenwich, CT: JAI Press.

Jolliffe, D.J., Farrington, D.P., Hawkins, J.D., Catalano, R.F., Hill, K.G. and Kosterman, R. (2003) 'Predictive, concurrent, prospective and retrospective validity of self-reported delinquency', *Criminal Behaviour and Mental Health,* 13: 179–97.

Junger, M. (1989) 'Discrepancies between police and self-report data for Dutch racial minorities', *British Journal of Criminology,* 29: 273–84.

Junger, M. (1990a) *Delinquency and Ethnicity: An Investigation on Social Factors relating to Delinquency among Moroccan, Turkish, Surinamese and Dutch Boys.* Deventer: Kluwer Law and Taxation.

Junger, M. (1990b) 'Studying ethnic differences in relation to crime and police discrimination: answer to Bowling', *British Journal of Criminology,* 30: 493–502.

Junger-Tas, J. (2001) 'Ethnic minorities, social integration and crime', *European Journal of Criminal Policy and Research,* 9: 5–29.

Kornhauser, R.R. (1978) *The Social Sources of Delinquency: An Appraisal of Analytic Models.* Chicago, IL: University of Chicago Press.

Kupersmidt, J.B., Griesler, P.C., DeRosier, M.E., Patterson, C.J. and Davis, P.W. (1995) 'Childhood aggression and peer relations in the context of family and neighborhood factors', *Child Development,* 66: 360–75.

Laub, J.H., Nagin, D.S. and Sampson, R.J. (1998) 'Trajectories of change in criminal offending', in A. Piquero and P. Mazerolle (eds) (2001) *Life-course Criminology: Contemporary and Classic Readings.* Belmont, CA: Wadsworth.

Laub, J.H. and Sampson, R.J. (2003) *Shared Beginnings, Divergent Lives; Delinquent Boys to Age 70.* Cambridge, MA: Harvard University Press.

Lazersfeld, P.F. (1966) 'Foreword', in J.C. McKinney (ed.) *Constructive Typology and Social Theory.* New York, NY: Meredith.

Le Blanc, M. (1997) 'A generic control theory of the criminal phenomena: the structural and dynamic statements of an integrative multilayered control theory', in T.P. Thornberry (ed.) *Development Theories of Crime and Delinquency.* New Brunswick, NJ: Transaction.

Le Blanc, M. and Loeber, R. (1998) 'Developmental criminology updated', in M. Tonry (ed.) *Crime and Justice: A Review of Research. Volume 23.* Chicago, IL: University of Chicago Press.

Loeber, R. and Farrington, D.P. (1999) *Serious and Violent Juvenile Offenders: Risk Factors and Successful Interventions.* Thousand Oaks, CA: Sage.

Loeber, R. and Farrington, D.P. (2001) *Child Delinquents: Risk Factors, Interventions, and Service Needs.* Beverly Hills, CA: Sage.

Loeber, R., Farrington, D.P., Stouthamer-Loeber, M., Moffitt, T. and Caspi, A. (1998) 'The development of male offending: key findings from the first decade of the Pittsburgh Youth Study', *Studies on Crime and Crime Prevention,* 7: 141–71.

Loeber, R. and Stouthamer-Loeber, M. (1986) 'Family factors as correlates and predictors of juvenile conduct problems and delinquency', in M. Tonry and N. Morris (eds) *Crime and Justice: An Annual Review of Research. Volume 7.* Chicago, IL: University of Chicago Press.

Loeber, R. and Wikström, P.-O.H. (1993) 'Individual pathways to crime in different types of neighborhoods', in D.P. Farrington *et al.* (eds) *Integrating Individual and Ecological Aspects of Crime.* Report 1993: 1. Stockholm: Allmänna Förlaget.

Lösel, F. and Bender, D. (2003) 'Protective factors and resilience', in D.P. Farrington, and J.W. Coid (eds) *Early Prevention of Adult Antisocial Behaviour.* Cambridge: Cambridge University Press.

Ma, N. (2006) 'On the juveniles of Macau: a study of Chinese youth's patterns of offending and victimisation.' Unpublished PhD thesis, University of Cambridge, Institute of Criminology.

Magnusson, D. (1988) *Individual Development from an Interactional Perspective: A Longitudinal Study.* Hillsdale, NJ: Lawrence Erlbaum Associates.

Martens, P.L. (1993) 'An ecological model of socialization in explaining offending', in D.P. Farrington *et al.* (eds) *Integrating Individual and Ecological Aspects of Crime.* Report 1993: 1. Stockholm: Almänna Förlaget.

Martens, P.L. (1997) 'Parental monitoring and deviant behaviour among juveniles', *Studies on Crime and Crime Prevention*, 6: 224–44.

Matza, D. (1990) *Delinquency and Drift.* New Brunswick, NJ: Transaction.

Maung, N.A. (1994) *Young People, Victimisation and the Police: British Crime Survey Findings on Experiences and Attitudes of 12 to 15 Year Olds.* London: Home Office Research and Planning Unit.

McCord, J. (2000) 'Developmental trajectories and intentional actions', *Journal of Quantitative Criminology*, 16: 237–53.

McDonald, L. (1969) *Social Class and Delinquency.* London: Faber and Faber.

McKinney, J.C. (1966) *Constructive Typology and Social Theory.* New York, NY: Meredith.

McQuoid, J. and Lockhart, B. (1994) 'Self-reported delinquency and other behaviours amongst young people in Northern Ireland.' CIRAC, Extern Organisation. Unpublished report.

McVie, S. (2003) 'Gender differences in adolescent development and violence: findings from the Edinburgh Study of Youth Transitions and Crime', in F. Dünkel and K. Drenkhahn (eds) *Youth Violence: New Patterns and Local Responses – Experiences in East and West.* Mönchengladbach: Forum Verlag Godesberg.

Merry, S.E. (1984) 'Rethinking gossip and scandal', in D. Black (ed.) *Toward a General Theory of Social Control. Volume 1. Fundamentals.* Orlando, FL: Academic Press.

Moffitt, T.E. (1993) 'Adolescence-limited and life-course-persistent antisocial behavior: a developmental taxonomy', *Psychological Review*, 100: 674–701.

Moffitt, T.E., Caspi, A., Rutter, M. and Silva, P.A. (2001) *Sex Differences in Antisocial behaviour: Conduct Disorder, Delinquency, and Violence in the Dunedin Longitudinal Study.* Cambridge: Cambridge University Press.

MORI (2002) *Youth Survey 2002: Research Study Conducted for the Youth Justice Board* (downloaded from http://www.youth-justice-board.gov.uk/ Publications/Scripts/prodList.asp?idcategory=2&curPage=6&sortField= description&eP= YJB).

MORI (2003) *Youth Survey 2003: Research Study Conducted for the Youth Justice Board by MORI* (downloaded from http://www.youth-justice-board.gov. uk/Publications/Scripts/prodList.asp?idcategory=2&curPage=6&sortField =description&eP= YJB).

MORI (2004) *MORI Youth Survey 2004* (downloaded from http://www. youth-justice-board.gov.uk/Publications/Scripts/prodList.asp?idcategory= 2&curPage=6&sortField=description&eP= YJB).

Nagin, D.S. (2004) 'Response to "Methodological sensitivities to latent class analysis of long-term criminal trajectories"', *Journal of Quantitative Criminology*, 20: 27–35.

Nagin, D.S., Farrington, D.P. and Moffitt, T.E. (1995) 'Life-course trajectories of different types of offenders', *Criminology*, 33: 111–39.

Nagin, D.S. and Land, K.C. (1993) 'Age, criminal careers, and population heterogeneity: specification and estimation of a nonparametric, mixed poisson model', *Criminology*, 31: 327–362.

Olafsson, J.O. (2004) 'Public violence in Iceland: disentangling the agency and structural effects.' Unpublished PhD thesis, University of Cambridge, Institute of Criminology.

Osgood, D.W., Wilson, J.K., O'Malley, P.M., Bachman, J.G. and Johnston, L.D. (1996) 'Routine activities and individual deviant behavior', *American Sociological Review*, 61: 635–55.

Ouston, J. (1984) 'Delinquency, family background and educational achievement', *British Journal of Criminology*, 24: 2–26.

Pentland, W.E., Harvey, A.S., Lawton, M.P. and McColl, M.A. (1999) *Time Use Research in the Social Sciences.* New York, NY: Kluwer Academic/Plenum Publishers.

Powis, B. and Walmsley, R.K. (2002) *Programmes for Black and Asian Offenders on Probation: Lessons for Developing Practice. Home Office Research Study 250.* London: Home Office Research, Development and Statistics Directorate.

Raudenbush, S.W. and Sampson, R.J. (1999) 'Econometrics: toward a science of assessing ecological settings, with application to the systematic social observation of neighborhoods', *Sociological Methodology*, 29: 1–41.

Reiss, A.J. Jr (1951) 'Delinquency as the failure of personal and social controls', *American Sociological Review*, 16: 196–207.

Reiss, A.J. Jr (1986) 'Why are communities important in understanding crime?', in A.J. Reiss Jr and M. Tonry (eds) *Communities and Crime*. London: University of Chicago Press.

Reiss, A.J. Jr (1988) 'Co-offending and criminal careers', in M. Tonry and N. Morris (eds) *Crime and Justice*. Chicago, IL. University of Chicago Press.

Reiss, A.J. Jr and Farrington, D.P. (1991). 'Advancing knowledge about co-offending: results from a prospective longitudinal study of London males', *Journal of Criminal Law and Criminology*, 84: 360–95.

Reiss, A.J. Jr and Rhodes, A.L. (1961) 'The distribution of juvenile delinquency in the social class structure', *American Sociological Review*, 26: 720–32.

Robinson, J.P. (1999) 'The time-diary method', in W.E. Pentland *et al.* (eds) *Time Use Research in the Social Sciences*. New York, NY: Kluwer Academic/Plenum Publishers.

Rutter, M. (1987) 'Psychosocial resilience and protective mechanisms', *American Journal of Orthopsychiatry*, 57: 316–31.

Rutter, M. and Giller, H. (1983) *Juvenile Delinquency: Trends and Perspectives*. Harmondsworth: Penguin Books.

Rutter, M., Maughan, R., Mortimore, P. and Ouston, J. (1979) *Fifteen Thousand Hours*. Wells: Open Books.

Sampson, R.J. (1986) 'The effects of urbanization and neighborhood characteristics on criminal victimisation', in R.M. Figlio *et al.* (eds) *Metropolitan Crime Patterns*. New York, NY: Criminal Justice Press.

Sampson, R.J. (1997) 'The embeddedness of child and adolescent development: a community-level perspective on urban violence', in J. McCord (ed.) *Violence and Childhood in the Inner City*. Cambridge: Cambridge University Press.

Sampson, R.J. and Groves, W.B. (1989) 'Community structure and crime: testing social-disorganization theory', *American Journal of Sociology*, 94: 774–802.

Sampson, R.J. and Laub, J.H. (1990) 'Crime and deviance over the life course: the salience of adult social bonds', *American Sociological Review*, 55: 609–27.

Sampson, R.J. and Laub, J.H. (1993) *Crime in the Making: Pathways and Turning Points through Life*. Cambridge, MA: Harvard University Press.

Sampson, R.J. and Laub, J.H. (1995) 'Understanding variability in lives through time: contributions of life-course criminology', *Studies on Crime and Crime Prevention*, 4: 143–58.

Sampson, R.J., Laub, J.H. and Eggleston, E.P. (2004) 'On the robustness and validity of groups', *Journal of Quantitative Criminology*, 20: 37–42.

Sampson, R.J. and Raudenbush, S.W. (1999) 'Systematic social observation of public spaces: a new look at disorder in urban neighborhoods', *American Journal of Sociology*, 105: 603–51.

Sampson, R.J., Raudenbush, S.W. and Earls, F. (1997) 'Neighborhoods and violent crime: a multilevel study of collective efficacy', *Science*, 277: 918–24.

Sarnecki, J. (1986) *Delinquent Networks. Report* 1986: 1. Stockholm: National Council for Crime Prevention.

Schoggen, P. (1989) *Behavior Settings*. Stanford, CA: Stanford University Press.

Short, J.F. Jr. and Nye, F.I. (1957) 'Reported behavior as a criterion of deviant behavior', *Social Problems*, 5: 207–13.

Smith, D., McVie, S., Woodward, R., Shute, J., Flint, J. and McAra, L. (2001) *The Edinburgh Study of Youth Transitions and Crime: Key Findings at Ages 12 and 13*. Edinburgh: University of Edinburgh.

Smith, D.J. (1997) 'Ethnic origins, crime, and criminal justice in England and Wales', in M. Tonry (ed.) *Ethnicity, Crime and Immigration: Comparative and Cross-national Perspectives. Crime and Justice: A Review of Research. Volume 21*. Chicago, IL: University of Chicago Press.

Thornberry, T.P. and Krohn, M.D. (2000) 'The self-report method for measuring delinquency and crime', in D. Duffee (ed.) *Criminal Justice 2000. Volume 4. Measurement and Analysis of Crime and Justice*. Washington, DC: National Institute of Justice.

Tittle, C.R. (1988) 'Two empirical regularities (maybe) in search of an explanation: commentary on the age/crime debate', *Criminology*, 26: 75–85.

Tittle, C.R., Villemez, W.J. and Smith, D.A. (1978) 'The myth of social class and criminality: an empirical assessment of the empirical evidence', *American Sociological Review*, 43: 643–56.

Tonry, M. (1997a) *Ethnicity, Crime, and Immigration: Comparative and Cross-National Perspectives*. Chicago, IL: University of Chicago Press.

Tonry, M. (1997b) 'Ethnicity, crime, and immigration', in M. Tonry (ed.) *Ethnicity, Crime and Immigration: Comparative and Cross-national Perspectives. Crime and Justice: A Review of Research. Volume 21*. Chicago, IL: University of Chicago Press.

Tonry, M., Ohlin, L.E. and Farrington, D.P. (1991) *Human Development and Criminal Behavior*. New York, NY: Springer-Verlag.

Torgersen, L. (1991) 'Patterns of self-reported delinquency in children with one immigrant parent, two immigrant parents and Norwegian-born parents: some methodological considerations', *Journal of Scandinavian Studies in Criminology and Crime Prevention*, 2: 213–27.

Tremblay, R.E. and LeMarquand, D. (2001) 'Individual risk and protective factors', in R. Loeber and D.P. Farrington (eds) *Child Delinquents: Development, Intervention and Service Needs*. Thousand Oaks, CA: Sage.

Wardak, A. (2000) *Social Control and Deviance: A South Asian Community in Scotland.* Aldershot: Ashgate.

Warr, M. (2002) *Companions in Crime. The Social Aspects of Criminal Conduct.* Cambridge: Cambridge University Press.

Wasserman, G.A. and Seracini, A.M. (2001) 'Family risk factors and interventions', in R. Loeber and D.P. Farrington (eds) *Child Delinquents: Development, Intervention and Service Needs.* Thousand Oaks, CA: Sage.

Wikström, P.-O.H. (1987) *Patterns of Crime in a Birth Cohort. Sex, Age and Social Class Differences. Project Metropolitan Research Reports* 24. Stockholm: Department of Sociology, University of Stockholm.

Wikström, P.-O.H. (1990) *Crime and Measures against Crime in the City.* Report 1990: 5. Stockholm: Allmänna Förlaget.

Wikström, P.-O.H. (1991) *Urban Crime, Criminals and Victims.* New York, NY: Springer-Verlag.

Wikström, P-O. H. (1996) 'Causes of crime and crime prevention', in T. Bennett (ed.) *Preventing Crime and Disorder: Targeting Strategies and Responsibilities.* Cambridge: University of Cambridge, Institute of Criminology.

Wikström, P.-O.H. (1998) 'Communities and crime', in M. Tonry (ed.) *Oxford Handbook of Crime and Punishment.* Oxford: Oxford University Press.

Wikström, P.-O.H. (2002) 'The Peterborough Youth Study. Adolescent crime in context: a study of gender, family social position, individual characteristics, community context, lifestyles, offending and victimisation.' Unpublished report to the Home Office. Cambridge: University of Cambridge, Institute of Criminology.

Wikström, P.-O.H. (2004) 'Crime as alternative: towards a cross-level situational action theory of crime causation', in J. McCord (ed.) *Beyond Empiricism: Institutions and Intentions in the Study of Crime. Advances in Criminological Theory.* New Brunswick, NJ: Transaction.

Wikström, P.-O.H (2005) 'The social origins of pathways in crime. Towards a developmental ecological action theory of crime involvement and change', in D.P. Farrington (ed.) *Integrated Developmental and Life-course Theories of Offending. Advances in Criminological Theory. Volume 14.* New Brunswick, NJ: Transaction.

Wikström, P.-O.H (2006) 'Individuals, settings and acts of crime: situational mechanisms and the explanation of crime', in P.-O.H. Wikström and R.J. Sampson (eds) *The Explanation of Crime: Context, Mechanisms and Development.* Cambridge: Cambridge University Press.

Wikström, P.-O.H., Ceccato, V., Oberwittler, D. and Hardie, B. (2006) *Crime and Behavioural Contexts* (forthcoming).

Wikström, P.-O.H., Clarke, R.V. and McCord, J. (1995) *Integrating Crime Prevention Strategies: Propensity and Opportunity.* Report 1995: 5. Stockholm: Fritzes.

Wikström, P.-O.H. and Loeber, R. (2000) 'Do disadvantaged neighborhoods cause well-adjusted children to become adolescent delinquents? A study of male juvenile serious offending, individual risk and protective factors, and neighborhood context', *Criminology*, 38: 1109–42.

Wikström, P.-O.H. and Sampson, R.J (2003) 'Social mechanisms of community influences on crime and pathways in criminality', in B.B. Lahey *et al.* (eds) *The Causes of Conduct Disorder and Serious Juvenile Delinquency.* New York, NY: Guildford Press.

Wikström, P.-O.H. and Torstensson, M. (1999) 'Local crime prevention and its national support: organisation and direction', *European Journal on Criminal Policy and Research,* 7: 459–81.

Wilson, J.Q. and Herrnstein, R.J. (1985) *Crime and Human Nature: The Definitive Study of the Causes of Crime.* New York, NY: The Free Press.

Wolfgang, M., Figlio, R.M. and Sellin, T. (1972) *Delinquency in a Birth Cohort.* Chicago, IL: University of Chicago Press.

Wootton, B. (1959) *Social Science and Social Pathology.* London: George Allen & Unwin.

Wright, B.R.E., Caspi, A., Moffitt, T.E., Miech, R.A. and Silva, P.A. (1999) 'Reconsidering the relationship between SES and delinquency: causation but not correlation', *Criminology,* 37: 175–94.

Index